IMAGES
of America

Rockbridge County
The Michael Miley Collection

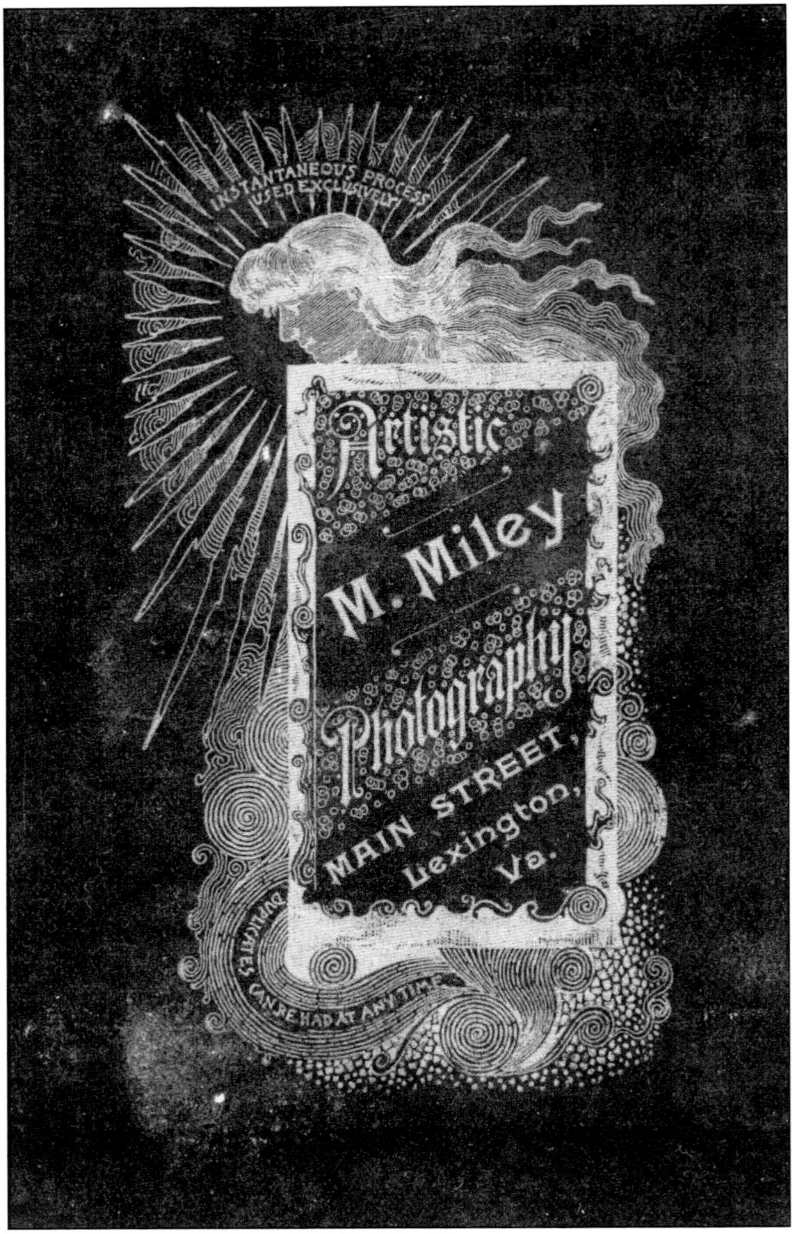

The photographer's imprint states, "Michael Miley Artistic Photography Main Street, Lexington, Va. Duplicates can be had at any time." This is the back mark that was used by Michael Miley to identify his photographs around 1890. Miley's back mark changed over the years to reflect his changing business names and associations. (Courtesy of Special Collections, Leyburn Library, Washington and Lee University.)

On the Cover: Before residence halls or dormitories were commonplace on college and university campuses, students were forced to find their own housing. Like other single men, students at Washington College in Lexington found accommodations by renting rooms in boardinghouses, sometimes referred to as ranches. In this engaging Boude and Miley photograph from 1869, students relax on the front porch of the J.W. Lindsay boardinghouse. (Courtesy of Seth McCormick-Goodhart.)

IMAGES
of America

ROCKBRIDGE COUNTY
THE MICHAEL MILEY COLLECTION

Richard A. Straw

ARCADIA
PUBLISHING

ISBN 978-1-4671-2019-7

Published by Arcadia Publishing
Charleston, South Carolina

Printed in the United States of America

Library of Congress Control Number: 2013932432

For all general information, please contact Arcadia Publishing:
Telephone 843-853-2070
Fax 843-853-0044
E-mail sales@arcadiapublishing.com
For customer service and orders:
Toll-Free 1-888-313-2665

Visit us on the Internet at www.arcadiapublishing.com

To all of the people who were given life forever through the lens of Michael Miley's camera

Contents

ACKNOWLEDGMENTS

When I first imagined an Arcadia book about Michael Miley, I knew little about him and knew little about Rockbridge County. I was sure that someone had certainly published a substantial number of his photographs, but no one had, and I continue to be a little mystified that so little attention has been paid to this artist. Now that the book is real, I must thank the many gracious and generous people who gave me the support and assistance necessary to complete this book. At the top of the list are Seth McCormick-Goodhart and Lisa McCown, who work in Special Collections at Washington and Lee University. Their knowledge and support of this project are really what made it possible. It is no exaggeration to say that without their help I would not have been able to do this work. They both gave freely of their time and energy to help retrieve photographs and to offer suggestions about books and other sources of information about Miley.

I especially owe Seth McCormick-Goodhart a huge debt of gratitude for his knowledge of 19th-century photography and for his tireless efforts to help identify places and people in the photographs. Most of what I know about Miley and his work I learned from him. I also wish to thank Tom Camden, the head of Special Collections at Washington and Lee, for his support of this project. Lissie Cain, my editor at Arcadia, was supportive of this book from the start, and I am grateful to her for that. I want to thank my colleague Johnny Moore for his astute comments on Miley's baseball photographs. Thanks finally to Yolanda Merrill, whose small exhibit of Miley photographs at W&L in 2012 introduced me to his work.

Four books were especially useful in my research into Miley and Rockbridge County: *The Architecture of Historic Lexington* by Lyle, Simpson, and Mann (1977); *Remarkable Rockbridge* by Charles A. Brodie (2011); *Michael Miley*, Exhibit Catalog (1980); and *General Lee's Photographer* by Marshall Fishwick (1954). I also read the typed transcripts of Henry Miley's memories of his father and the manuscript "The Mileys and Color Photography," written by Harrington Waddell in December 1941.

With one or two noted exceptions, Michael Miley took all of the photographs included in this book. Unless otherwise specified, all of the photographs in this book are courtesy of Special Collections, Leyburn Library, Washington and Lee University, and are used with permission.

Introduction

Rockbridge County, Virginia, could be a place where only ghost stories are told. Ghosts of Civil War soldiers slogging up and down the valley, perhaps on their way to or from Gettysburg; Hunter's raiders on their way out of Lexington after burning part of VMI; the ghosts of both Robert E. Lee and Thomas "Stonewall" Jackson, their posthumous energy spread thin over the landscape by those who revere their images and those who wish they would just go away forever; or the ghosts of countless ordinary people, farmers, blacksmiths, millers, canal and furnace workers, tradesmen, teachers, students, children, shopkeepers, wives and husbands, moms and dads. But in Rockbridge County today, the past is not a ghost story. It is instead a vibrant and frequently called upon part of everyday life that exists to inform, inspire, and, most importantly, to anchor those who call this county and these communities home to something solid and real, to a place.

The photographs of Michael Miley presented in this book have contributed significantly to that strong sense of the past that permeates life in Rockbridge. In addition, these images, which still speak to viewers over 100 years after they were made, continue to enlighten and guide us into the future by keeping the past close at hand. Some of these images are well known, as they have been reproduced in many publications. For example, the photographs of Robert E. Lee, iconic in some respects, have defined his appearance in the historical imagination. Others, like Miley's views of the Maury River and House Mountain, sustain that strong sense of historical continuity and vivid sense of place that are so present in Rockbridge life even today.

Many of the photographs reproduced in this volume appear in print for the first time, never having been seen before outside the small circle of family and friends who would have viewed them upon their creation. The identities of many of the individuals in the photographs have been obscured by time. My interest in Miley is in his role as an artist rather than as a photographer who took photographs of famous people. His Lee photographs, for example, exist not only as languid reminders of the awesome dedication that thousands, perhaps millions, felt for this man, but they also reveal hidden aspects of this leader's character and life, features under the veneer that only a gifted artist like Miley could reveal to us. It is my hope that these photographs will help to meld into the minds of all who view them the historical connection between the vision of Michael Miley, the images of the familiar and unfamiliar places he recorded for us, and life today and tomorrow in Rockbridge County. There is only one Rockbridge County in the United States of America. Unique in more ways than this, it is a rural place (only 37 people per square mile) with a cosmopolitan feel, many visitors (some who choose to stay a lifetime), and a landscape of awesome beauty that is still largely pastoral. In many ways defined by its geography, its people, and its history, Rockbridge County gets a hold on its residents and will not let go.

Between 1710 and 1775, as many as 250,000 Scotch-Irish people migrated to America from the northern counties of Ireland, usually referred to as Ulster. They were largely Presbyterian and, like migrants then and now, they were looking for a better life in a new place. The first white settlers wandered into the area that would become Rockbridge County sometime in 1737 and established settlements in rich bottomlands and, later, up the creeks that came down from the surrounding mountains. Over time, many small farming communities were established, some of which are still around, some that exist only as names on highway signs or as clusters of houses along back roads. Sharing much in common with other Scotch-Irish and German settlements in the backcountry, the early white inhabitants of Rockbridge County were no doubt hardworking farmers and craftsmen who through years of movement and settlement established a rural, semi-self-sufficient way of life on the frontier that is identified today as an integral part of Appalachian history and culture.

Rockbridge County was carved from parts of Augusta and Botetourt Counties in 1777. By the antebellum era, it had established itself as an important agricultural and iron-producing region in Virginia. Enslaved persons were used extensively in the county in farming, but, in particular, pig iron furnaces like those at Buffalo Forge, in the southern part of the county, used large numbers of African American enslaved laborers to establish Rockbridge County as a vital cog in the industrial wheels of the South. Iron ingots and agricultural products were shipped to Richmond on canals and rivers that helped to establish the importance of water resources in the county. Today, the Maury River continues to be widely used, not as the commercial thoroughfare it once was, but as an important part of the recreational and outdoor life so vital to the county's citizenry.

Rockbridge County's Civil War heritage is well known and well documented. At the center of that history is Lexington, the county seat. A number of the photographs in this book reflect that heritage, as do many of the buildings that make up Lexington's past and present. Thomas "Stonewall" Jackson's home is a popular tourist attraction, as are the campuses of the Virginia Military Institute and Washington and Lee University. Lee Chapel and the Jackson statue and burial site make Lexington what some have called "the shrine of the South." Established as it is, Lexington's Civil War heritage is as controversial as it is persistent. As this community has changed in the past 30 years, many questions have been raised about the Civil War's legacy and how its history should be folded into its contemporary image of itself as a cultural and educational center.

At the end of the Civil War, both Michael Miley and Robert E. Lee were without jobs. Miley had spent the last two years of the war in a prison. Lee spent the last two years of the war trying to hold his army together in the face of mounting odds against him, finally accepting defeat in April 1865. By the end of the next year, both Lee and Miley were in Rockbridge County, Lee of course as president of Washington College and Miley as a budding businessman with a burgeoning interest in and an exceptional talent for photography. Lee had come to a small struggling college and succeeded in putting it on a sound financial and educational path. Michael Miley had come home.

Miley was born on July 19, 1841, on a farm just over the border in Rockingham County. His family soon moved onto another farm in Rockbridge County, a short distance north of Lexington. Marshall Fishwick, in his short study of Miley published over half a century ago, suggests that Miley's later propensity to photograph the many examples of natural beauty in Rockbridge County had its genesis in the carefree life of a mountain youth, able to wander the hills and valleys learning from nature, history, and life itself. While it is difficult to document the connections between youthful curiosity and adult vocations in Miley's case, it seems apparent. His body of photographic work is full of landscapes, mountain vistas, stormy skies, and flooding rivers. Even many of his photographic studies of human subjects show a frivolity and free spirit that could easily have been borne of a youth spent outdoors, happy and lighthearted.

What is known of Miley's life comes primarily through the memories of his son, Henry, who learned his father's techniques, took over the business after Michael died in 1918, and recorded his recollections of his father in 1941. When the Civil War began, Michael Miley enlisted and served under Stonewall Jackson. Miley was captured and spent the final two years of the war as a prisoner of war at Fort Delaware. It is unclear when Miley returned to his home in Rockbridge County after Appomattox, although it is known that he was living in Staunton and learning photography from John Burdette prior to his move to Lexington sometime in late 1866.

While Miley had no personal contact with Robert E. Lee during the war, it is no doubt more than a coincidence that Miley chose to move to Lexington at nearly the same time as Lee. His relationship with Lee during the four years that Lee was president of Washington College and the many photographs Miley took of Lee, his family, and his friends suggests that knowledge of Lee's arrival in Lexington was a motive for his move there as well. According to his son's memories of his father, Michael Miley had enormous respect for Lee and considered him, according to biographer Marshall Fishwick, "the greatest man that ever lived."

In Lexington, Miley first worked with an itinerant photographer from Augusta County named Adam H. Plecker, who was the classic 19th-century photographer with a traveling road show of props and equipment that he would take from town to town, setting up his operation, advertising in the local paper, and making photographs of whoever could pay the small fee. Still only 25 years old, Miley had gained experience with two established practitioners. Miley wanted to settle down and start his own studio, but because he was without funds, he needed a partner. From late 1866 to 1870, John C. Boude backed Miley financially. According to Seth McCormick-Goodhart of W&L Special Collections, there is no evidence that Boude assumed more than just a financial role in the business. Miley did all the photographic work until he was able to buy out Boude's share of the concern in 1870. Miley spent the remaining years of his life, until his death in 1918, photographing the famous and the ordinary inside and out of his studio at the corner of Main and Nelson Streets in Lexington.

From the evidence of Miley's personality and demeanor, he was an artist and creative technician first and foremost, experimenting with photographic methods and materials and certainly an innovator in the field, but he was also so individualistic and even iconoclastic that he eschewed a type of ambition that might have turned his methods into capital. He was primarily concerned with artistic achievement and either failed to see or more likely consciously rejected opportunities that might have brought him wider acclaim and possibly substantial income. He died a poor man, in artistic obscurity, and was laid to rest in the town cemetery, his grave marked only by a small stone inscribed with just his name and the dates 1841 and 1918.

This small book is filled with many images that are representative of Miley's most creative work. While Miley garnered the bulk of his income from the prosaic task of making thousands of portraits of W&L and VMI students, he considered himself a photographic artist, and that vision is reflected in the images reproduced here. Miley seemed to be everywhere in Lexington and Rockbridge County, taking photographs at will of people, situations, and scenes that interested him. Many of his photographs have the appearance of having been made for his enjoyment alone, and any other purpose for most of his artistic work is unknown. Miley was as spontaneous in his work as the equipment and technology of the day would allow, leaving his studio on the spur of the moment if he felt a particular sky, light, or cloud formation might evolve into a photographic opportunity. In one famous photograph of Robert E. Lee's funeral procession on Main Street in Lexington, he shot the scene by awkwardly positioning his camera outside the open window of his second-floor studio.

His most distinguished and sensitive works are his landscapes, stunning and dramatic, which show his fondness for Rockbridge County landmarks such as the Maury River, House Mountain, and Natural Bridge, and his environmental portraits. An environmental portrait is a portrait executed in the subject's environment, such as a home or workplace, and typically illuminates the subject's life and surroundings. By photographing a person in his or her natural surroundings, it is thought that the photographer will be better able to illuminate their character, and therefore portray the essence of personality instead of focusing on a mere likeness of their physical features. By photographing a person in natural surroundings, the subject will be more at ease and more conducive to expression, as opposed to being placed in a studio, which can be a rather intimidating and artificial experience. In some of his best environmental portraits included here, it is easy to imagine Miley directing his subjects to do something funny or saying to them, "Do not look at me, look at something else." The results are works of sublime character that show a deep commitment to examining human nature.

The surroundings and background are key elements in Miley's work and are used to convey further information about the people or subjects being photographed. Rather than being superfluous or unintended, the background and surroundings become an integral part of Miley's images. In fact, the details that convey the message from the surroundings, whether they are furniture or wall hangings in his studio or buildings, streets, sky, clouds, light, people, or even the position of his camera, can often be quite small and yet still significant and revealing. Miley possessed an extraordinary talent and artistic vision, and his legacy is that he has left us with a nearly unparalleled record of both everyday life and the physical beauty of Rockbridge County, which will continue to anchor its residents in the past as they evolve through the present into the future.

One

Michael Miley, Photographer

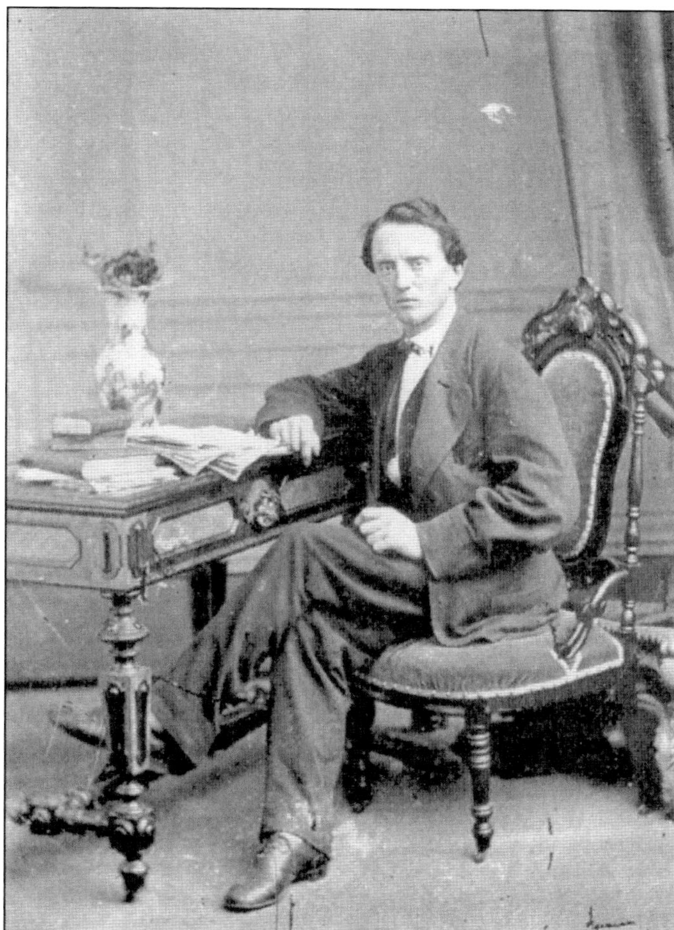

When Michael Miley returned to Rockbridge County sometime after the end of the Civil War in 1865, he had apparently made the decision to become a photographer. No information exists as to how he arrived at this decision, but he soon went to Staunton, where he found work with the photographer John Burdette. There is some speculation that he was influenced by the photography of Mathew Brady, but neither Miley nor his son commented on how Michael Miley decided on photography as a career. In this earliest known photograph of Miley, he is posed in typical Victorian fashion in Burdette's studio. John Burdette took the photograph of the 25-year-old Miley.

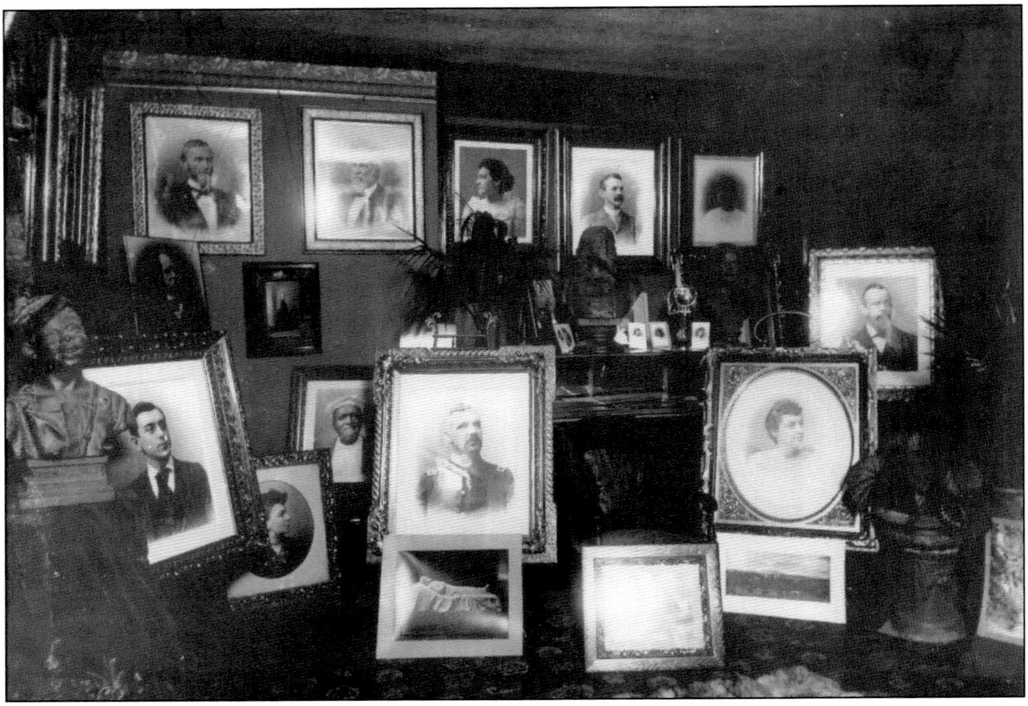

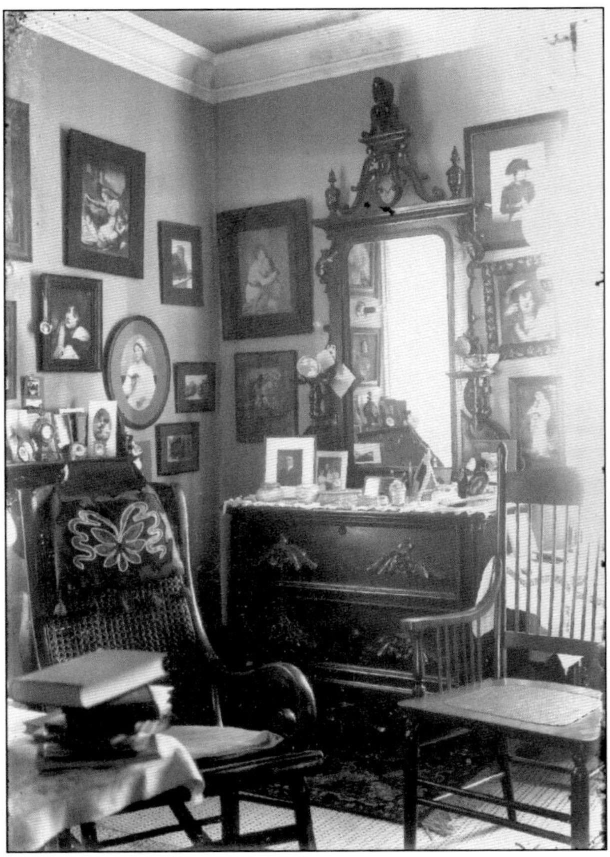

While a completely accurate identification of the subjects of these two photographs is impossible to make, it is probable that they were taken either in Miley's home or studio. It is certain that Miley made the images, though no date was provided. The style is high Victorian, and the furniture in one of the photographs seems to be the same as pieces that appear in other Miley studio photographs. The artwork displayed on the walls is typical of the late 19th century, showing Romantic scenes and images, European in feel and subject matter. It would be reasonable to assume that the photograph above could have been used by Miley for advertising purposes, either in print or as a display of his services and style, since many of the photographs presented are examples of Miley's portraiture and show individuals from various walks of life from Lexington.

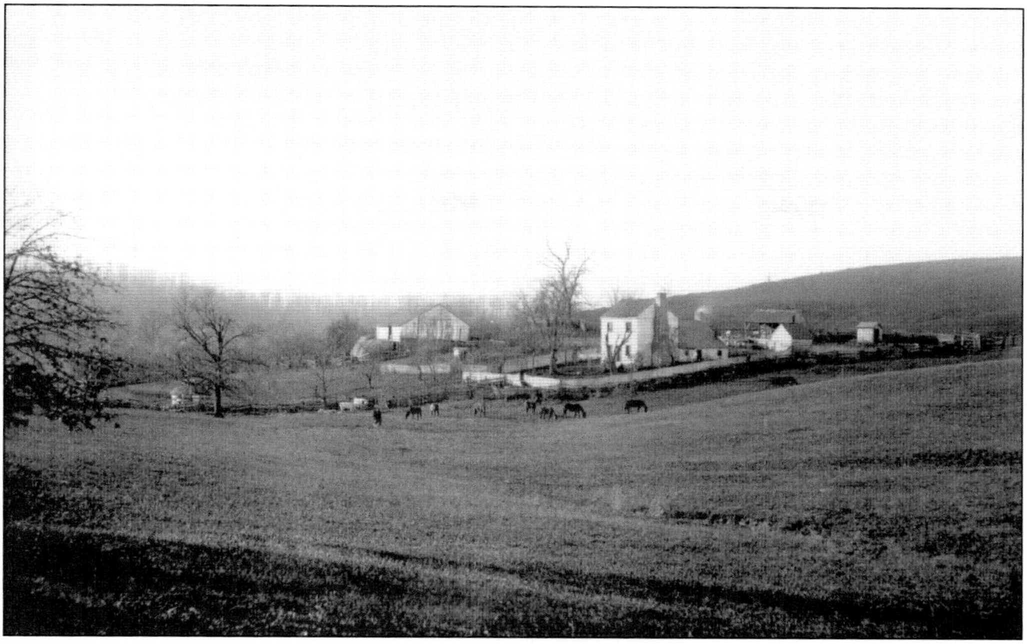

The Miley homestead is above. It was to this farm that Miley's family moved while he was still a very young boy, probably in the 1840s. The homestead was along the route used for centuries by buffalo, Native Americans, and then backcountry settlers to travel south and west. The farm was located about three miles from the village of Fairfield along the Brownsburg road and is typical of the semi-self-sufficient farmsteads that were common in Virginia at this time.

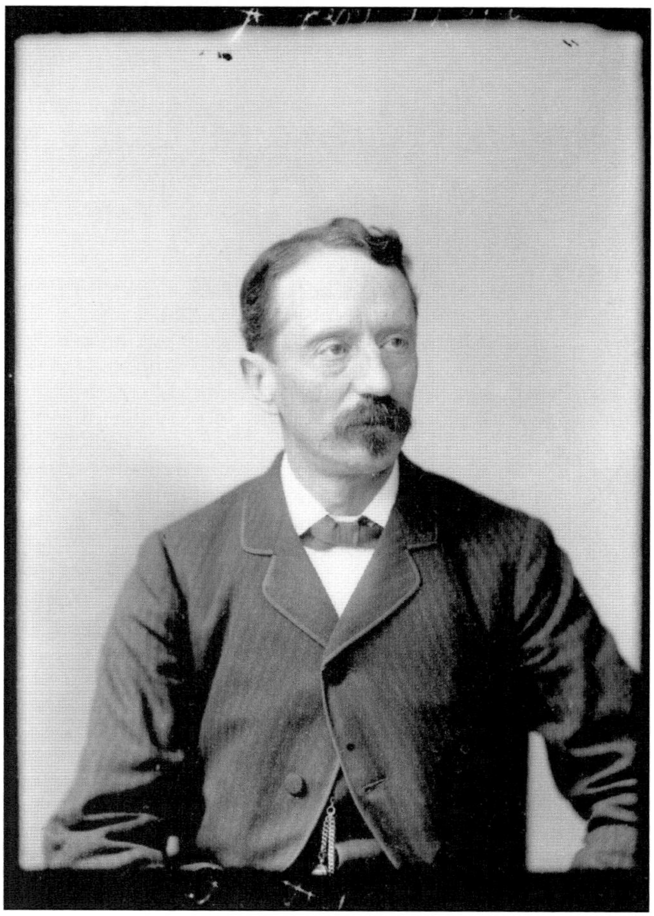

This formal portrait of Michael Miley was most certainly taken by his son Henry about 1910. Miley was married to Martha Mackey of Rockbridge County, and they had three sons. Henry, their second son, graduated from Washington and Lee in 1894 and joined his father in business. After this date, Miley's photographic imprint read, "M. Miley and Son, Carbon Studio, Lexington, Va."

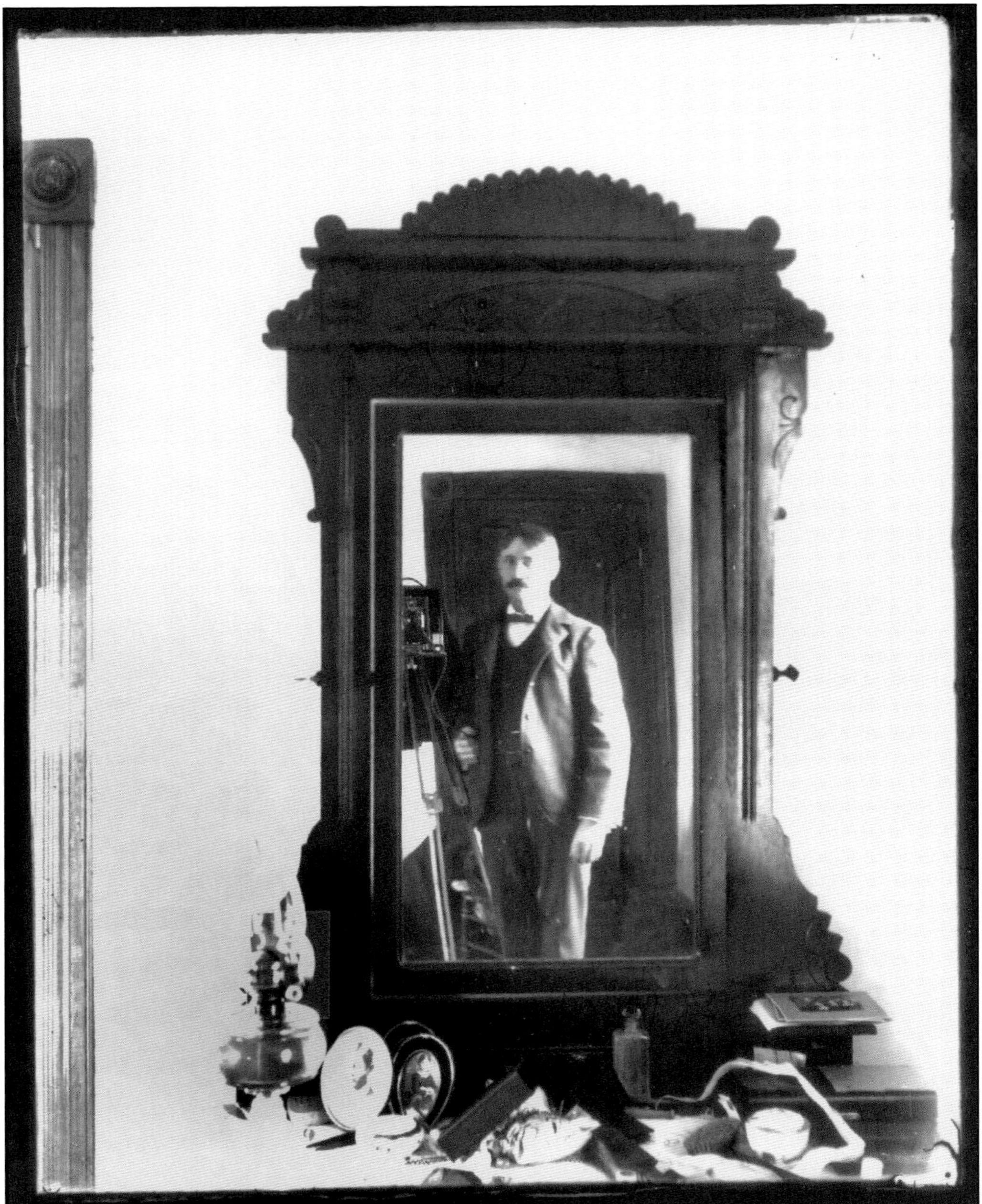

Nothing is known about this extremely interesting self-portrait other than that Michael Miley took it. His clothing and appearance and the camera he is using suggest that it might have been taken around 1880. His hairstyle and general appearance is younger than in the portrait from 1910 on the previous page. The general appearance of the bureau's top in the photograph's foreground suggests that either the photograph was taken on the spur of the moment or that a very casual look was desired. It gives an appearance of disarray, or at least of daily living. It is a small peek, perhaps, into Miley's private world.

Two

Environmental Portraits

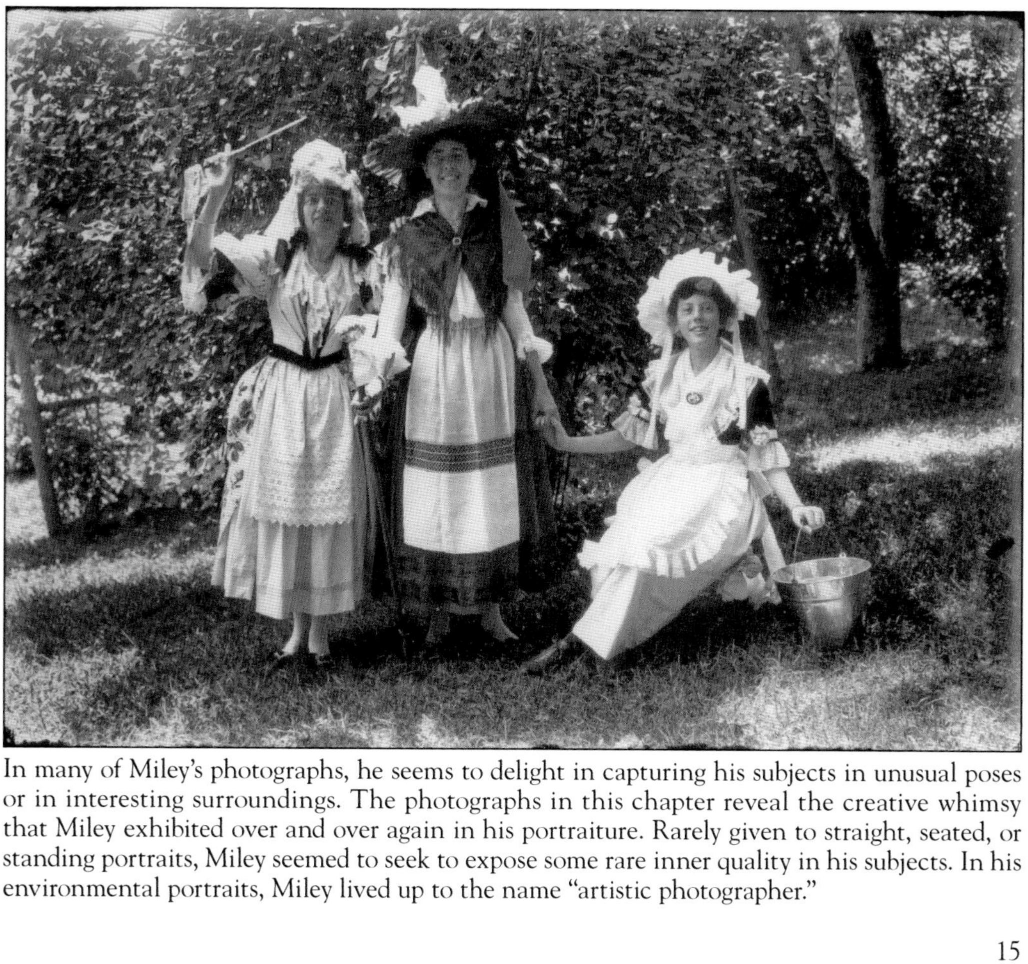

In many of Miley's photographs, he seems to delight in capturing his subjects in unusual poses or in interesting surroundings. The photographs in this chapter reveal the creative whimsy that Miley exhibited over and over again in his portraiture. Rarely given to straight, seated, or standing portraits, Miley seemed to seek to expose some rare inner quality in his subjects. In his environmental portraits, Miley lived up to the name "artistic photographer."

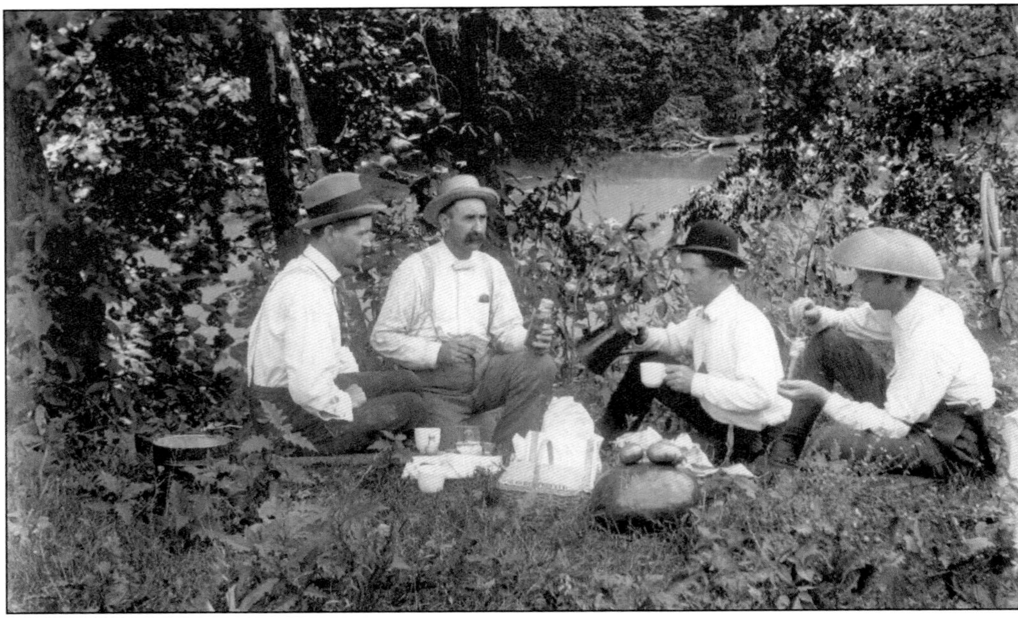

These two photographs, upon first looking at them, appear to be rather plain scenes of two groups of men enjoying a fine picnic. They are both taken beside the Maury River in familiar-looking locales. The photograph below shows the canal dam in the background, possibly at the forks of the South and Maury Rivers. The photograph above could have been taken at any spot along the current Chessie Trail. Both photographs were taken around 1900. A close examination of the photographs reveals some interesting details. The hats are intriguing, particularly the one that could very well be a bowl simply turned upside down on the gentleman's head (above, far right). This man is spearing olives from a jar while two tomatoes sit atop a watermelon. In both photographs, the men have a well-laid table complete with picnic baskets, saltshakers, and cushions to sit upon. Two fine picnics, indeed. The man in the bowl-shaped hat is F. Howard Campbell.

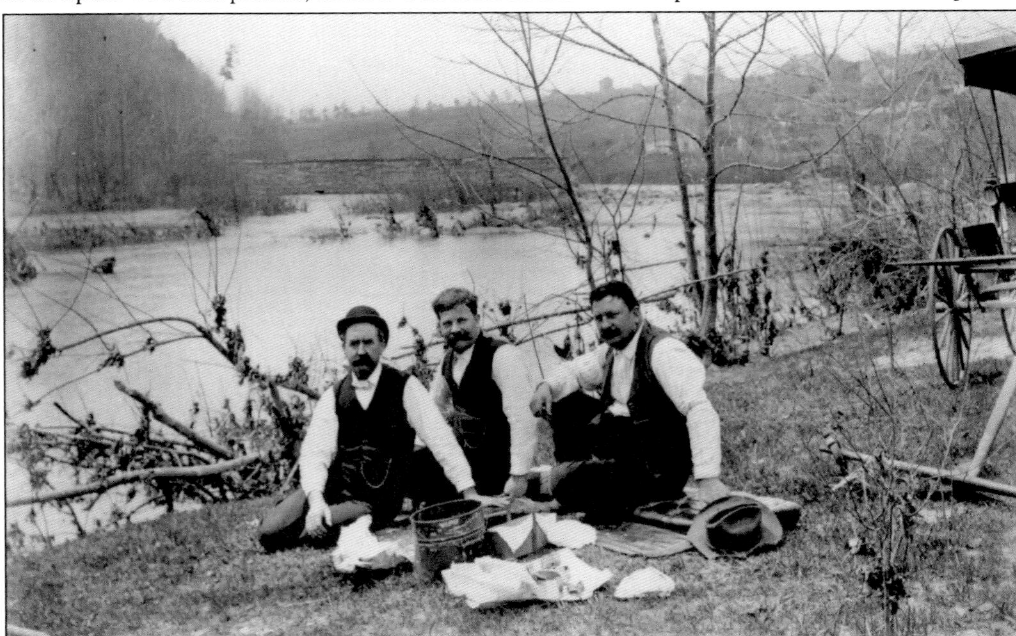

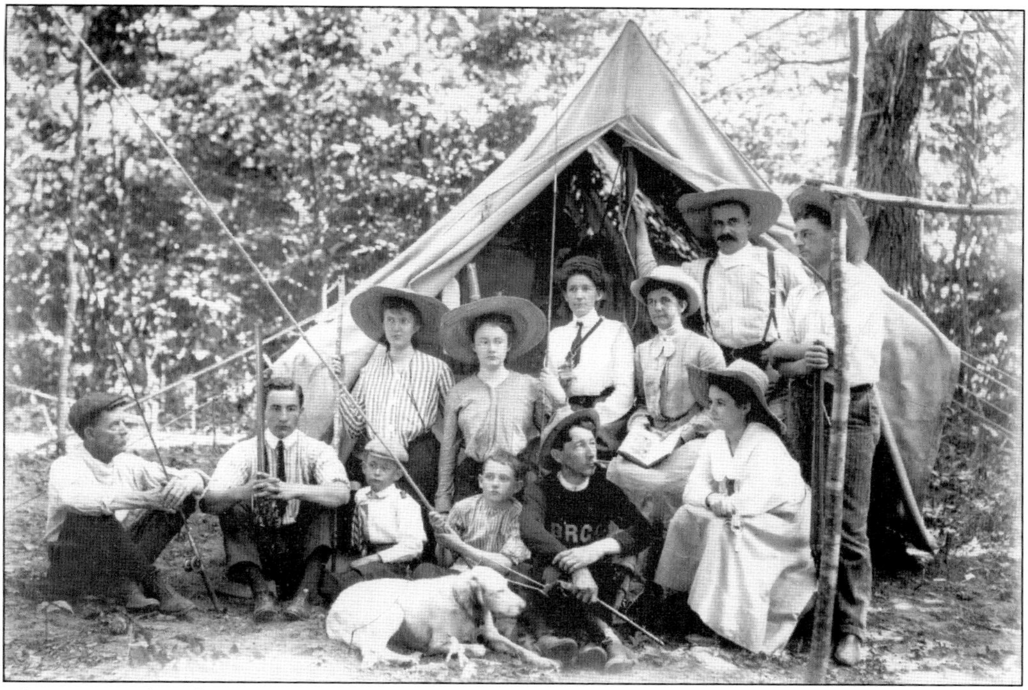

These two Miley photographs have a decidedly Western look to them; they were taken somewhere in Rockbridge County to document a large camping event. The subjects of the photographs are unidentified, but considering the clothing, staff, and accouterments surrounding them, it is safe to say that they represented some of the wealthier citizens of the community. It could be suggested that at least some of the people are in costume, although this could have simply been fashionable camping attire of the day.

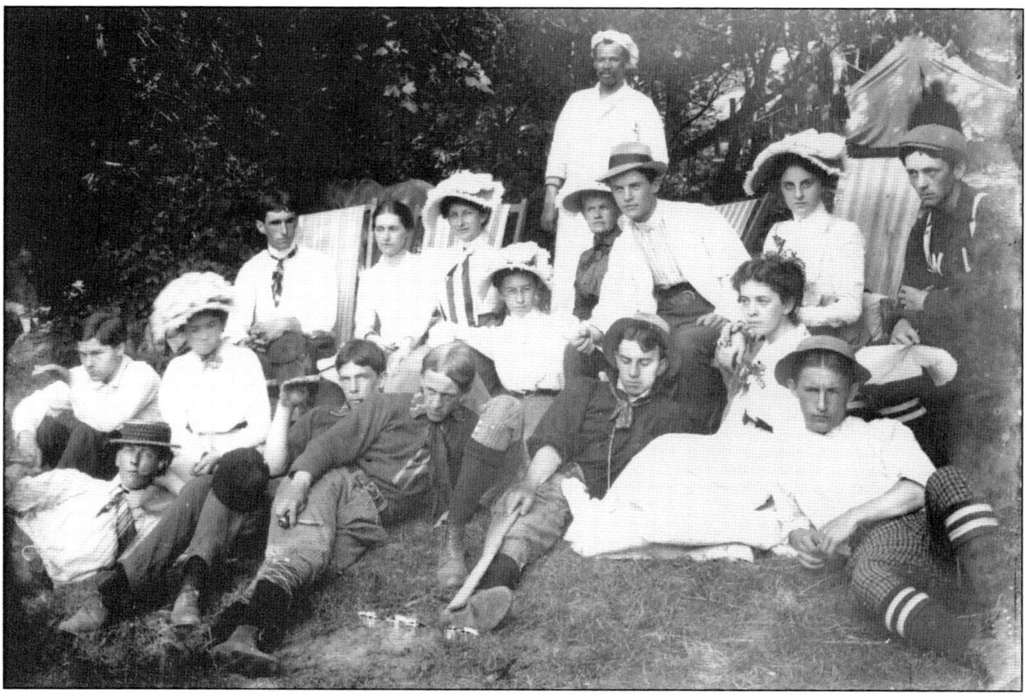

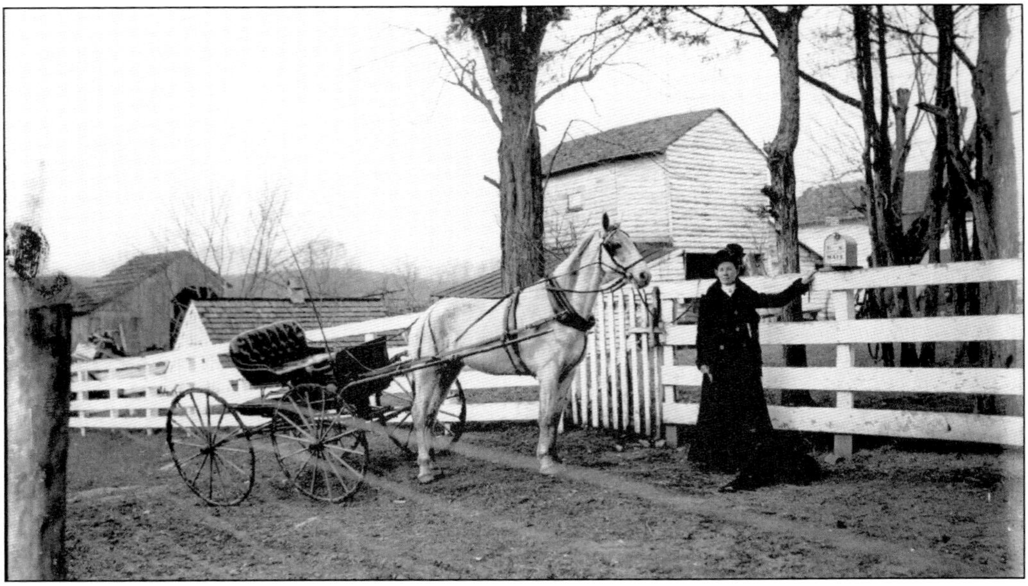

These two additional photographs illustrate Miley's ability to capture a moment in time in challenging circumstances. While neither photograph is identified and nothing is known about why he took them, the results are nevertheless engaging. Both photographs reveal the importance of surroundings as integral parts of photographs taken outside. Rather than being negligible aspects of the scene, where these people are gives structure and meaning to it. The photograph above shows a young woman standing beside her mailbox, which has a small American flag sticking up and a lock on it. Below, a group of men are posed with a dog on an outcropping of rock. Miley is below them, and four of the five are looking down at his camera. One of the men has his eyes rolled to his left, looking up and away.

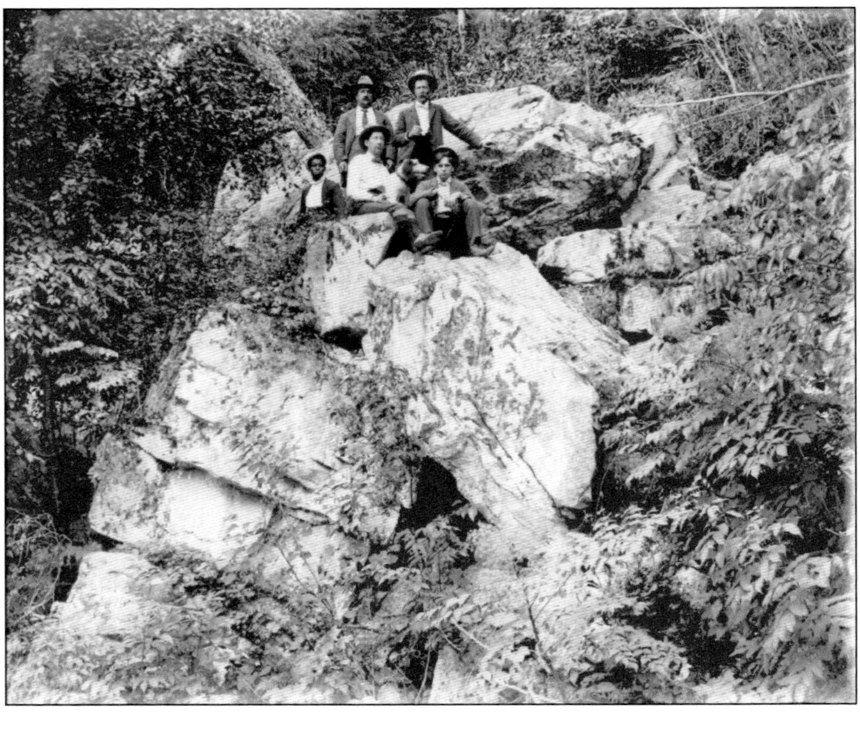

Miley's photographs of this young girl are so much more engaging to the eye and interesting to think about than if they had been posed in a studio. He brought her out on the porch with a lovely cane-bottom chair for a prop. She looks exquisite with her hat, coat, and lace-up boots. She is unidentified, as is the occasion, though it is clear that she is dressed in her finest. Though it is hard to see, she is wearing at least four rings on her fingers. It is reasonable to assume that due to the length of time required to make exposures at this time, many mistakes were made and photographs had to be retaken. Given Miley's wit, one wonders if the photograph below of the girl rolling her eyes was a mistake or if perhaps Miley intentionally captured her in a typical gesture.

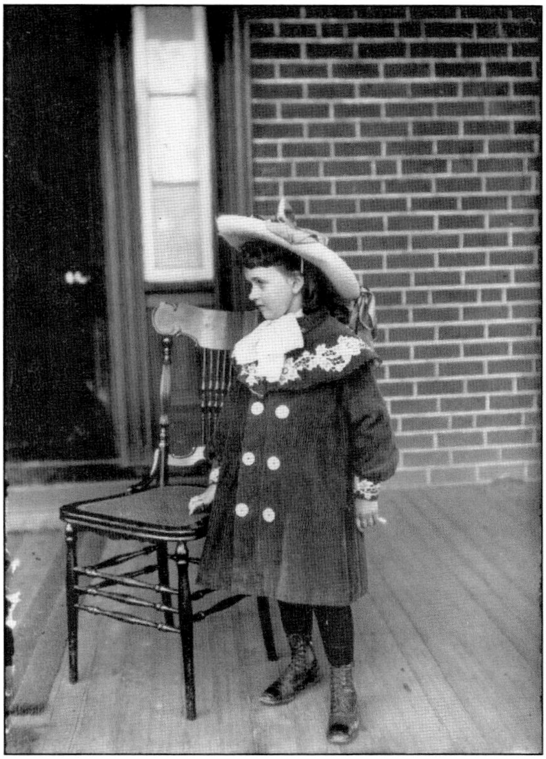

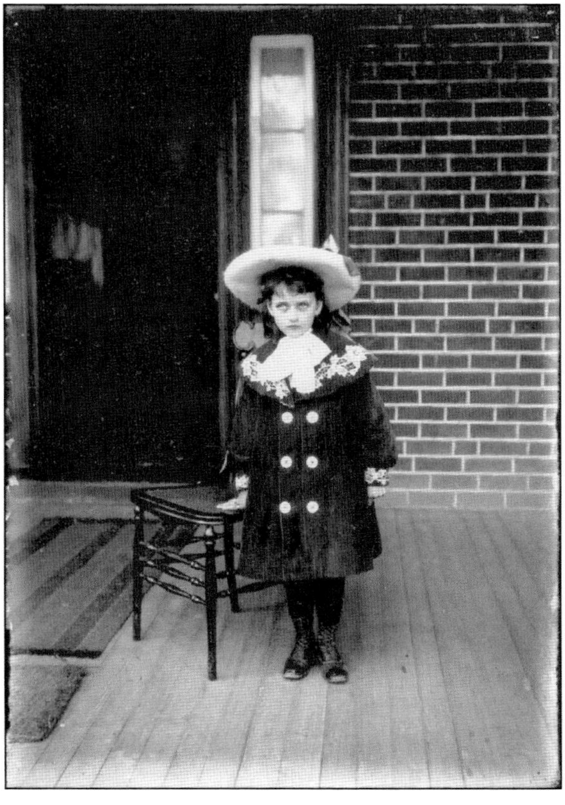

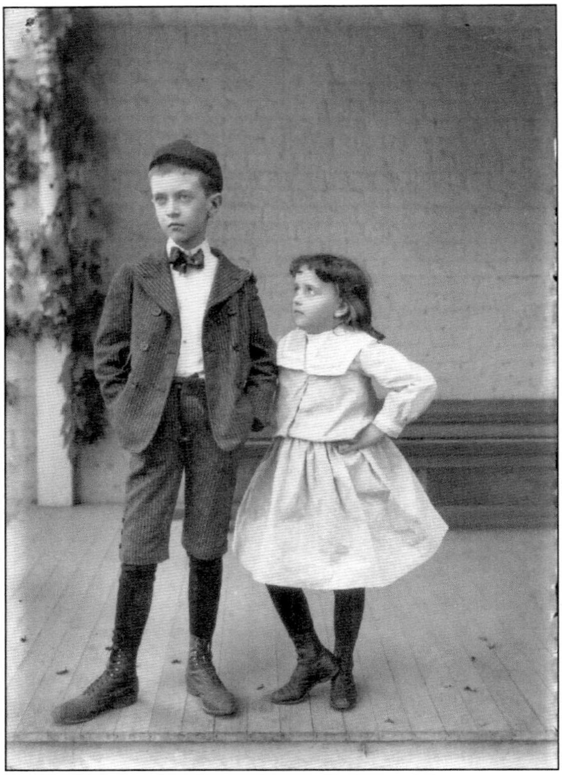

Here again are two views of the same pair of children. The little girl is certainly Beatrice Miley, and the boy appears to be one of Miley's sons, although this is not certain. The two views also reflect what could either be a mistake and reshoot or two photographs reflecting the different moods of the children. Below, the children are posed and looking at the camera, while Miley perhaps asked them to look away for the photograph at left. The boy looks distracted and the girl just a little irritated. The dog below may have been Miley's as well, as it appears in a number of his images.

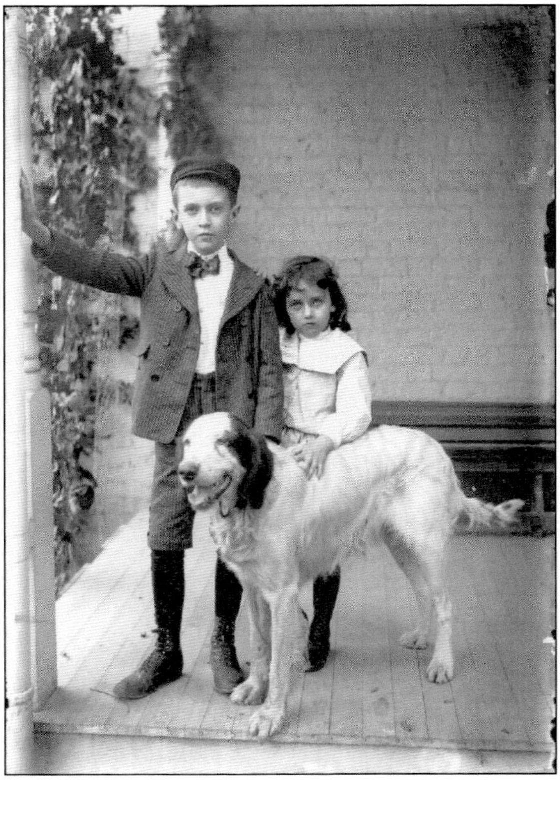

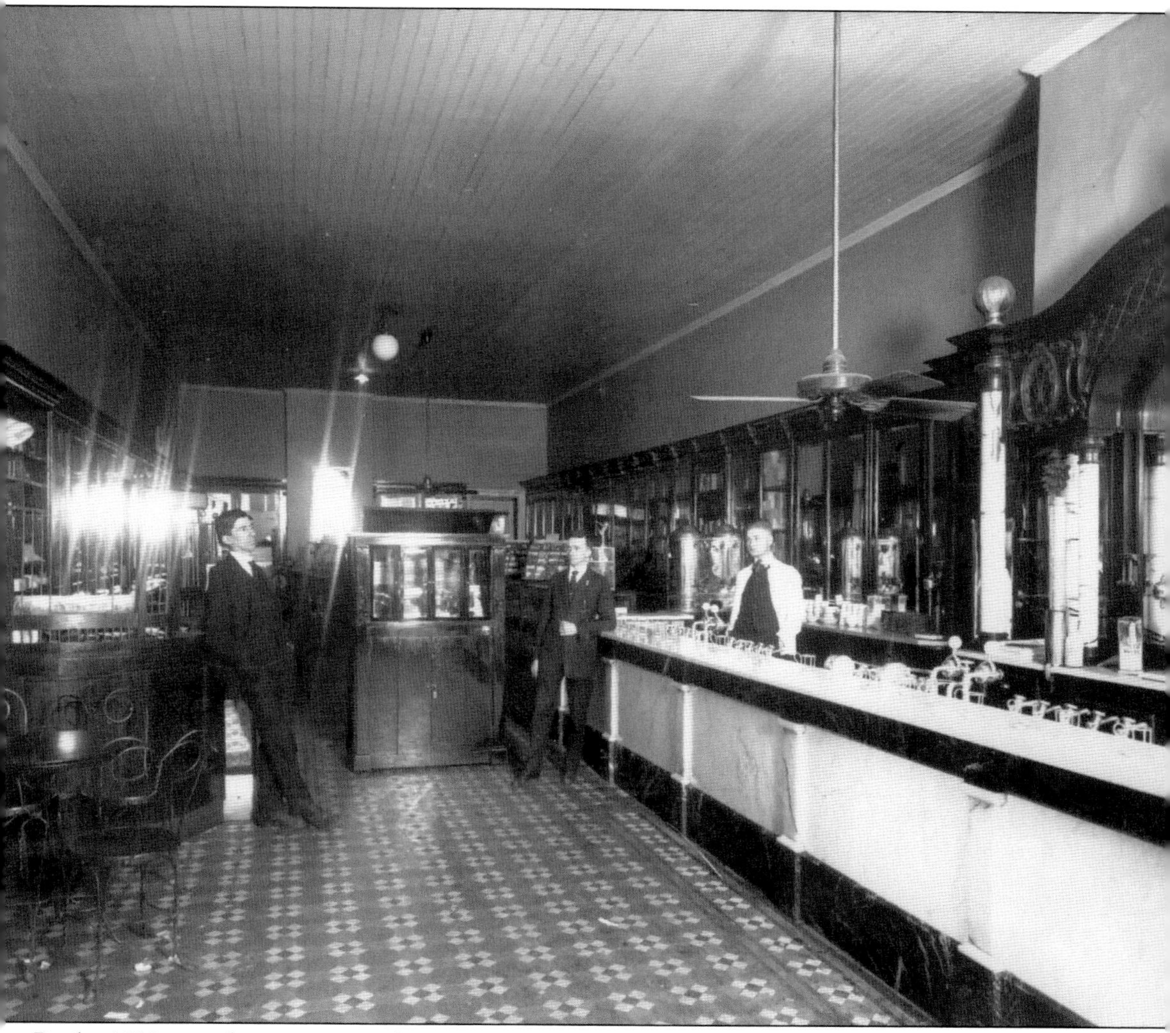

By the 1890s, nearly every town of any size in America had a store like this one. Having evolved from the old country crossroads stores, the new general merchandise stores of the era served many purposes, not the least of which was to provide a relaxing and cordial atmosphere in which to enjoy a soda from the newly installed fountain. Fizzy drinks became the rage during this period of time, and the most popular soda fountain in Lexington was located in the McCrum Building on Main Street. Soda fountains were proper places for young ladies to go to cap off an afternoon stroll, and they were always popular meeting places. The interior of McCrum's survived largely intact until the 1960s. In this photograph from about 1890, the owner and two employees are pictured in a scene that would have greeted thousands over the decades. Cleveland Davis, the owner of the store, is the man leaning against the wall on the left.

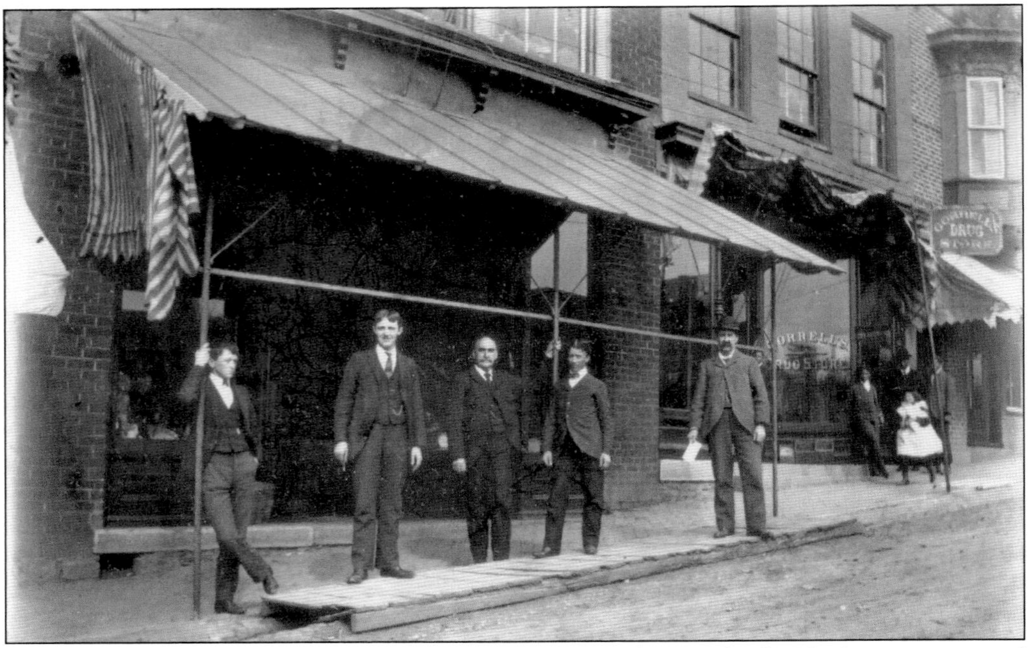

These two similar photographs suggest the spontaneity that Michael Miley's environmental portraiture contains. In an era when taking photographs of any kind involved setting up almost as much equipment as it takes today to make a movie, Miley somehow created the impression in many of his photographs that he was just passing by and asked interesting looking people to pose for him. Robert S. Anderson, in the center of the above photograph, poses in front of his china store. Everyone is exceptionally well dressed, but a quick look around at the surroundings reveals a shabbiness and run-down appearance that is ubiquitous in outdoor photographs of this era. Looking carefully at people's clothing and at the streets and buildings exposes the difficulty of life and the mess and dirt that was a part of daily life at this time, around 1890.

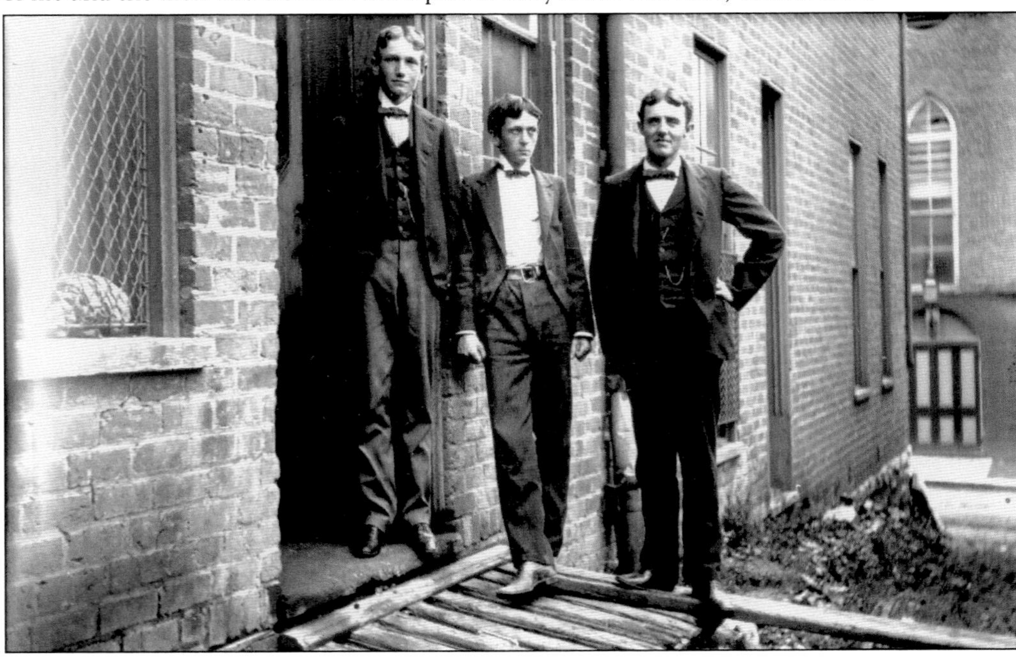

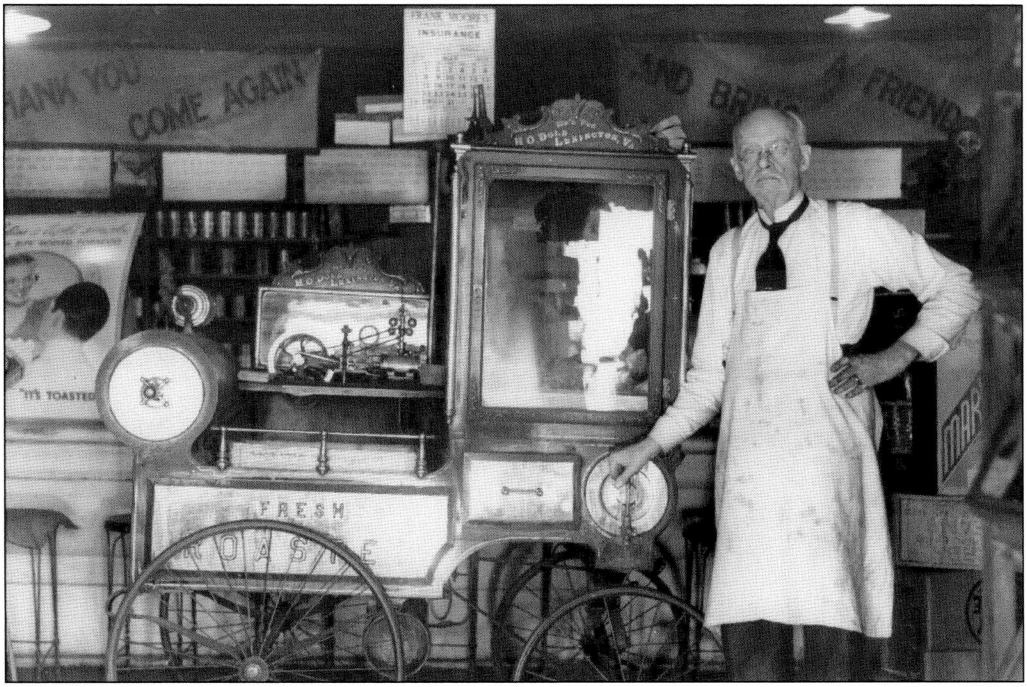

These two photographs, taken by Henry Miley, reflect the style and conceptual philosophy taught to Henry by his father. In photograph above, a Lexington landmark, H.O. Dold, stands beside his peanut roaster in his Main Street store. The calendar on the wall behind him shows that it is May 1939. Both machines read "Mfd for H.O. Dold, Lexington, Va." The building he owned was in his family for 114 years. The photograph below shows the interior of Pettigrew's general merchandise store and Mr. and Mrs. Joseph Pettigrew. Their establishment graced a Washington Street location for many years as well, and they were well established when Henry Miley immortalized them in their natural environment around 1920.

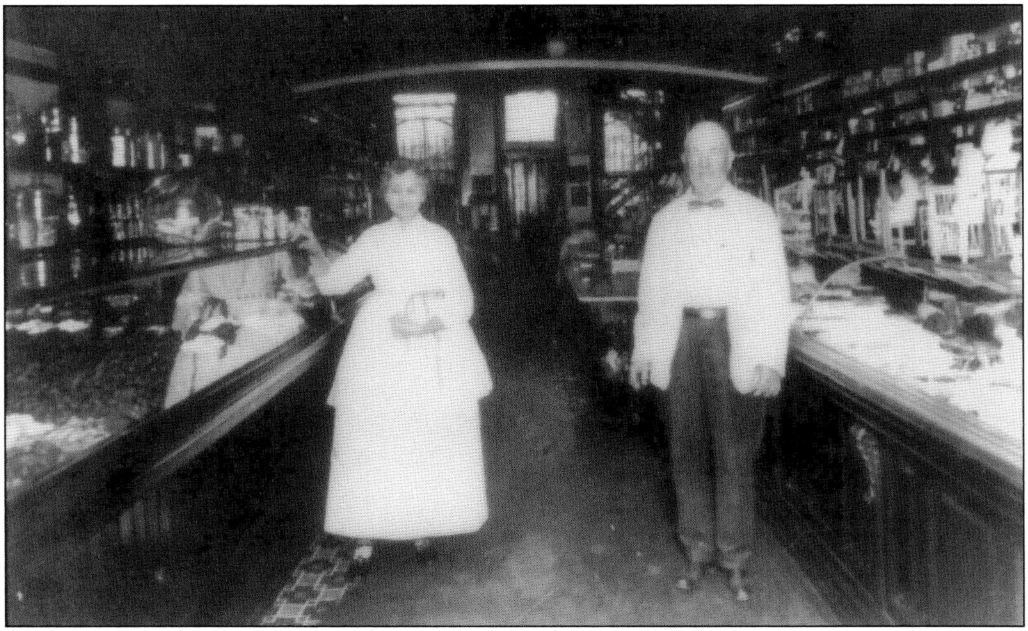

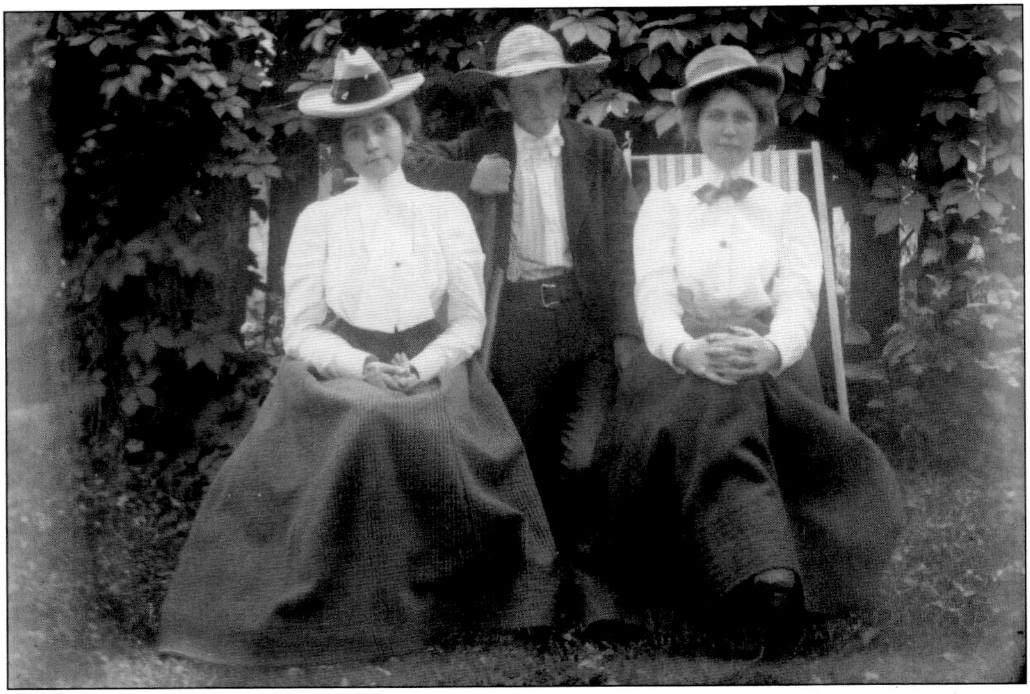

We are used to seeing people in vintage and historical photographs wearing hats, as people wore hats back then, but the sheer variety and character of the hats on Michael Miley's subjects is remarkable, not to mention so much fun. Miley had to have thought of these accessories as vital to imparting to the viewer or the subjects themselves a sense of frivolity and a generous openness about what photographs could be used to communicate. The friends, family, and locals who posed for him must have shared in his sense of artistic license. They all appear willing participants and seem to be thoroughly enjoying themselves in the process. His photographs, like these and others in this book, belie the image of dour and overly serious people usually associated with Victorian-era studio photography. In the above image, Mary Campbell Moore is on the left.

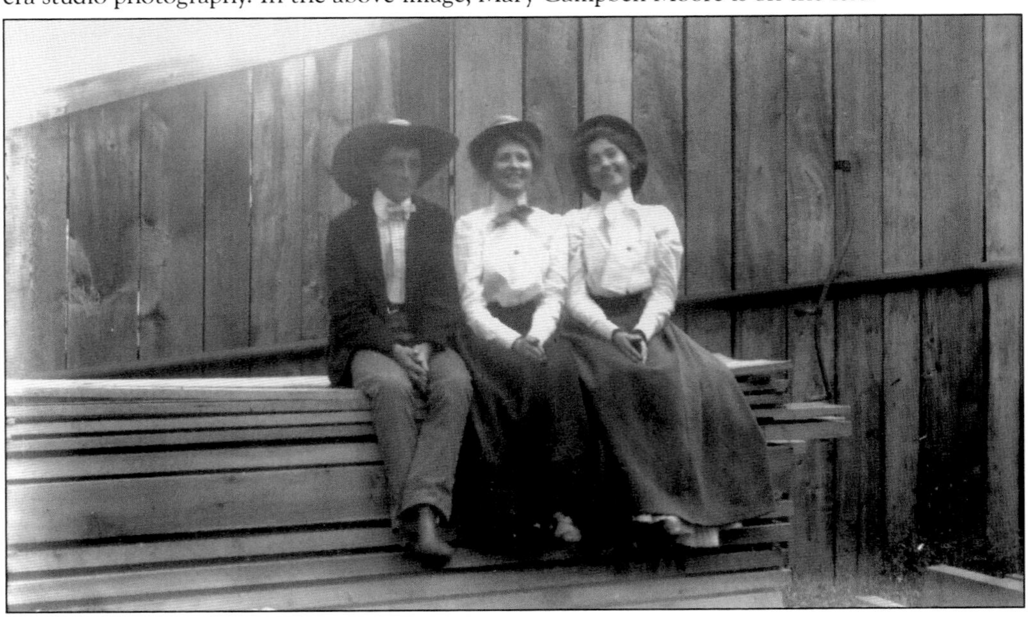

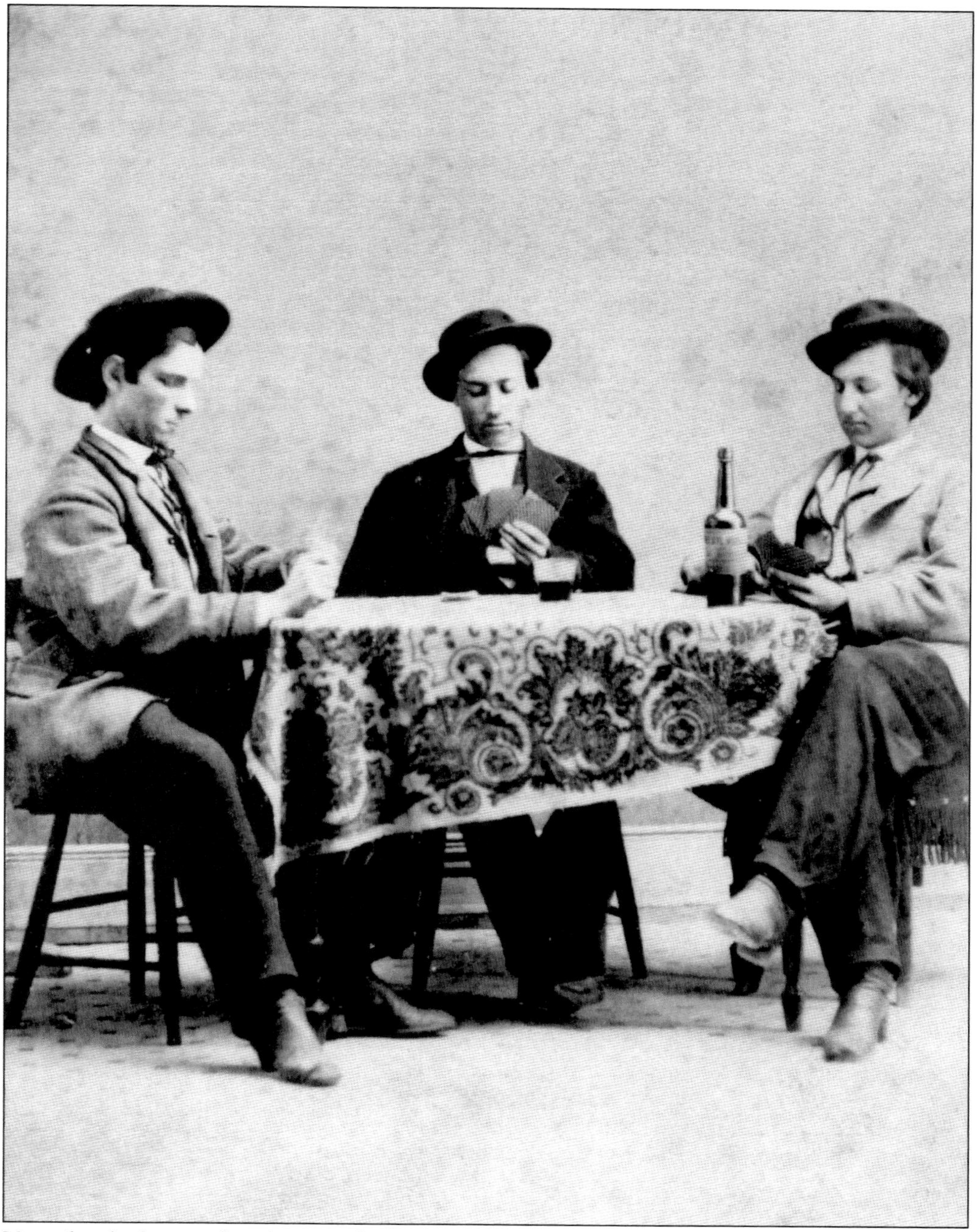

Upon first looking at this photograph, it might not occur to the viewer that the subjects are college students, except perhaps for the bottle of rye whiskey sitting on the table. Looking more like Western heroes or Eastern dandies, their clothes were typical attire for the stylish Washington College student in 1869, when this photograph was taken. While the individuals in the photograph are identified, the location is not. The sparse surroundings could suggest that it was set up as a studio shot, but then again, college students are not known for their decorating prowess. Unfortunately, as with so many of Miley's photographs, not much is known about this one except that it shows three young college men playing cards, drinking, and enjoying life. From left to right are C.M. Hawkins, T.S. Norfleet, and H. Cromelin. The photograph is attributed to Boude and Miley.

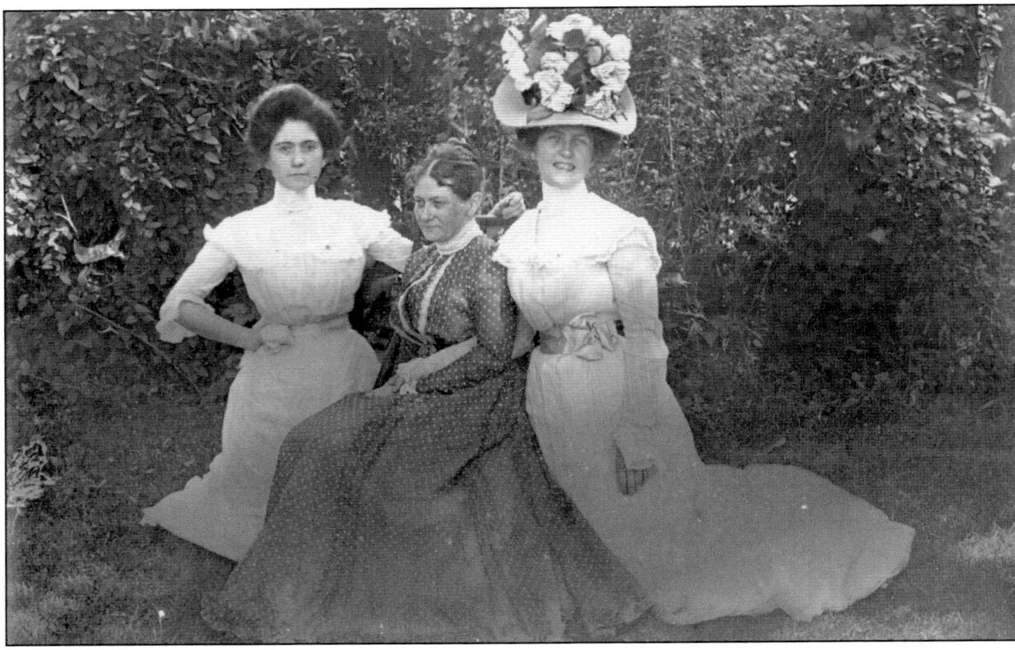

In these two photographs that capture the feminine mystery that Miley clearly admired, he again juxtaposes his subjects and directs their view in unusual ways. In both photographs, two of the three subjects look directly at the camera and seem fully engaged in what is happening. The third individual in each is looking away from the camera, obviously distracted. In the photograph above, Mrs. L.W. Moore, Mary's mother, is in the center. Mary Campbell Moore, on the left, reflects a good example of the Gibson Girl effect, that stylized and iconic ideal of feminine beauty created by the artist Charles Dana Gibson and popularized in advertising sketches and artworks between 1890 and 1900. Below, the coquettishness displayed by Ms. Moore suggests a degree of comfort in front of the camera rarely seen in this era.

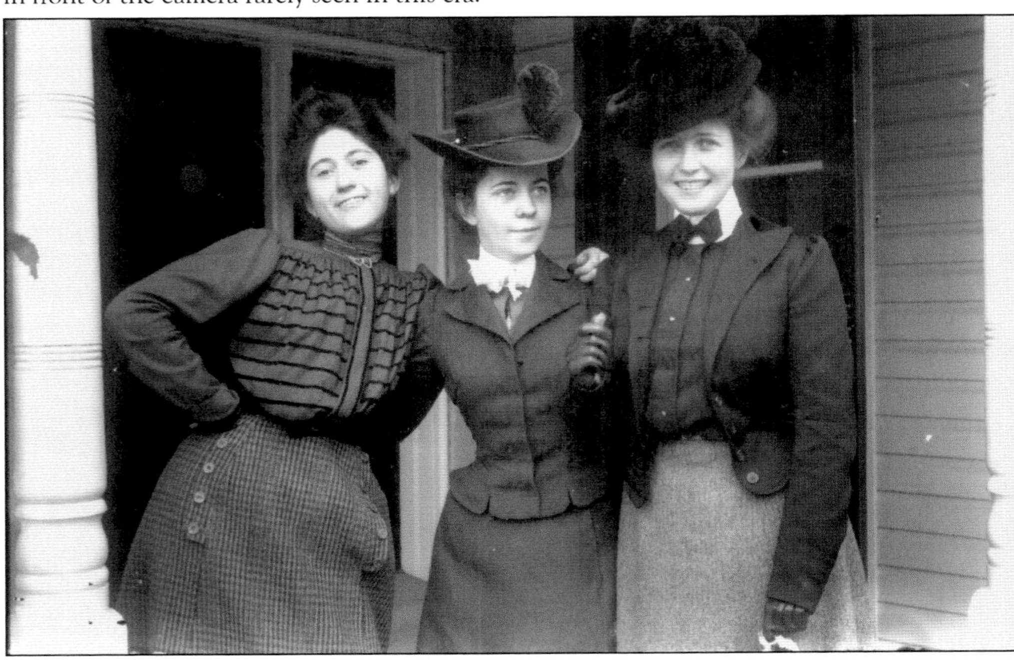

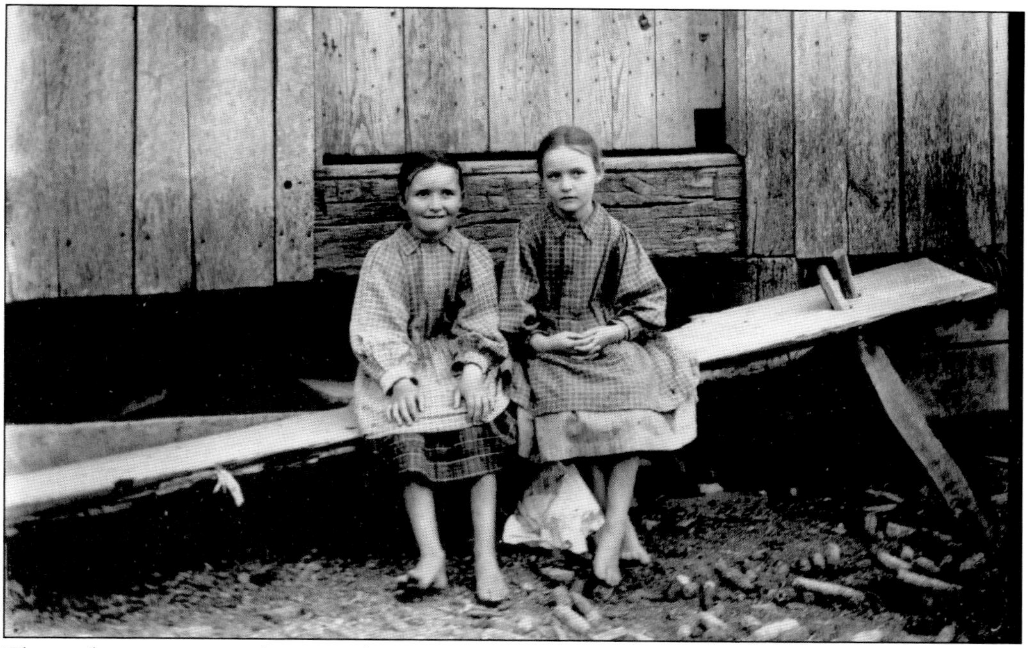

The striking contrasts that exist between every aspect of these two photographs could not be more pronounced. The two farm girls above appear timid, shy, even frightened, as they sit on a bench in front of a corncrib, barefoot and dirty. The photograph below suggests a life of softness and security; the girls are scrubbed, their dresses are immaculate, and their hair is curled with lovely bows and ribbons secured. The cause of the blur in the eyes of the blonde girl is unknown, but it was no doubt caused by a slight movement at the time the exposure was made.

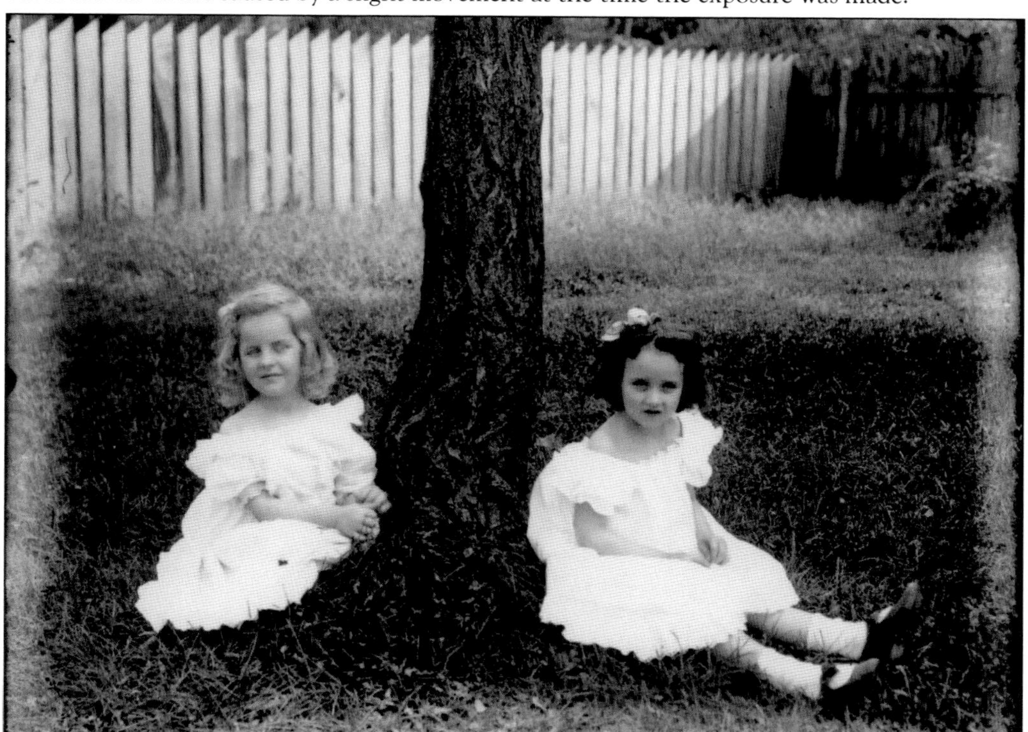

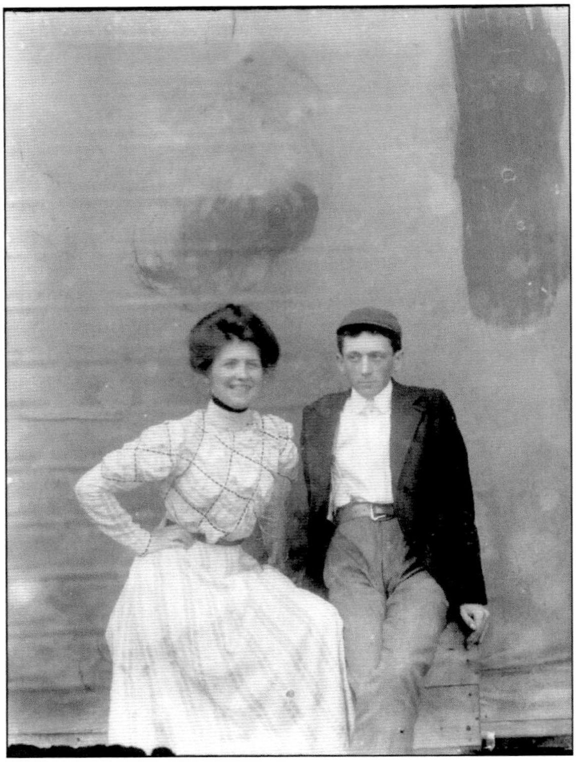

Given the large number of photographs in the Miley collection that exhibit minor or major eccentricities in posing or positioning of subjects, it is not hard to imagine the photographer giving directions to the young couples in these photographs that allowed them the freedom to be themselves. Miley's knack was his ability to set up a conventional shot and then add a quirk or twist that made the image so much more appealing and interesting to look at.

In both of these photographs, Miley has his subjects seated in awkward positions. At left, again one of the subjects is looking away from the camera, giving the viewer the distinct impression that something else is going on in the scene besides the photographic session. Below, Miley may have suggested to this couple to perhaps do something different or funny with their legs and feet. They are both sitting in unusual ways and seem completely aware of it. One of Miley's favorite subjects, Mary Campbell Moore, appears here and in several other photographs in this book.

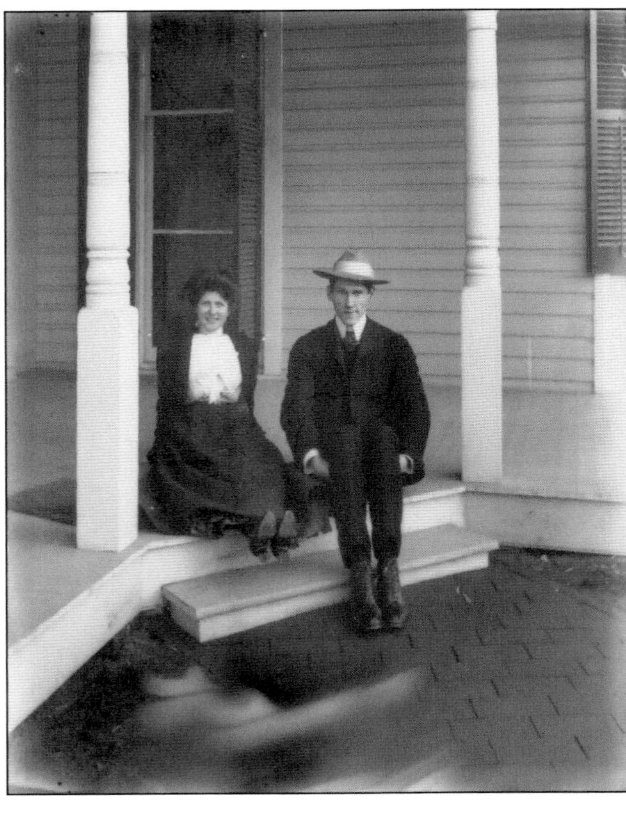

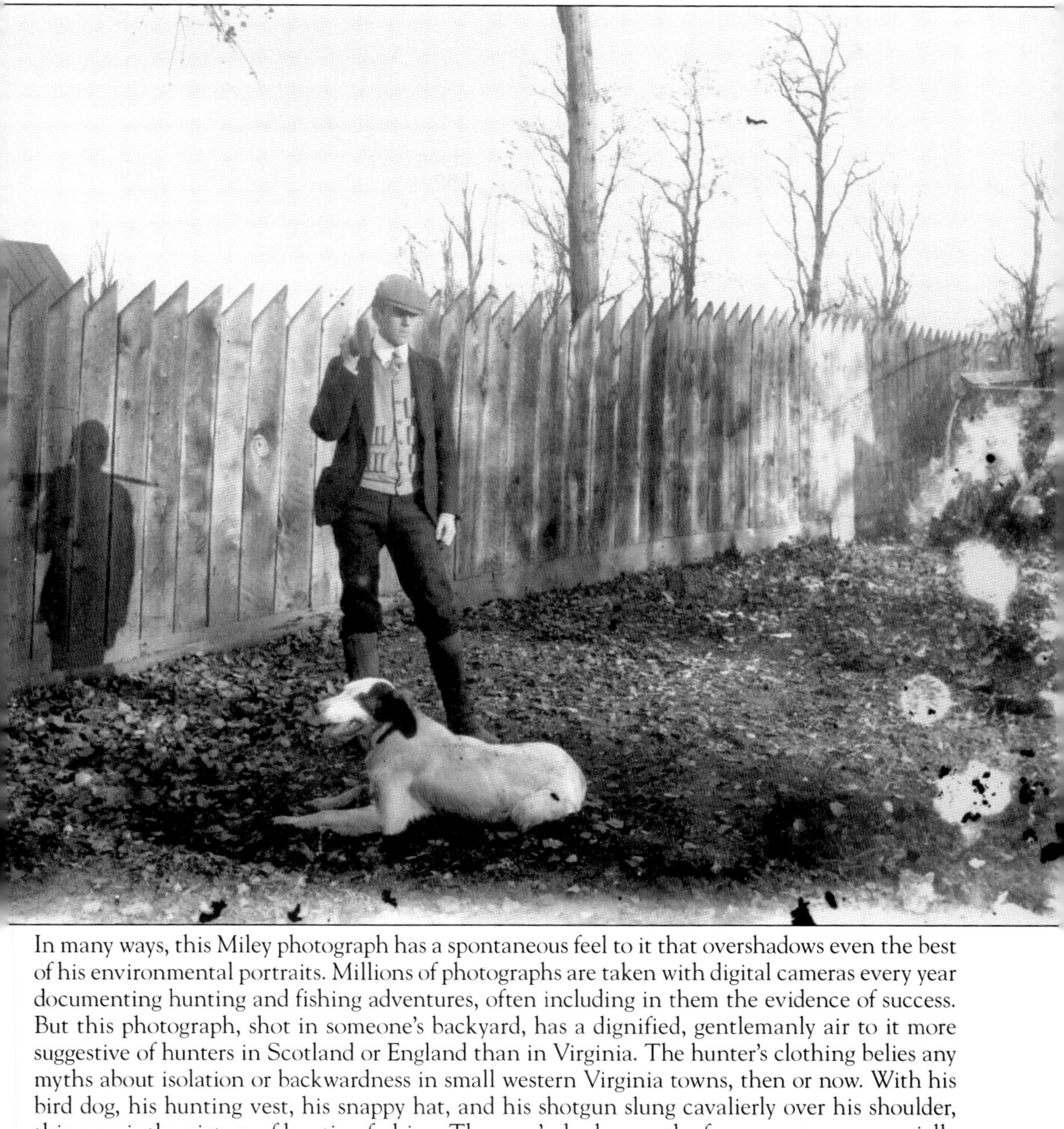

In many ways, this Miley photograph has a spontaneous feel to it that overshadows even the best of his environmental portraits. Millions of photographs are taken with digital cameras every year documenting hunting and fishing adventures, often including in them the evidence of success. But this photograph, shot in someone's backyard, has a dignified, gentlemanly air to it more suggestive of hunters in Scotland or England than in Virginia. The hunter's clothing belies any myths about isolation or backwardness in small western Virginia towns, then or now. With his bird dog, his hunting vest, his snappy hat, and his shotgun slung cavalierly over his shoulder, this man is the picture of hunting fashion. The man's shadow on the fence creates an especially effective and masculine line, as does his obedient companion, who bears a striking resemblance to Miley's own dog, or at least to a dog that appears in many of his photographs.

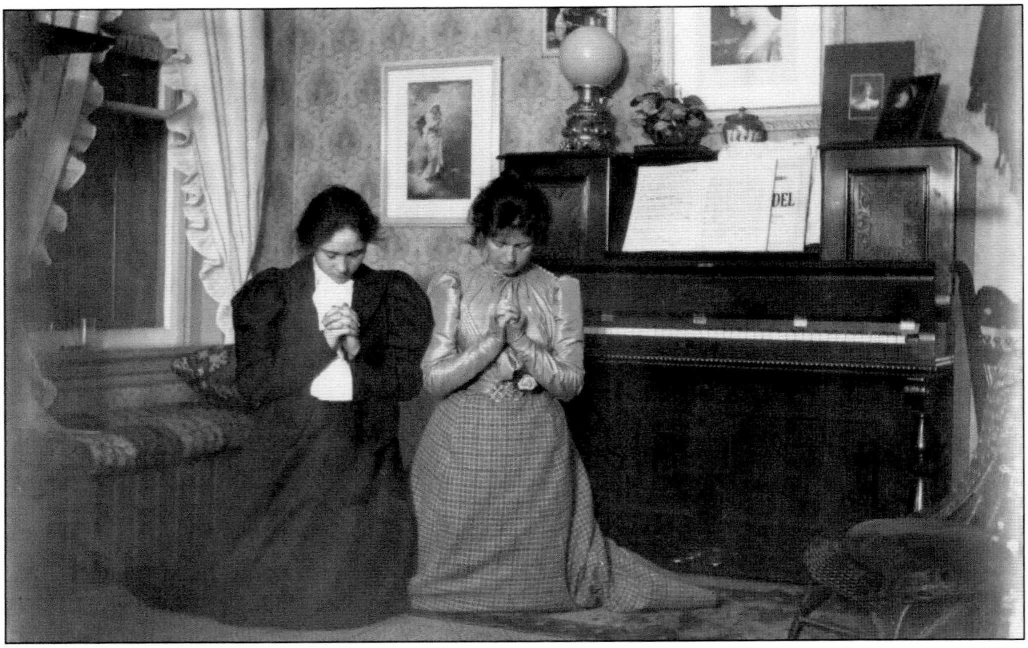

These two photographs reflect attempts by Miley to create scenes of domestic life around 1900. Stylized and with many aspects of the scene carefully manipulated in theatrical fashion, the photographs evoke notions of family and devotion that were particularly important in the face of the dramatic social and cultural changes that swept the United States in the late 19th century. Domestic tranquility and spiritual devotion are the obvious themes of these two settings, created in the style of the popular pictorialist photography of the day. Pioneered by photographer Alfred Stieglitz, pictorialism is often seen as an attempt by photographers to imitate painting. The emphasis was on pure composition, creating a beautiful look to the photographs and emphasizing the gorgeousness of putting things together in the photograph in the most visually pleasing manner.

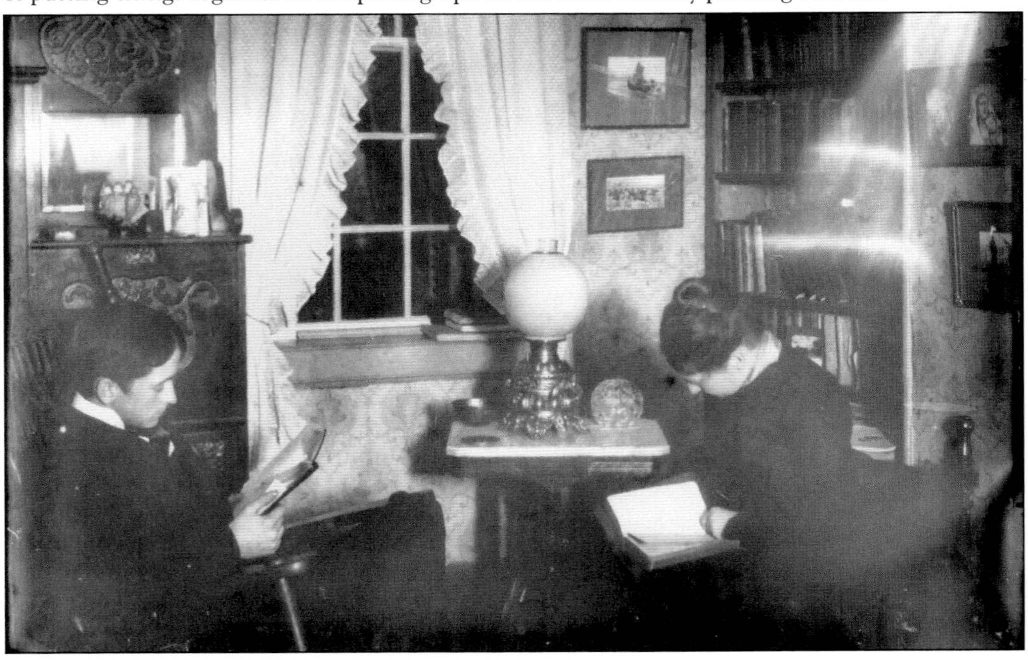

In these two photographs, one could easily ascribe titles to them that would seal an unspoken bond between them and the expressive purposes of painting. They seek to impress the viewer with ideas that flow from the composition and look of the image as much, if not more so, than the particular subject. In these two photographs, the unknown identities of the two women are not nearly as significant as the ideas the scenes are designed to generate. The woman at right is stately, wearing an exquisite gown and seated in a way designed to bring the viewer's eyes to the loveliness of her arm, neck, face, and hair. Below, viewers may be confused as to what the subject is looking at, unable to distinguish between the importance of the china collection and her odd hand position. What could she be gazing out at, or perhaps shielding her eyes from?

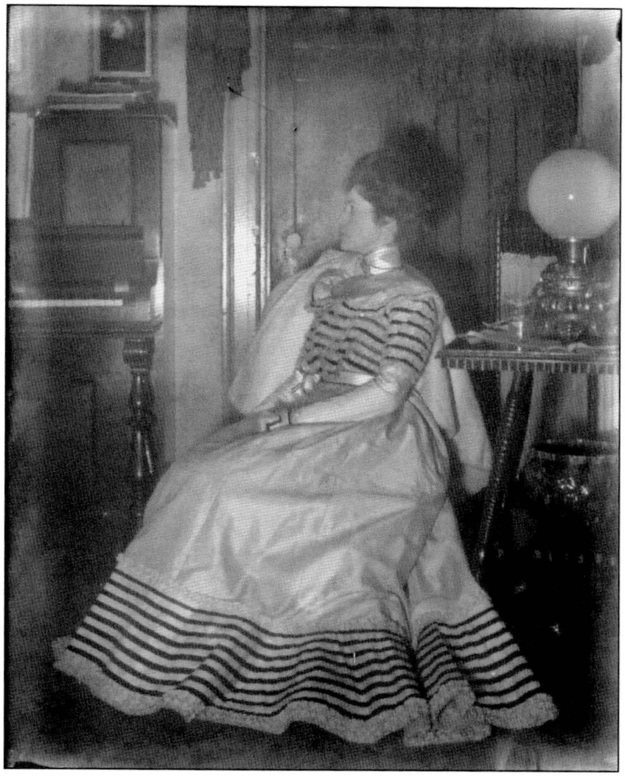

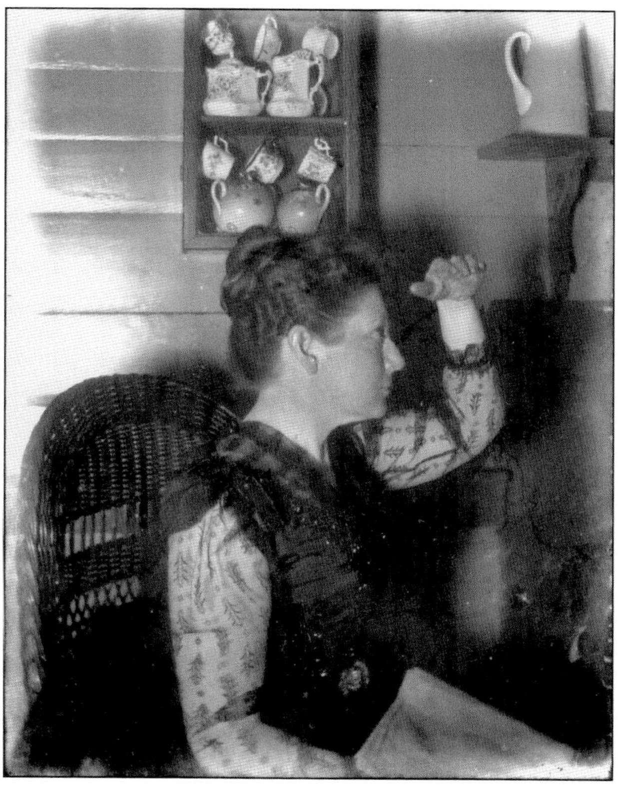

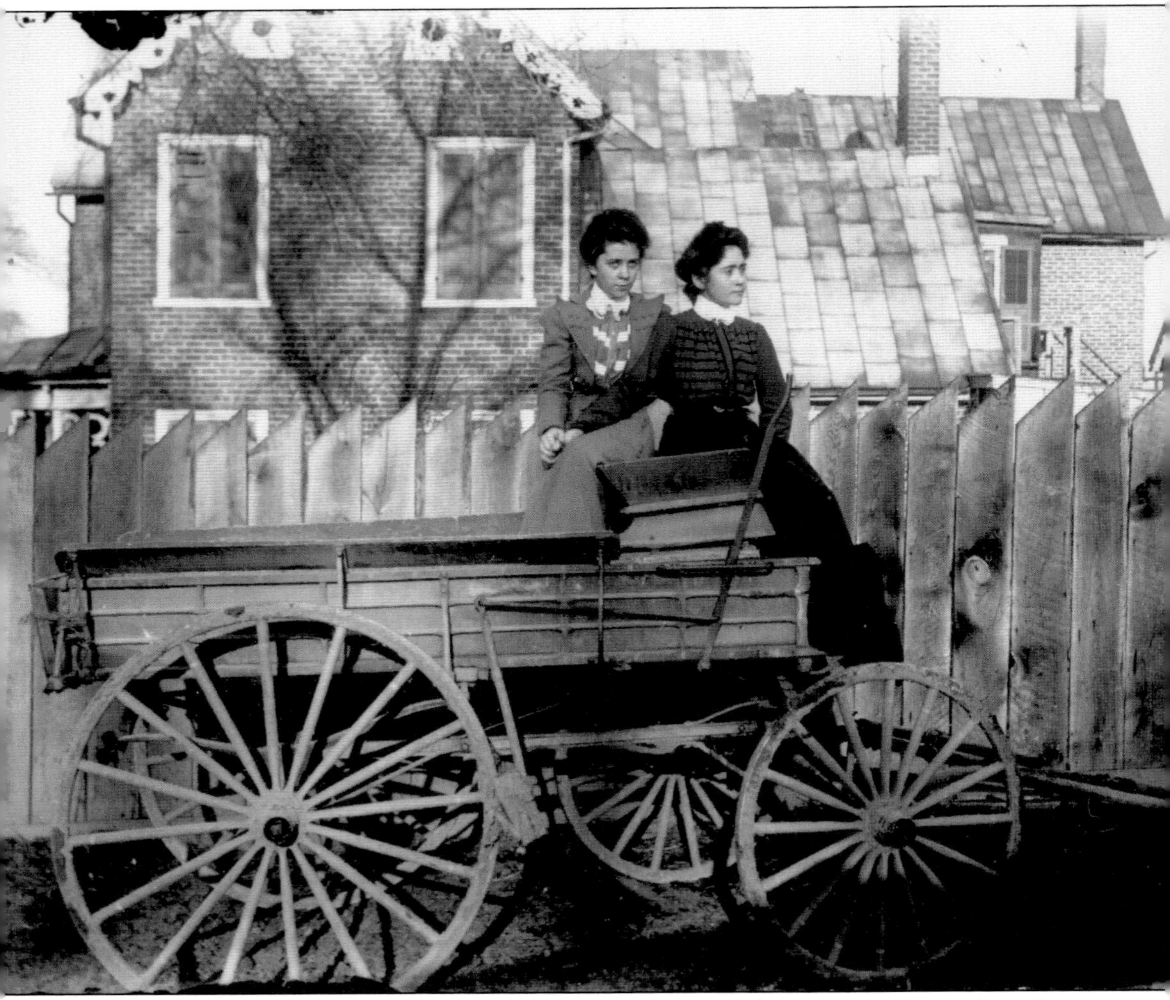

Even in Miley's less obviously pictorialist photographs, some theme or underlying idea inherent in the photograph's composition and style can be discerned. From everything known about Miley, from his various imprints to the way he conducted his business and personal affairs, it is known that he considered himself to be and worked as an artist. Leading from that conclusion, it is fair to assume that very few, if any, details of photographs like this were left to chance and not set up or manipulated by him. This photograph suggests counsel, the giving and receiving of advice, and some distance or perhaps disagreement. The women are touching, consoling, ignorant of the camera's presence, giving the appearance of still photographs shot on a film set. Did Miley create this scene in his imagination and then create it for his camera? It is impossible to know. The feeling of the image is very private.

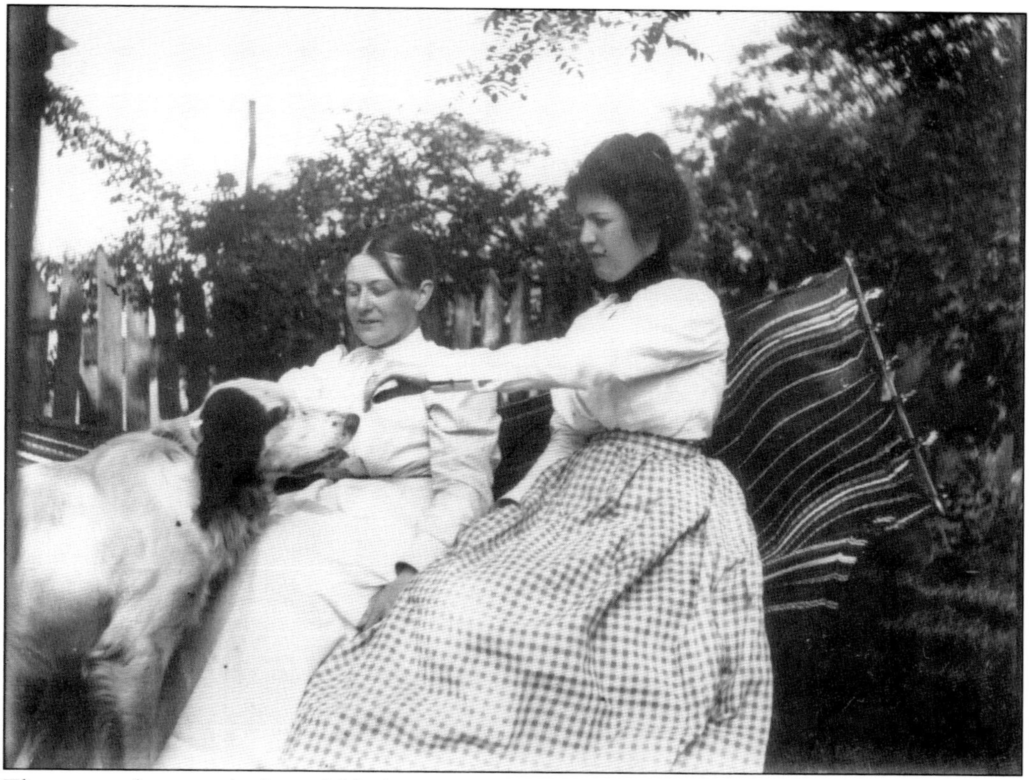

These two photographs leave Miley's pictorialism behind in favor of the spontaneous, look-and-shoot photography that emerged in the early 20th century along with technological innovations that allowed cameras to be made more portable and photographic processes to be simplified. After looking at so many Miley photographs, one can be forgiven for saying of the photograph above, "There's that dog again." Perhaps the two women were visiting Miley, sitting in the hammock in his backyard, and he was able to capture them simply playing with the dog. It shows nothing profound; just life. At right, was he passing this window and asked the two women if they minded him making their photographs? Personalities make themselves known even after the passage of so much time, and there are clear differences in this photograph, with a hint of a smile from the woman on the right and perhaps a look of near disdain from the woman on the left.

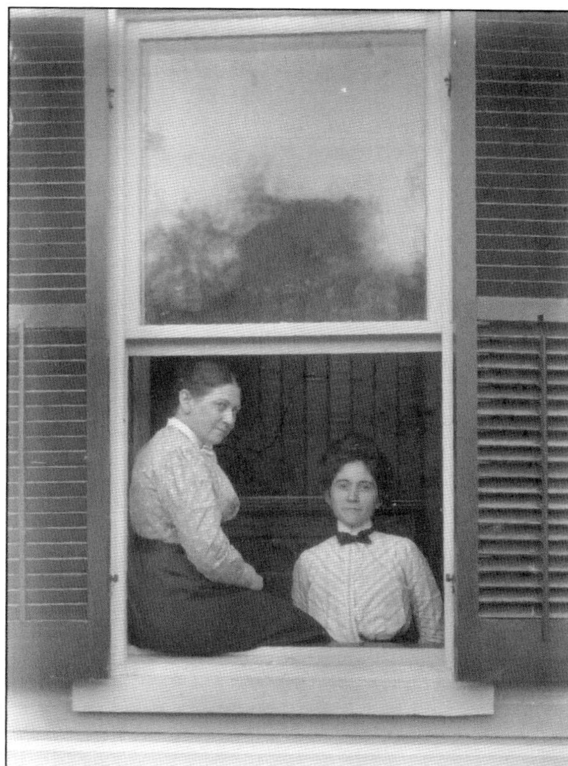

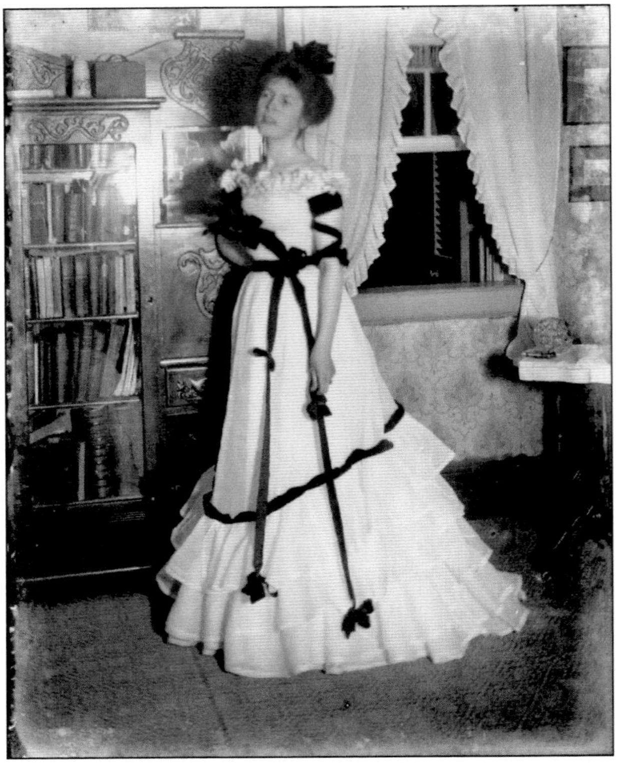

A beautiful woman (one of Miley's favorite subjects) is seen here dressed in an elegant and flowing gown, but what are the dark ribbons? Is she singing or rehearsing a recitation? Her expression suggests longing. There is the feeling of movement in the photograph. Is this a costume for a production of some type? There is no identification of the occasion, but this appears to be another image of Mary Campbell Moore. The photograph is likely from around 1890 because of the almost perfect rendition of Gibson Girl styling and graciousness.

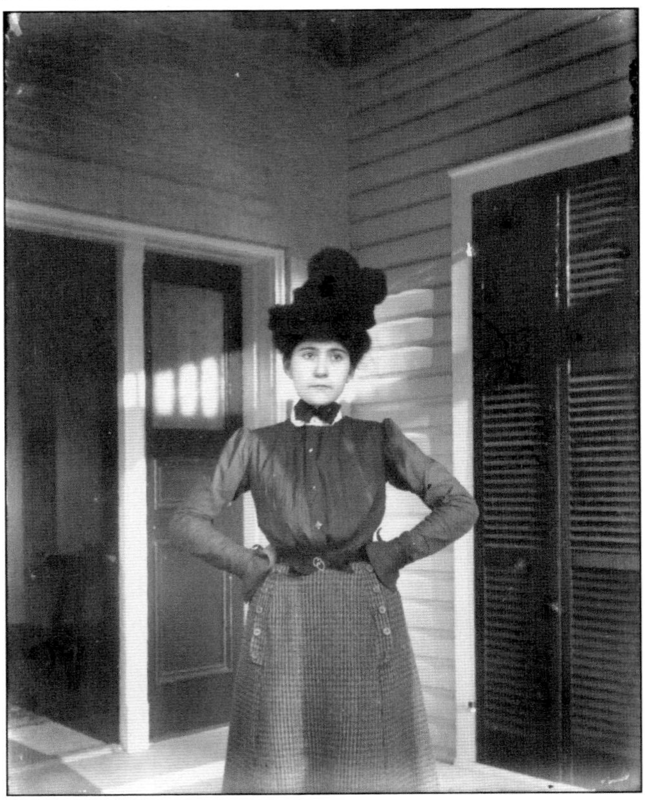

It would be wonderful to know what prompted this photograph. One can imagine the subject saying to Miley, "Okay, just one more but then we have to go." There is, of course, no evidence that suggests anything of the sort, but she certainly has an exasperated expression on her face. Judging from details in the background, this is the same front porch seen in several other photographs. A lovely detail of this young woman's outfit is the pin of intertwined hearts attached at her waist.

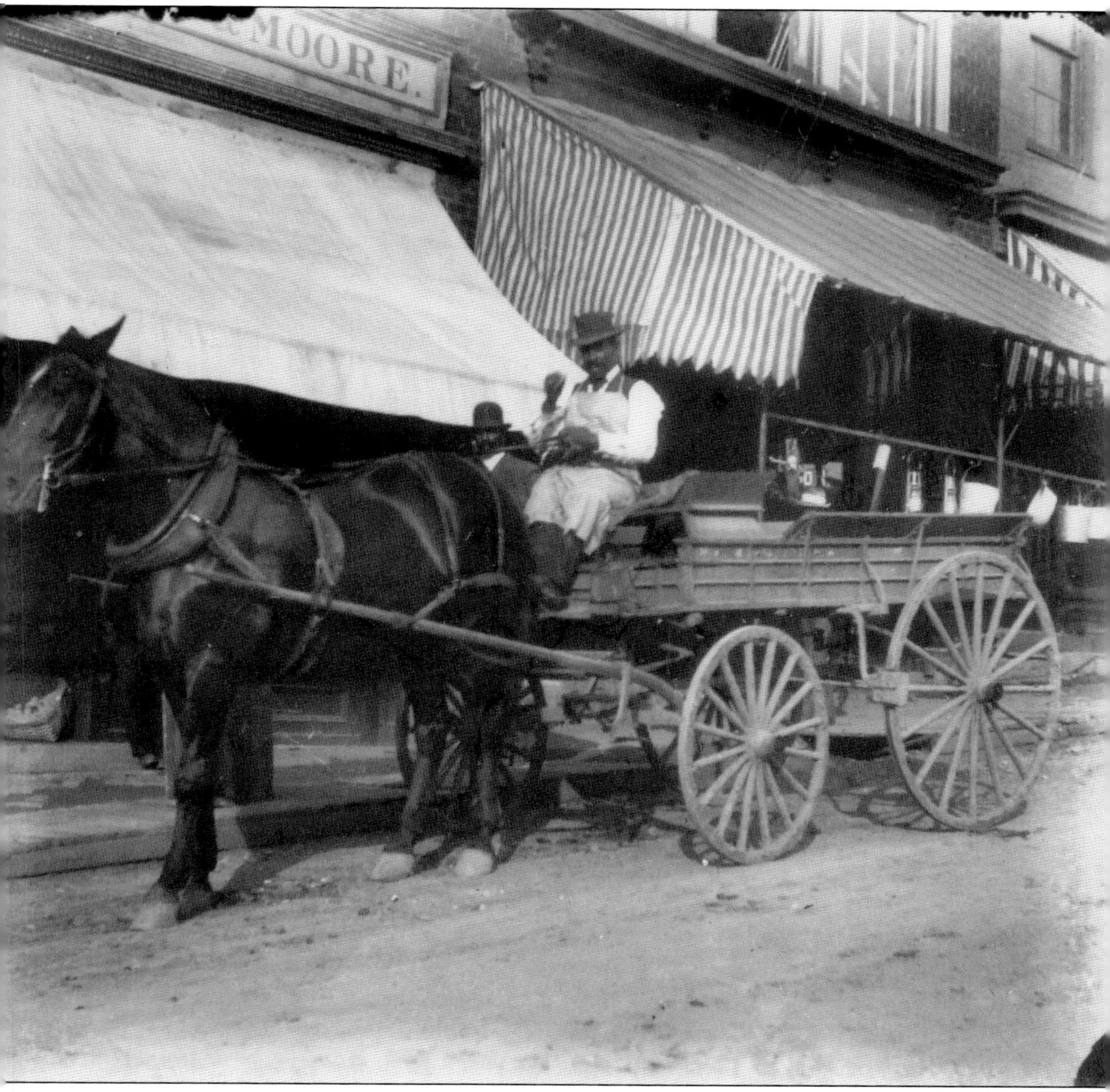

Wagons, buggies, buckboards, carriages, carts, and other assorted horse-drawn conveyances were a ubiquitous part of life in the 19th century. In towns like Lexington, horses and what they left behind were everywhere and presented special hazards when crossing streets and getting in and out of carriages. This fine example of a grocer's buckboard with its driver on top sits in front of a Main Street dry goods and grocery store around 1870.

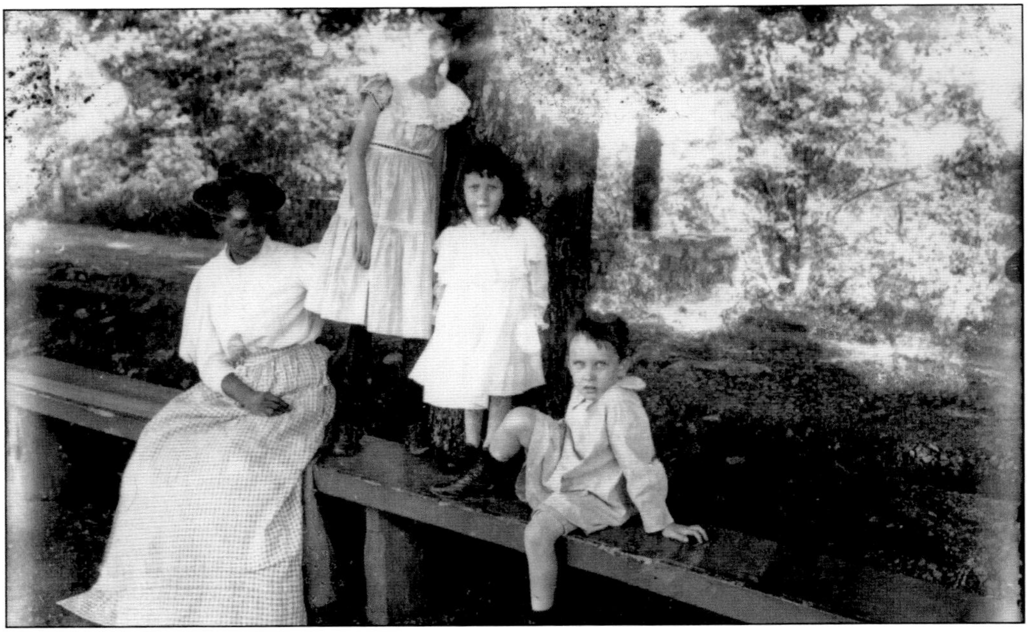

Two very different families from two classes are represented in these striking photographs from around 1870. Miley seemed to have a real desire to include a great many African American citizens of Rockbridge County in his photographs. In a few photographs, they are the focal point, but, in many more, they are present as they were in life: working, living, and contributing to the community. Above, a woman who is clearly old enough to have been enslaved is the nanny or nursemaid of these three children. Below, another family, with the mother and father and their 10 children, lines up dutifully in front of their house to have their photograph taken. This was perhaps a rejected photograph that Miley kept and printed precisely because it is not perfect. The little girl in the front may have ruined the photograph, but from another perspective, she brings life to the image.

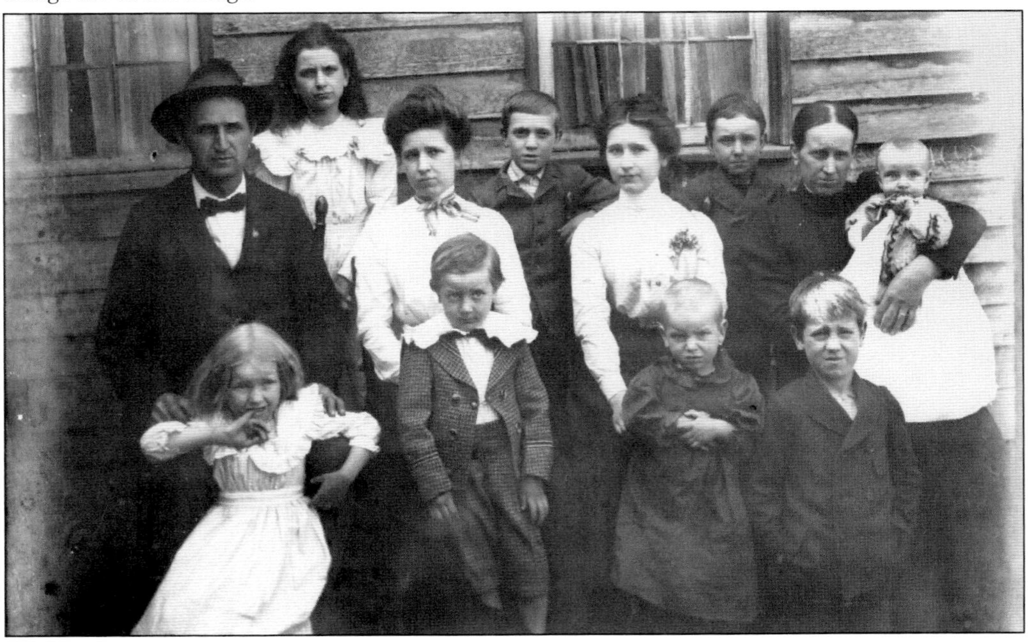

Three

Studio Photography

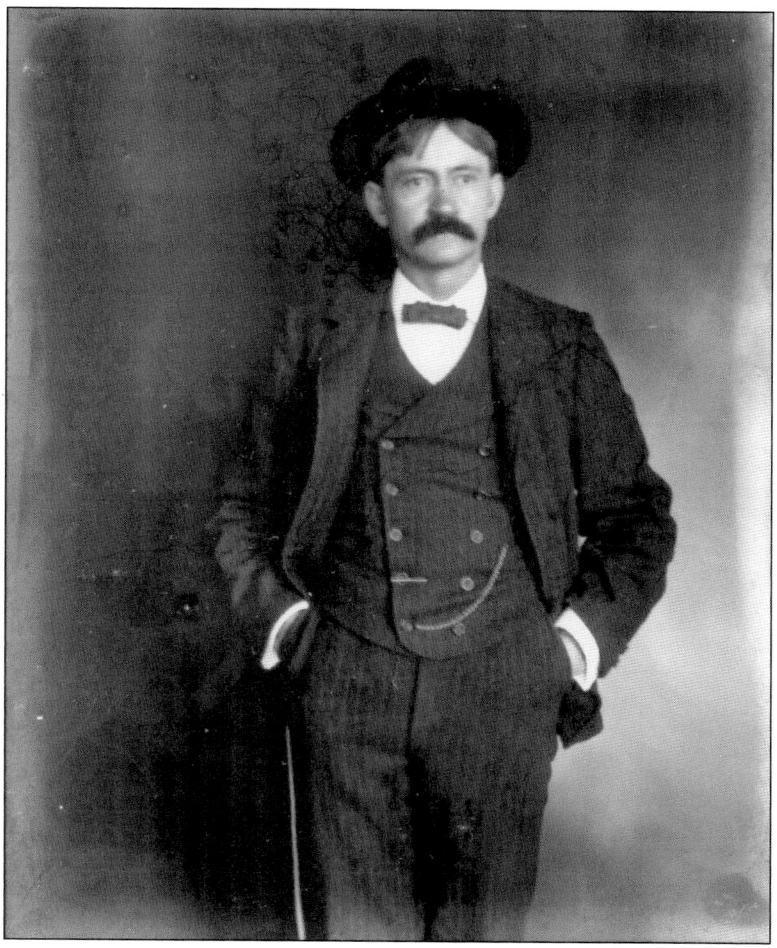

This is an excellent example of what a well-dressed man would have worn to have a formal portrait made by Miley, or any other professional photographer, in his studio between 1900 and 1910. The term "dude" became commonplace to describe such a man around this time. The man's hairstyle, matching three-piece suit, bow tie, pocket watch, chain, and extravagant moustache reflect his interest in style and projecting an up-to-date look.

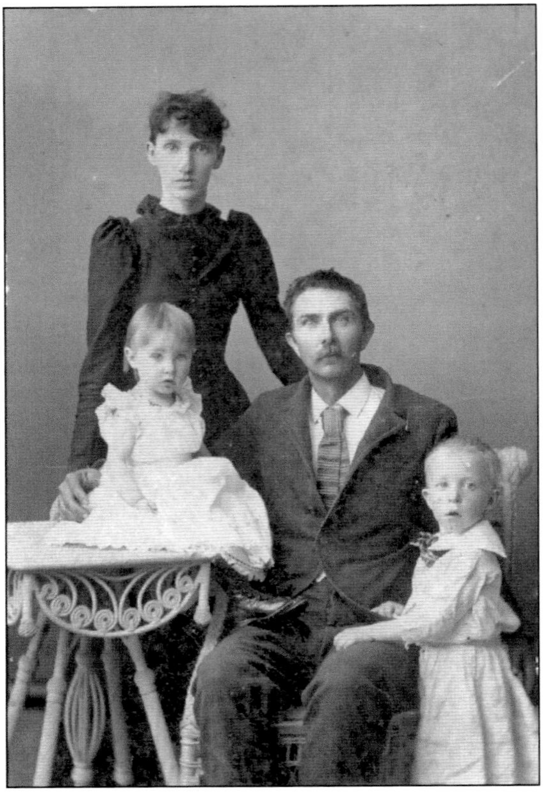

Michael Miley's studio work can be divided into three categories: photographs he took of members of the community who would have come to his studio to be photographed on a special occasion or to simply record their lives; photographs that he made of the famous friends and family of Robert E. Lee; and the thousands of photographs that he took of Washington and Lee college students and Virginia Military Institute cadets. The young family pictured here are Susie and Jim Black with their children Willie and Annie.

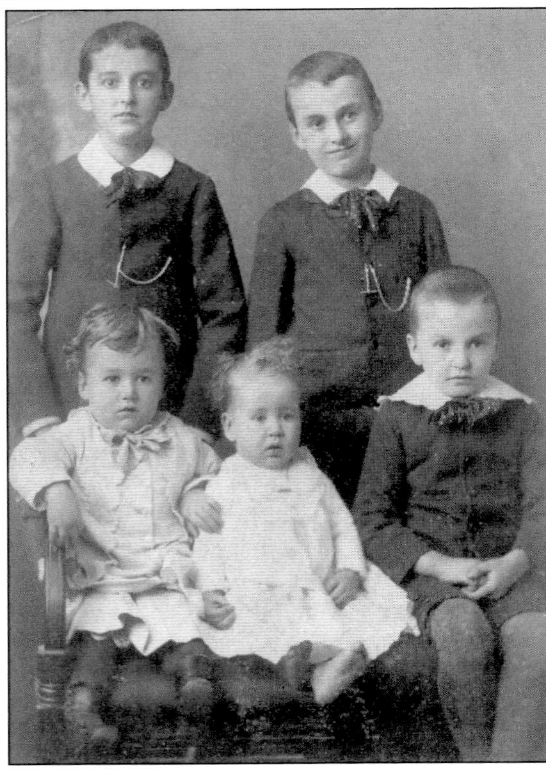

More than one source suggests that the contracts Miley had with W&L and VMI were responsible for the bulk of his income and that this work made it possible for him to pursue his more artistic interests on his own. The group of children on the right is unidentified. Both photographs were taken between 1875 and 1885.

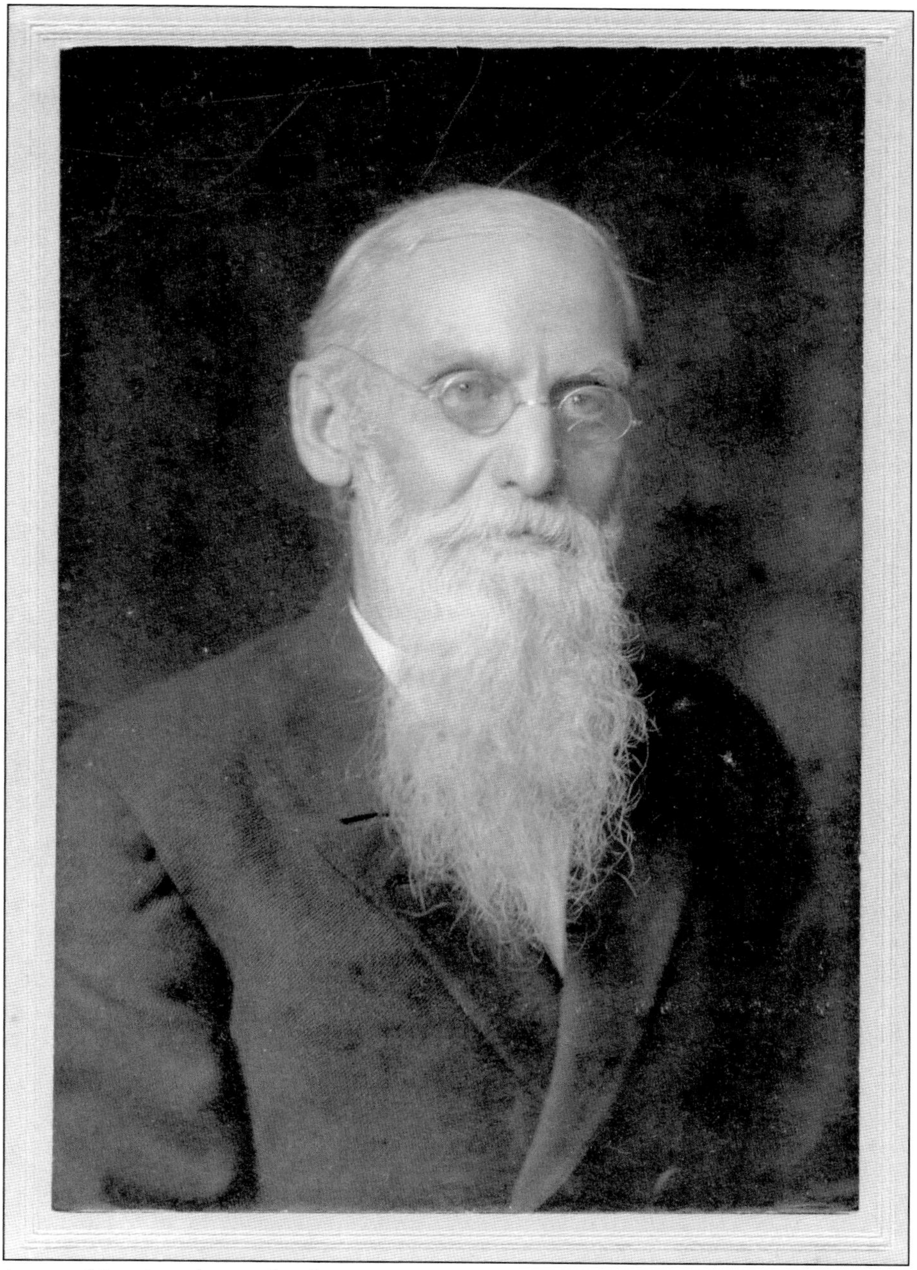

Bringing a subject into his studio for a portrait sitting meant that Miley could much more easily control the conditions under which the photograph was taken than those he did outside. But sacrificing the kind of spontaneity that is characteristic of his environmental photographs did not mean that Miley sacrificed artistic expression in the reproduction of his subject's likenesses. By manipulating light, camera position, exposure time, expression, and posture, the artist is capable of creating likenesses that are both highly accurate as well as expressive and memorable. This distinguished gentleman is Rev. Dr. Daniel A. Penick, who was the minister at New Monmouth Presbyterian Church in the Kerrs Creek district of Rockbridge County from 1873 to 1903. By the time this portrait was made, duplicates of photographs like this one could be made easily and inexpensively in the photographer's studio.

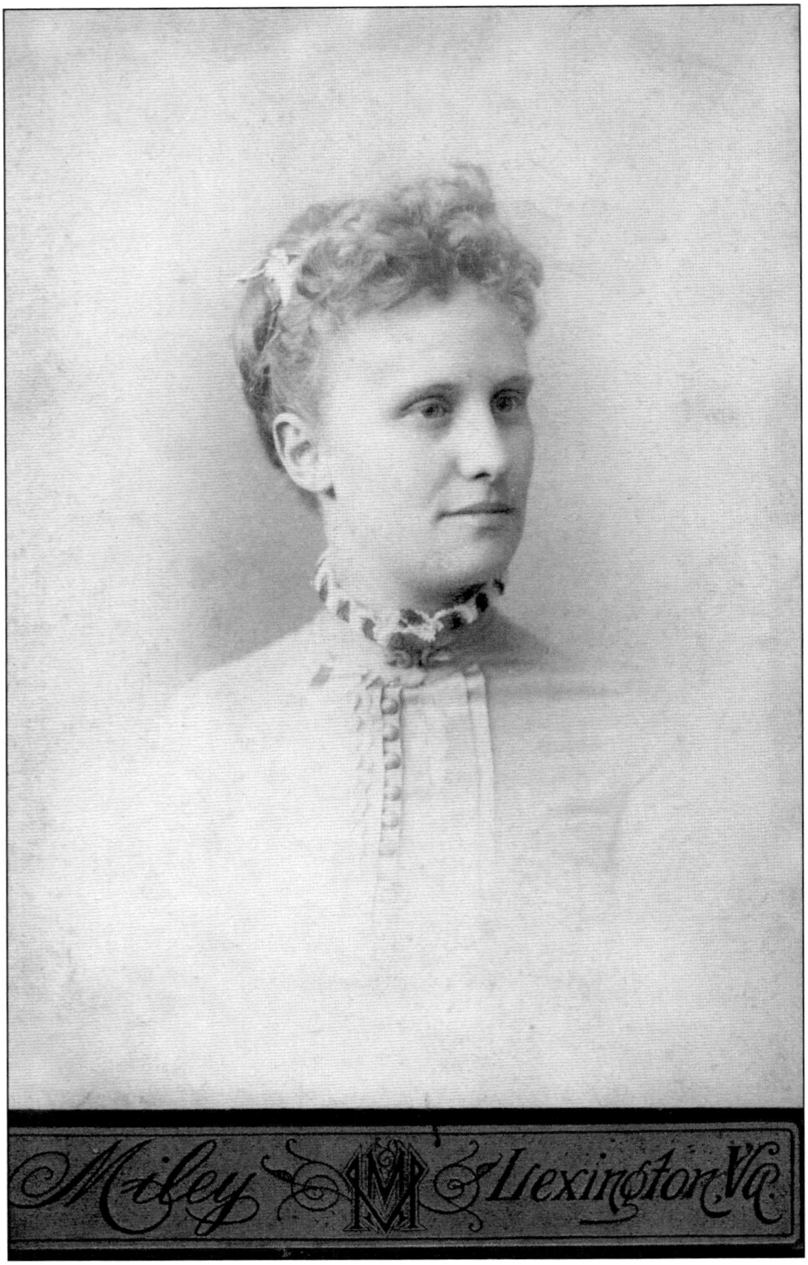

This is an excellent and beautifully preserved example of a *carte de visite*. The CdV, as it was typically abbreviated, was a type of small photograph patented in Paris in 1854. It was a thin paper print mounted on a thicker paper card that could be carried easily and shown to others. By the 1860s, the method had spread throughout the world and was an extremely popular means of displaying and collecting photographs in Victorian parlors. Each photograph was the size of a visiting card and was traded among friends and visitors. The popularity and low cost of these cards led directly to the publication and collection of photographs of many famous people, though they were also popular among ordinary people, as this Miley photograph indicates. The cards also become a convenient and inexpensive way of advertising as Miley's imprint on the front of this *carte de visite* illustrates.

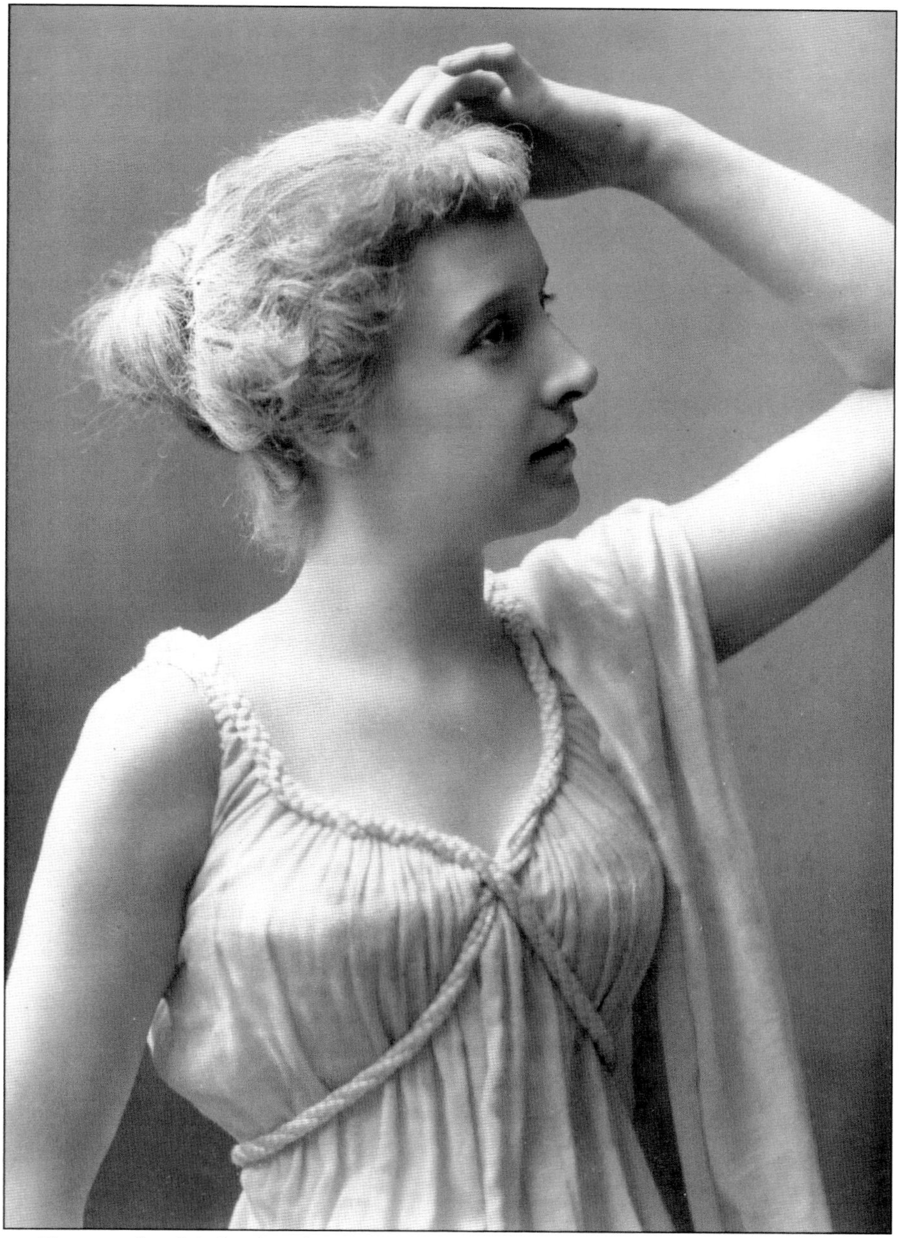

In the oral history that Michael Miley's son Henry wrote in 1941, Henry rather emphatically stated that his father was fascinated by beautiful women and took every opportunity to photograph them in and out of his studio. Henry also mentioned that Miley sought out beauty for beauty's sake "and made a lot of photographs in his studio just because he considered the subject beautiful in some way." Miley did not have to search far to discover this young woman, who, in her Romanesque outfit, could be modeling for a cameo, an item of jewelry very popular during the Victorian era. The young woman is Gertrude Jaccheri, perhaps in her late teens or early twenties when Miley created this highly stylized image. According to the 1880 US Census, Jacheri was born in Lexington in 1869 to Pompeo and Christina Jaccheri, who were both born around 1835. Her father, an Italian immigrant, came to America before 1860; her mother was born in North Carolina. Many members of her family are buried in Jackson Memorial Cemetery in Lexington.

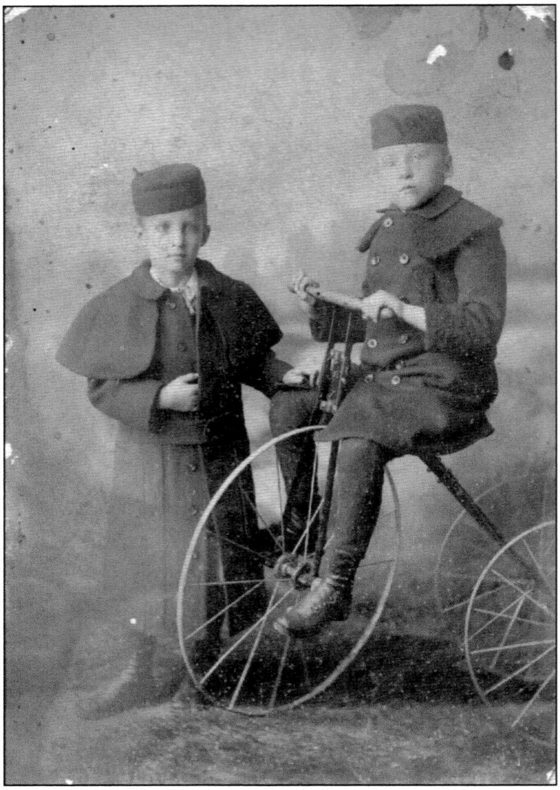

As a professional photographer who considered himself an artist, Miley must have experienced the tension between needing to make a living and the desire to create something beautiful, meaningful, and lasting. After 1870, he was married and soon had three sons to bring up.

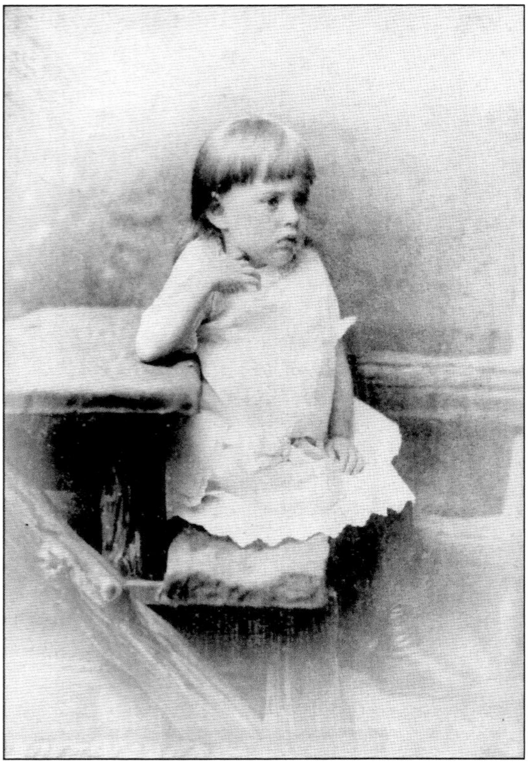

Though he never made a great deal of money, Miley owned a substantial house at 108 White Street in Lexington and could afford to travel to photography conventions as far away as Philadelphia and New York. Photographs like these two and others in this chapter that were clearly taken in a studio showcase his technical expertise and his ability to capture perfect and charming likenesses of his clients. The subjects of these photographs are, unfortunately, unidentified.

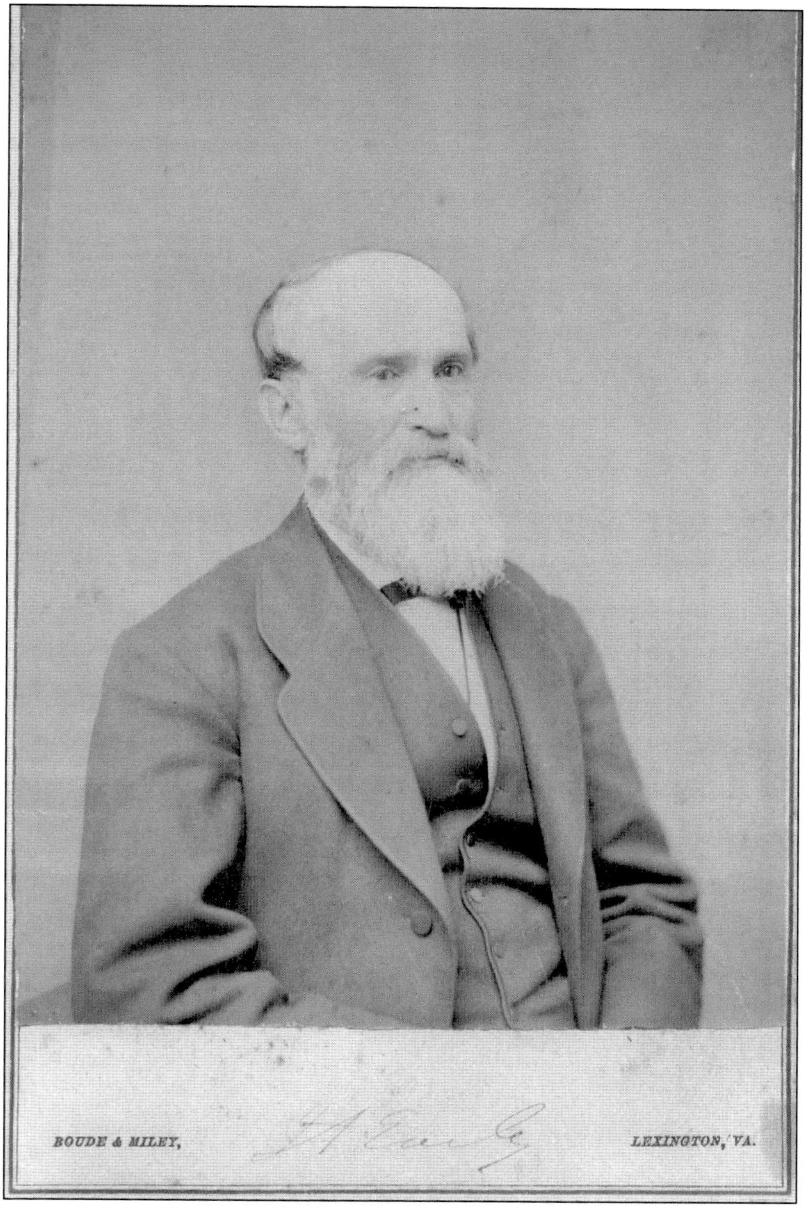

This is a very rare original autographed Boude and Miley *carte de visite* of the important Civil War general Jubal Early taken sometime between 1867 and 1870. As far as can be ascertained, this photograph has never been published. Early visited Robert E. Lee in Lexington on more than one occasion, spoke at Lee's funeral in 1870, and returned to Lexington in 1891 for the unveiling and dedication of the Stonewall Jackson monument in the Presbyterian cemetery. Born in Franklin County, Virginia, in 1816, Early practiced law, served in the Virginia House of Delegates, and fought in the Mexican-American War all before he reached 40 years old. Like many others from western Virginia, he was a reluctant secessionist until Virginia seceded, but once that action was taken, he embraced the cause with zeal largely unmatched in the South. Following Appomattox, Early fled to Texas, then to Cuba and Mexico, and then to Toronto, Canada, where he lived until 1869. An unreconstructed promoter of the Confederate cause until the very end, he died in Lynchburg in 1894.

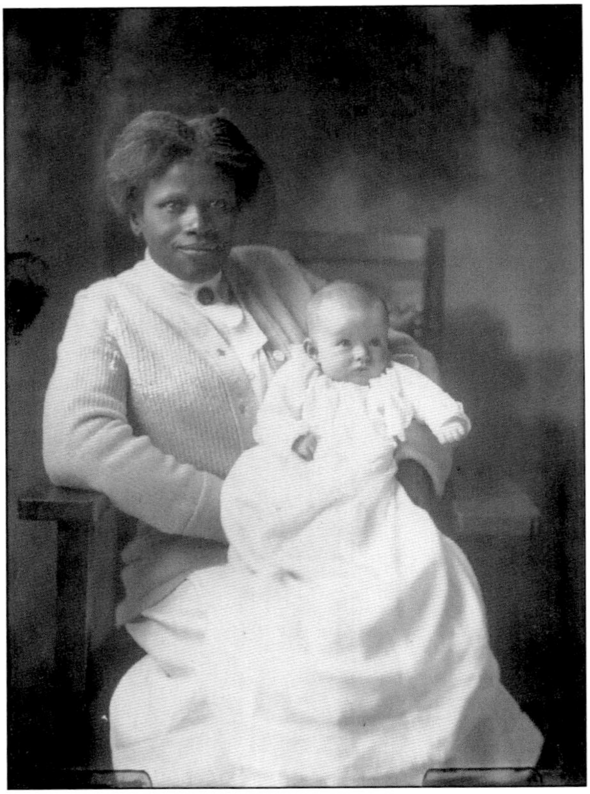

Nothing is known of Miley's views on race, since neither he nor his son ever commented on the topic. He photographed many African American citizens of Lexington and Rockbridge County, and nothing in his photographs could be construed in any way to imply sentiments of white supremacy. On the contrary, these photographs suggest dignity and substance. The baby in this c. 1885–1900 photograph was identified as "Bessie."

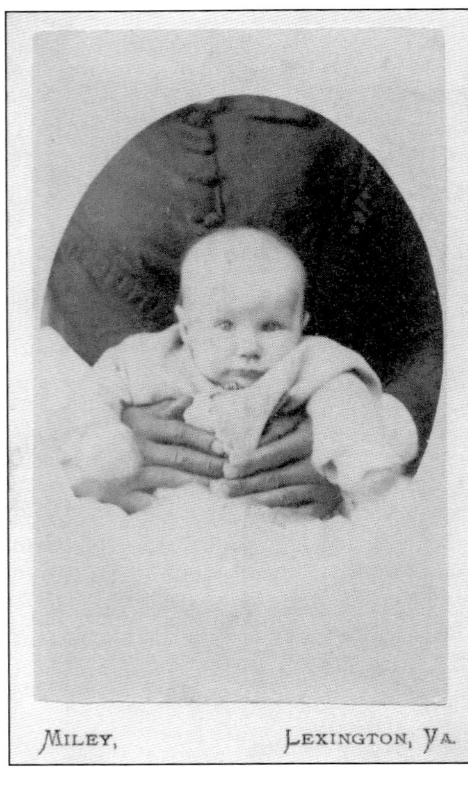

Elizabeth White, in the image on the right, was the daughter of Lexington businessman Gustavos A. White. The photograph is a CdV from around 1870–1873.

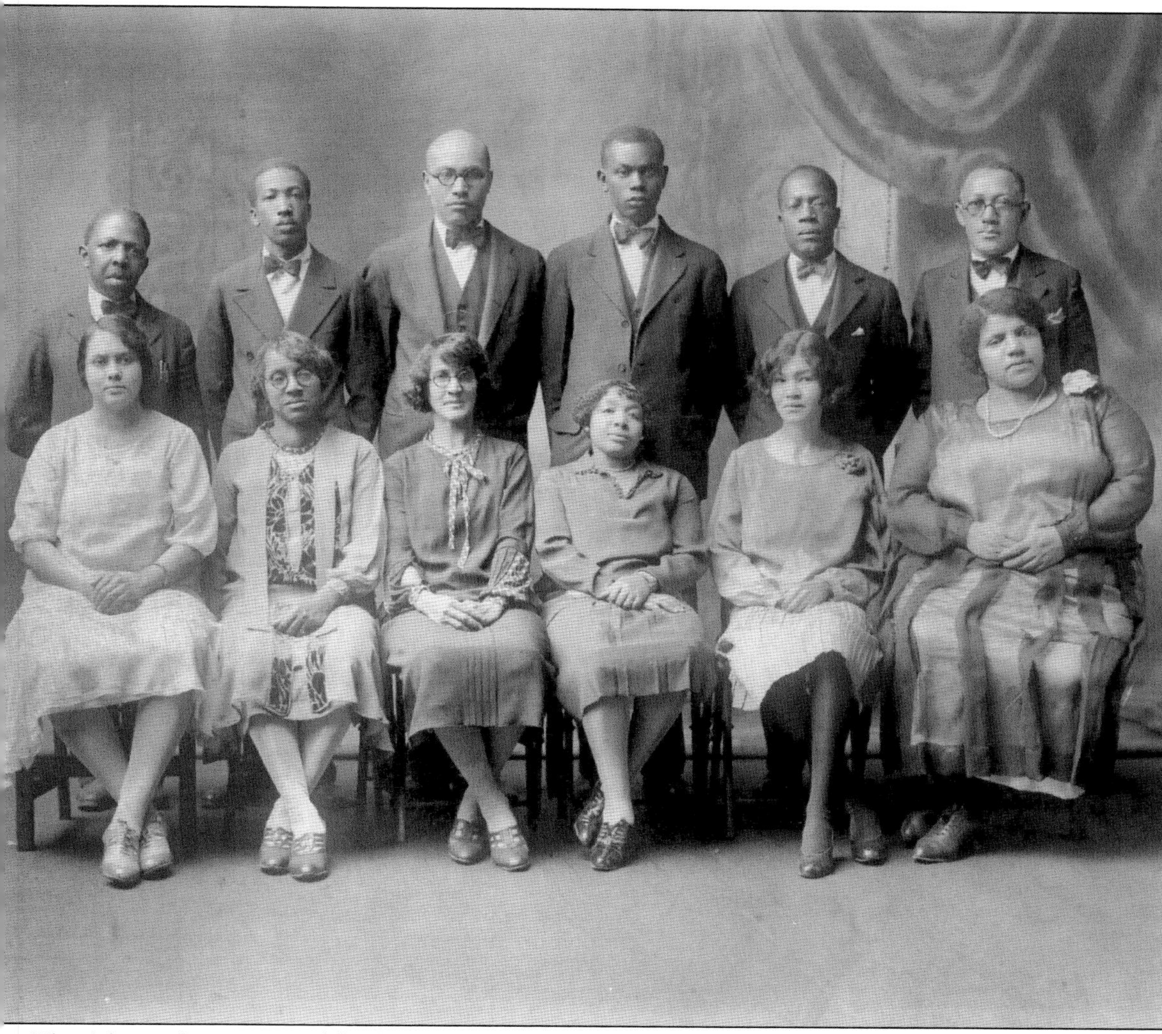

The African American middle class in small Southern towns like Lexington generally consisted of a few ministers, some small-businessmen, possibly a doctor or a dentist, and the usual group of teachers. One of the most prominent black families in Lexington in the early 20th century was the Walkers, Harry and Eliza. They were deeply involved in the African American community and Harry Walker was a businessman to be reckoned with in both the white and black communities. In 1911, he purchased one of Lexington's oldest Main Street buildings and converted it into Lexington Meat Market, which supplied meat and groceries to all the residents of the town. Eliza Walker was as accomplished and active as her husband. Trained as a nurse and midwife, she was also very interested in music and developed several music programs in town. Their home, known as Blandome, became a meeting place and even a bed and breakfast for black travelers to the area. Eliza founded the singing group seen here, called the Charity Nightingales, and had this photograph taken by Henry Miley about 1920. Eliza Walker is sitting third from the left.

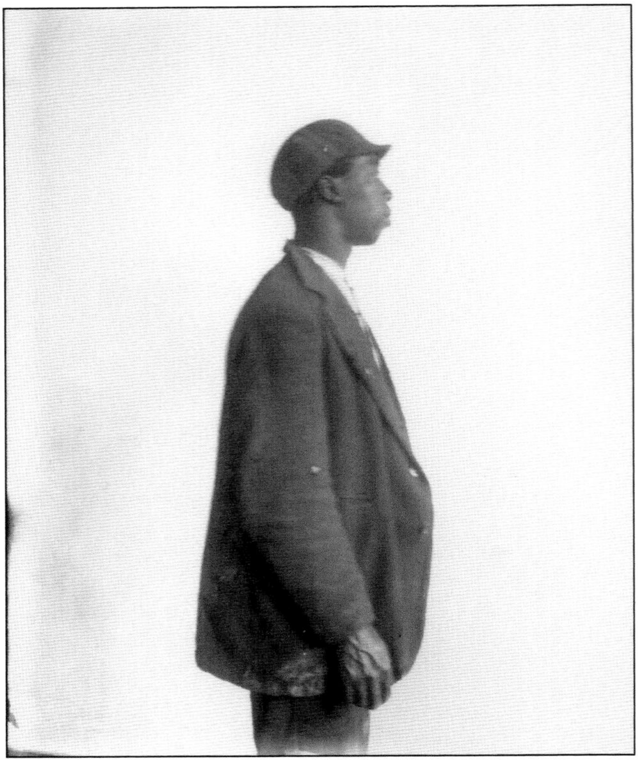

The interesting aspect of this portrait is that it is of a working person, ordinary by the appearance of his clothes, rough and standing in an uncomfortable position. Against the stark background, all of the man's features stand out. Was Miley interested in this contrast, in the dusty look that the whole photograph possesses, in the veins of the man's hands, in the details of his hat and coat? It is a photograph rich in detail and nuance, and there is not another like it in his work.

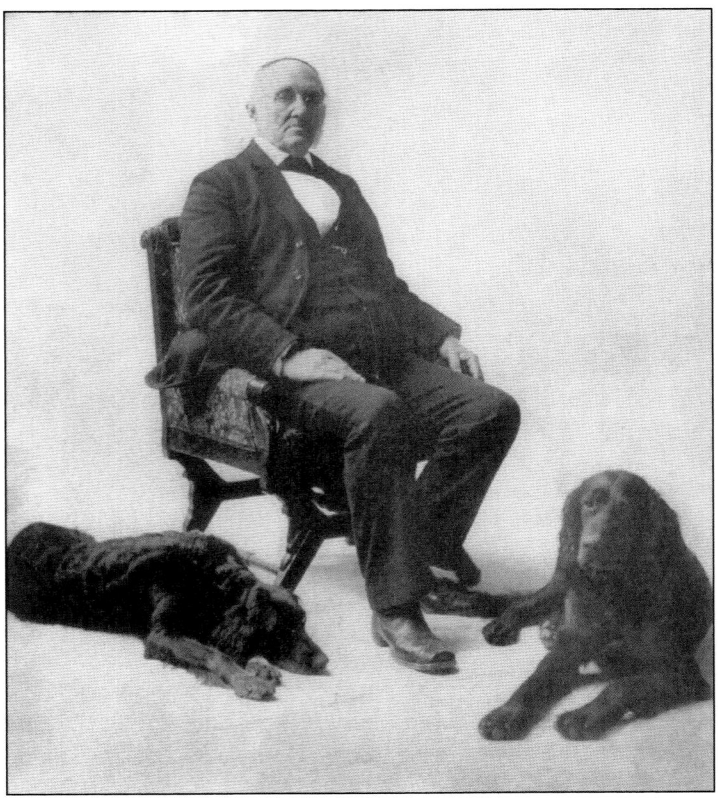

This is a hybrid photograph, part studio and part environmental, of Lexington mayor J.W. Houghawout with two of his hunting dogs around 1882. An avid hunter who would sound his hunting horn on the town's Main Street, the mayor of postwar Lexington was a sufficiently eccentric figure for Miley to pose in the company of his hunting dogs. All three figures, cloaked in black and heavy-limbed, assume related poses that lighten the formality of this portrait.

This is a very rare autographed large format photograph signed by Virginia's Civil War governor John Letcher, who was born in Lexington in 1813. He founded the *Valley Star* newspaper about 1840. In 1851, he was elected to the US House of Representatives, and he served four terms before running successfully for governor of Virginia in 1859. As the secession crisis deepened, Letcher urged moderation while opposing secession until after Virginia left the Union on April 17, 1861. After the war, he served for many years on the board of visitors of the Virginia Military Institute. He died in Lexington in 1884 and is buried in the Presbyterian cemetery.

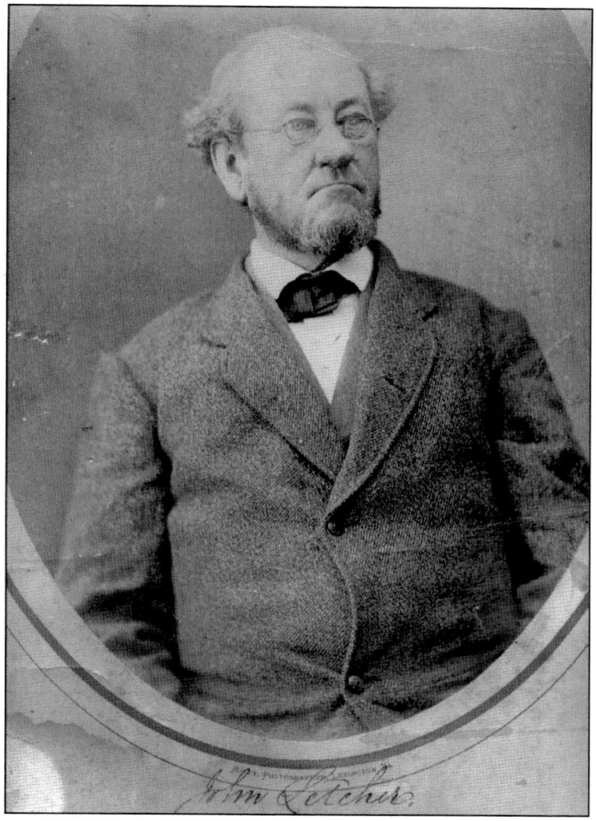

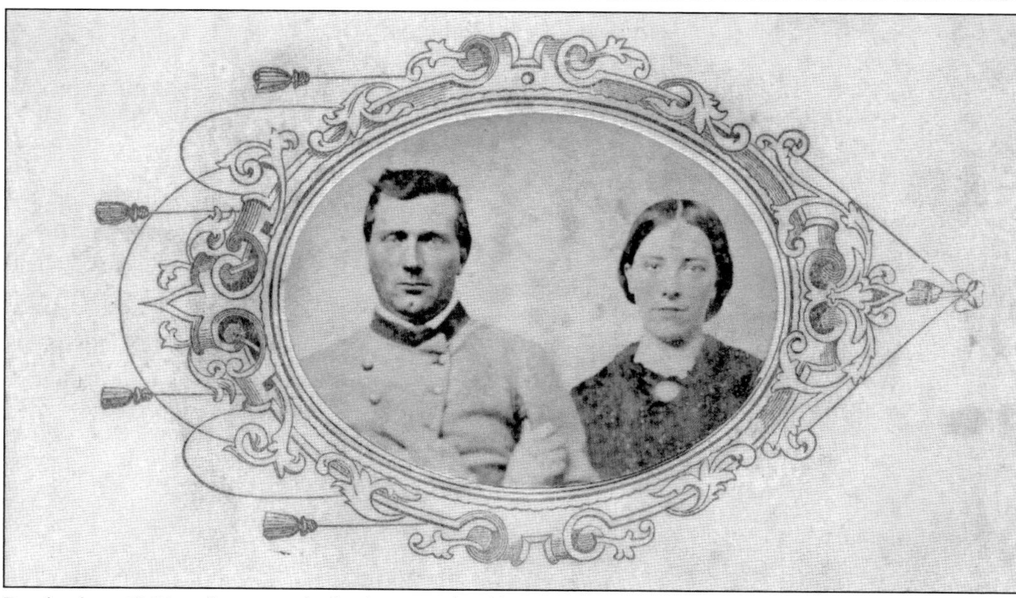

By the late 1860s, photograph duplication had become commonplace and was a good part of the business of studio photographers. This is a copy of a cased ambrotype or tintype photograph that Miley made of his brother Lt. Jacob Miley with his wife, Anne Eliza (Beard), sometime around 1867. The original was made before 1864, for in that year Lieutenant Miley died of wounds received at the Battle of Spotsylvania. (Courtesy of Seth McCormick-Goodhart.)

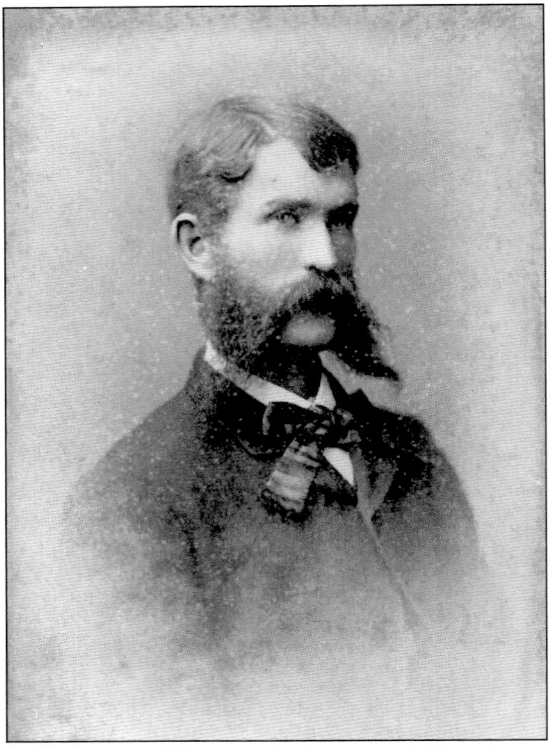

These two photographs are wonderful examples of the art of studio photography and represent the kind of commercial artistry that Miley excelled at. He must have displayed his work in his studio, and, along with the portraits of Robert E. Lee, it is easy to imagine works such as these hanging on the walls as examples of his finest studio portraiture.

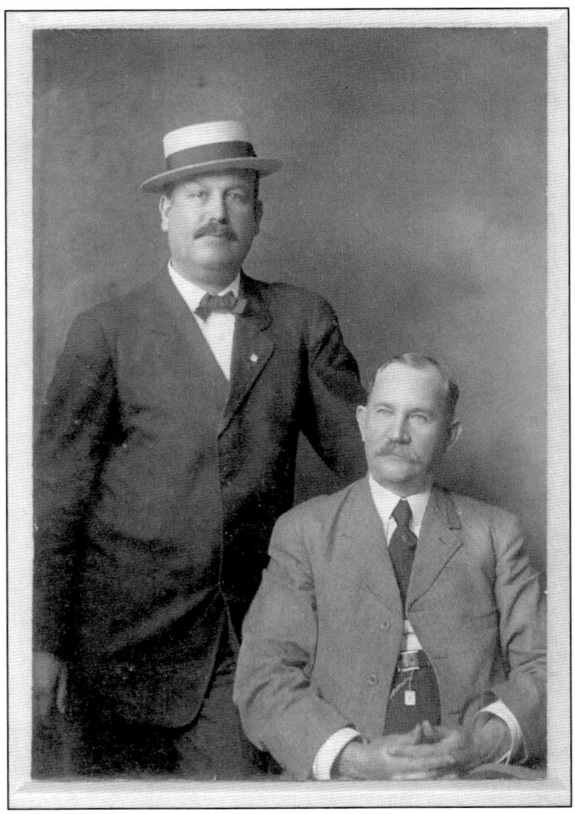

The high quality of the photographs, the clarity, and the personality and character that shine through in each would have provided powerful incentives for people to have their own portraits made by this master of the craft. In 1907, a fire devastated the store beneath Miley's shop and studio, destroying many of his negatives, papers, notes, and accounts. While much of his older work was saved, this loss has made it extraordinarily difficult to identify large portions of his work.

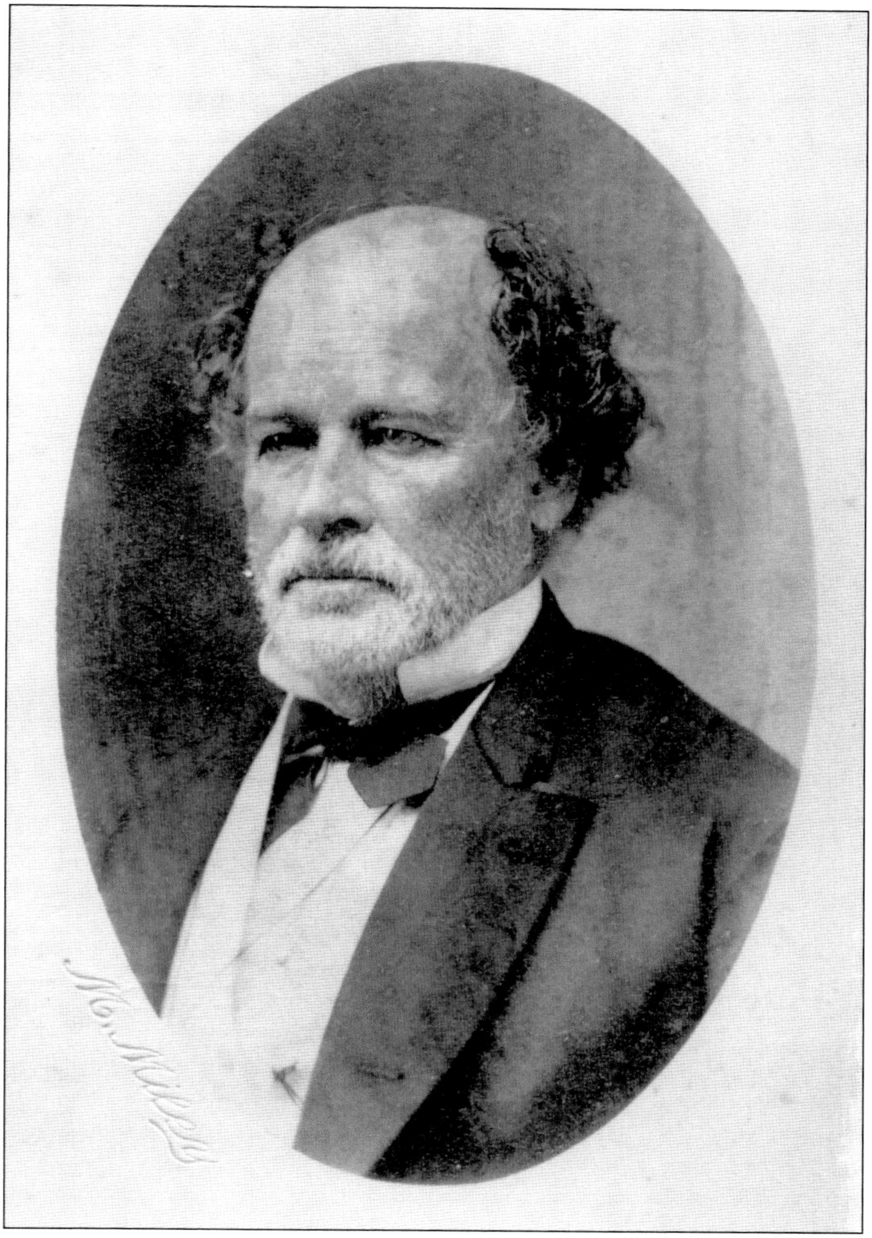

This is another well-preserved Miley *carte de visite* showing the image of Matthew Fontaine Maury taken in Miley's studio in 1871 or 1872. A man distinguished by his accomplishments in many areas, Maury was memorialized locally when the North River was renamed after him. Maury was born in 1806 in Fredericksburg and spent his youth dreaming of the sea. From 1825 to 1834, he sailed the world. In 1855, he published *The Physical Geography of the Sea*, which is now credited as the first textbook on modern oceanography. In April 1861, after Virginia seceded from the Union, Maury resigned from the US Navy and assumed command of the navy of the Confederate states. In 1868, he accepted the position of professor of meteorology at Virginia Military Institute. In the fall of 1872, Maury became ill during one of his lecturing tours and died several months later. He was temporarily buried in Lexington, but his body was later moved to Hollywood Cemetery in Richmond, where it remains today. (Courtesy of Seth McCormick-Goodhart.)

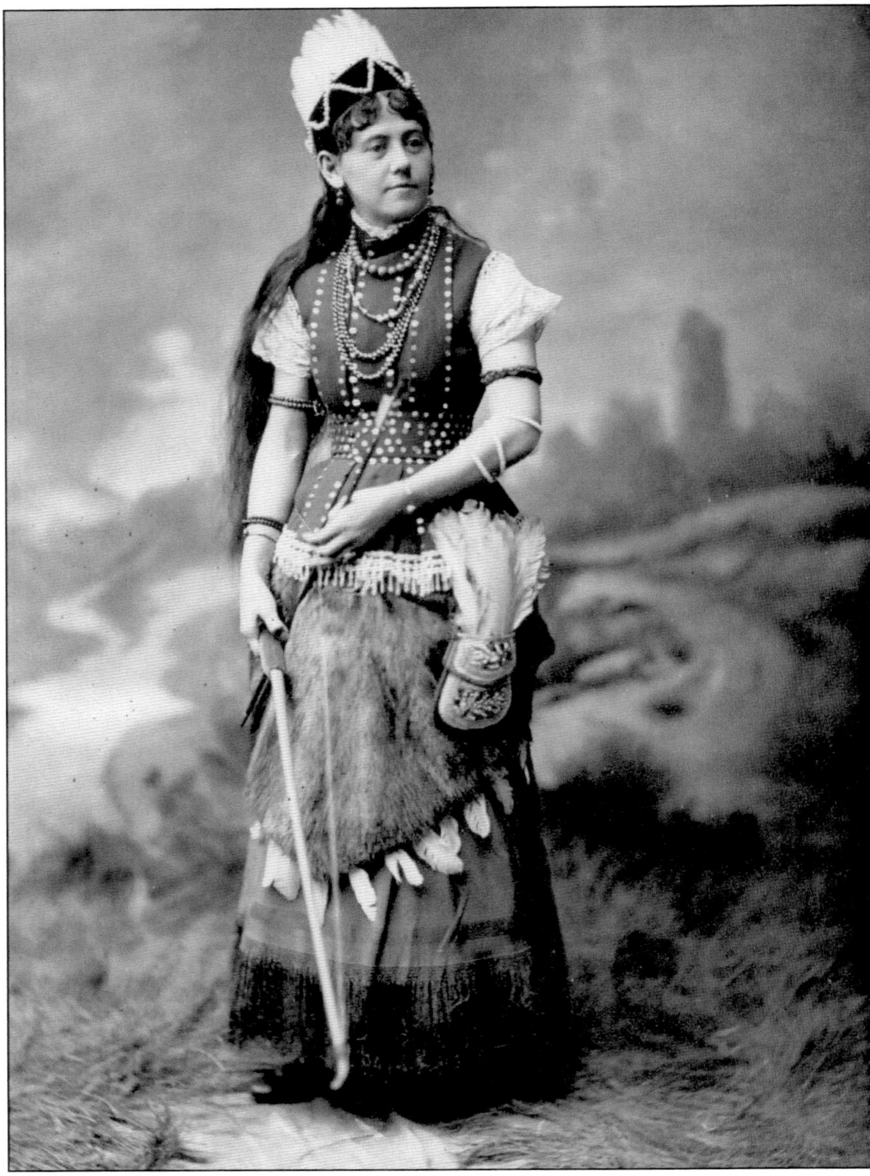

In this photograph, Miley captures all the charm of Miss Annie Joe White, the legendary librarian at Washington and Lee, in full Pocahontas regalia all set for the Fancy Dress Hop in 1876. White served the faculty and students at W&L from 1895 to 1922 and is widely regarded as the founder of the Fancy Dress Ball, still held annually at the university. A theme was announced for the ball in time for costumes to be ordered, and, over the years, themes such as "King Arthur and the Knights of the Round Table" and "Arabian Nights" were popular. Since the college was all male until recently, young men brought dates onto campus from near and far, many coming by train from other southern states and from as far away as Texas. In 1928, the *New York Times* described the ball as "the South's outstanding collegiate social event." In 1929, over 2,000 revelers attended, dressed as everything from clowns to cavaliers, and in 1952, *Life* magazine reported that the ball had been held annually since 1907, interrupted only from 1944 to 1946 because of World War II. Her full name was Anne Robertson White, but her tombstone in the town cemetery reads "Annie Joe White."

Four

W&L AND VMI

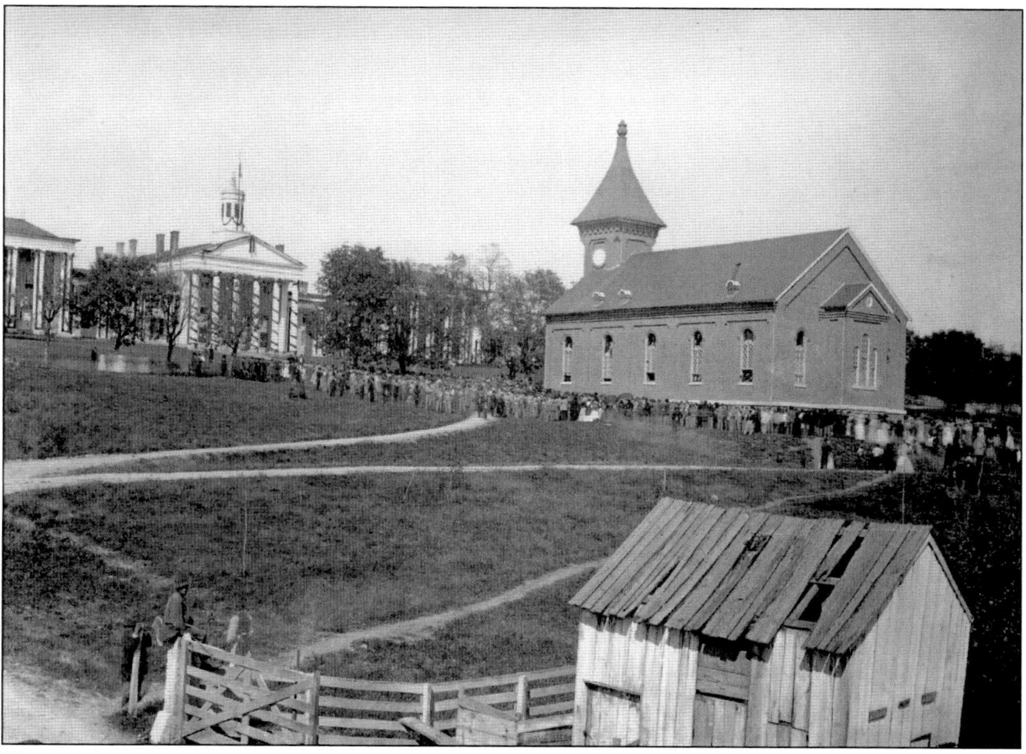

There is no more important shared single event in the history of these two colleges than the funeral of Robert E. Lee, seen here on October 15, 1870. At 10:00 a.m., starting at the Lee home, the procession moved through town and both campuses to the sound of solemn music and arrived back at Lee Chapel for the 1:30 p.m. service. According to one VMI cadet, so much black crepe was draped over buildings and men that more had to be sent for from Lynchburg.

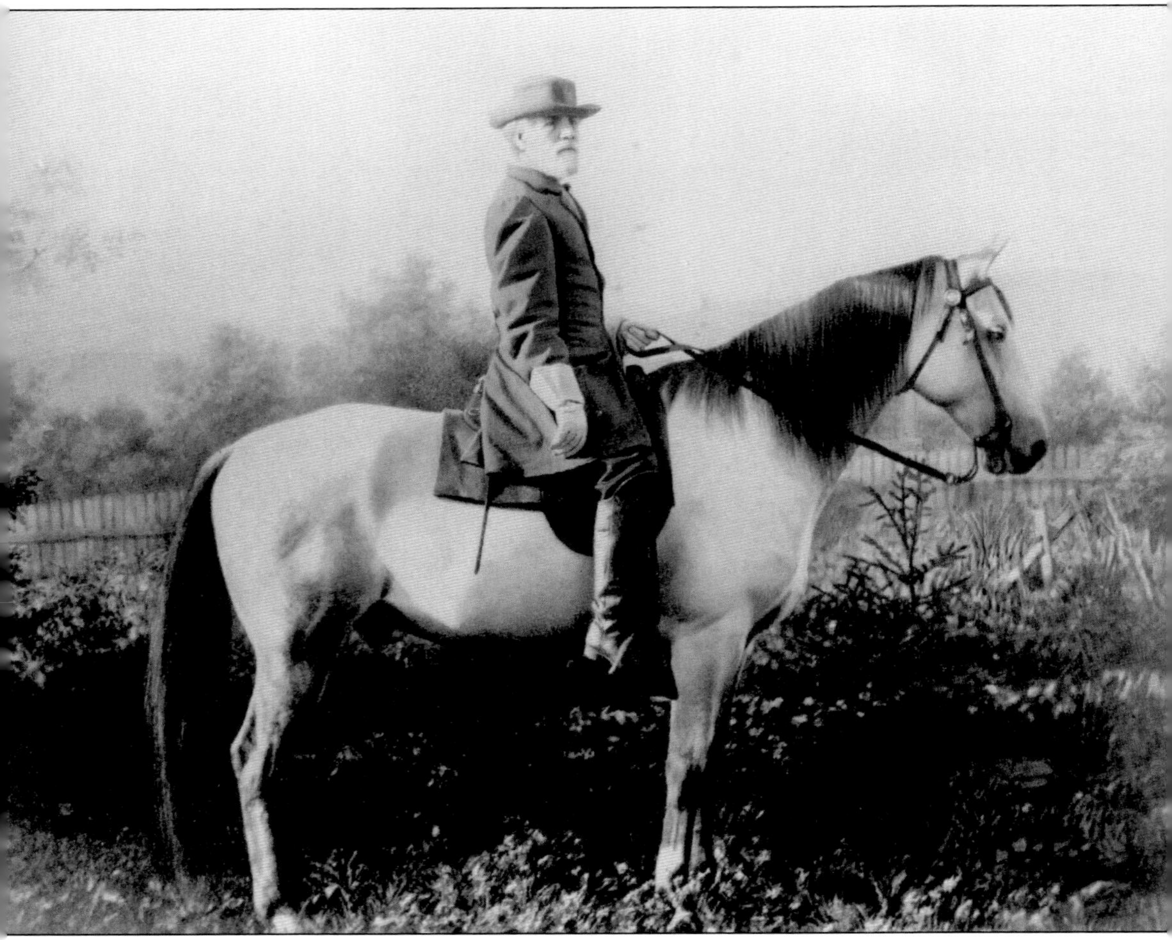

While there is a quality to this photograph that suggests it could have been done in a studio, it was actually shot, at Robert E. Lee's request, in the garden behind Lee's home on the W&L campus in September 1868. Henry Miley claims that this photograph was the most commercially successful of any his father made. The photograph was turned into a lithograph by the A. Hoen Company of Baltimore and sold as an inexpensive print all over the South. Robert E. Lee did not attend Confederate reunions and, after Appomattox, was ambivalent about being portrayed as a soldier. In this photograph, he is in uniform but his officer's insignias have been removed. Lee had owned this horse, Traveller, since 1862, and the year after Lee died, Traveller contracted tetanus and had to be killed. Originally buried on the campus grounds, the horse's bones were dug up and moved several times before finally being returned to the college in 1907. In 1971, a century after the horse died, his bones were buried next to the Lee Chapel, where a grave marker placed by the United Daughters of the Confederacy marks his final resting place.

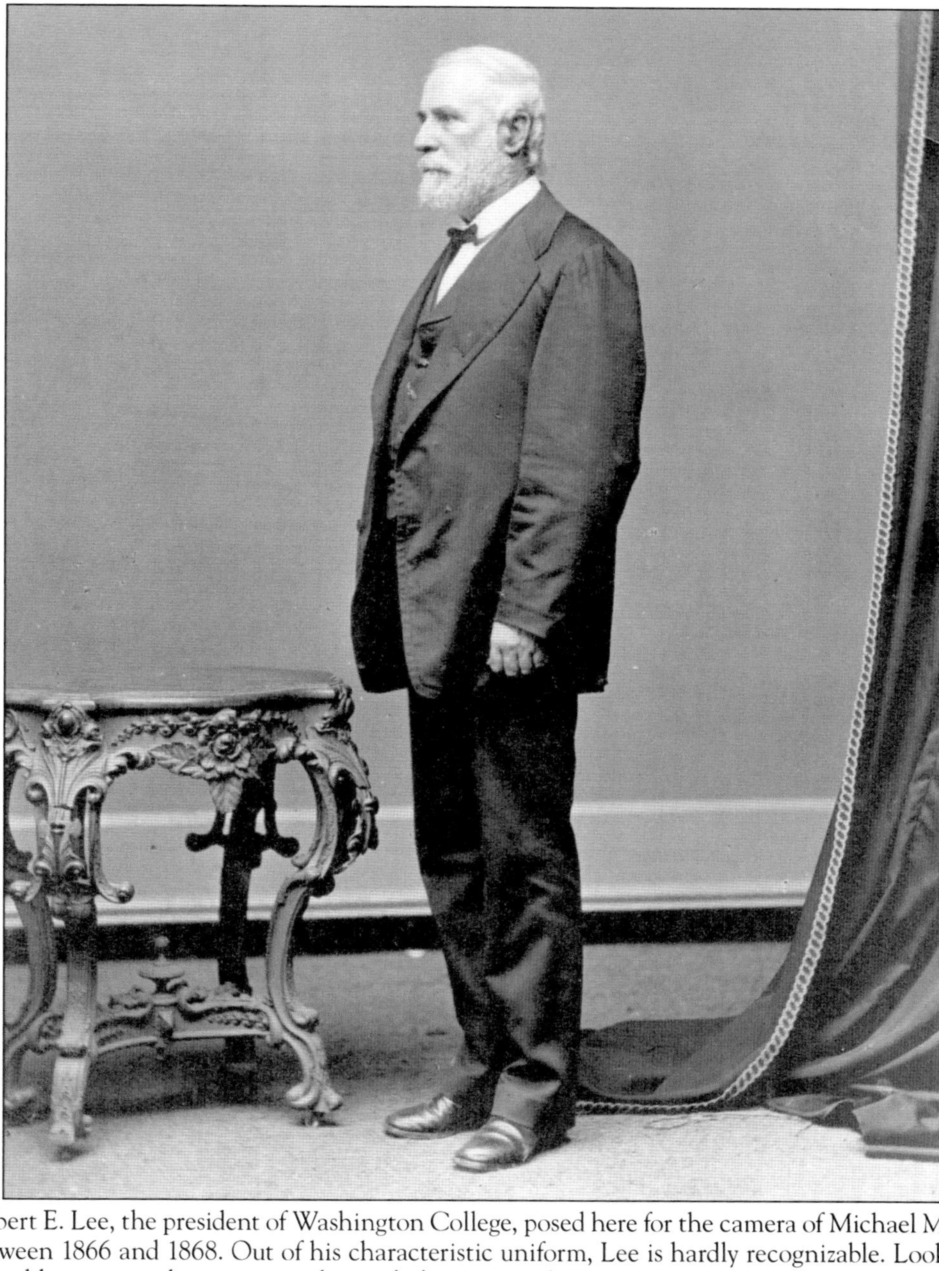

Robert E. Lee, the president of Washington College, posed here for the camera of Michael Miley between 1866 and 1868. Out of his characteristic uniform, Lee is hardly recognizable. Looking more like an aging businessman than a dashing general, Lee was about 61 years old at this time. Tall and considered handsome his whole life, his snow-white beard and hair reveal the effects of the constant stress and anxiety he lived with during the war years. This is an original carbon print on Miley & Son Studio mat. This photograph of Lee as a college administrator complements the one that shows the general on horseback. The two images by Miley serve to emphasize Lee's pursuit of two careers. Here, the subject is shown in his civilian work clothes, as the new president of Washington College. Lee is posed standing because this was a public photograph produced for distribution. He appears somber, dignified, and tired. Lee had assumed a job that was far less lucrative than many offered to him following the war, but one that he felt would help restore the South.

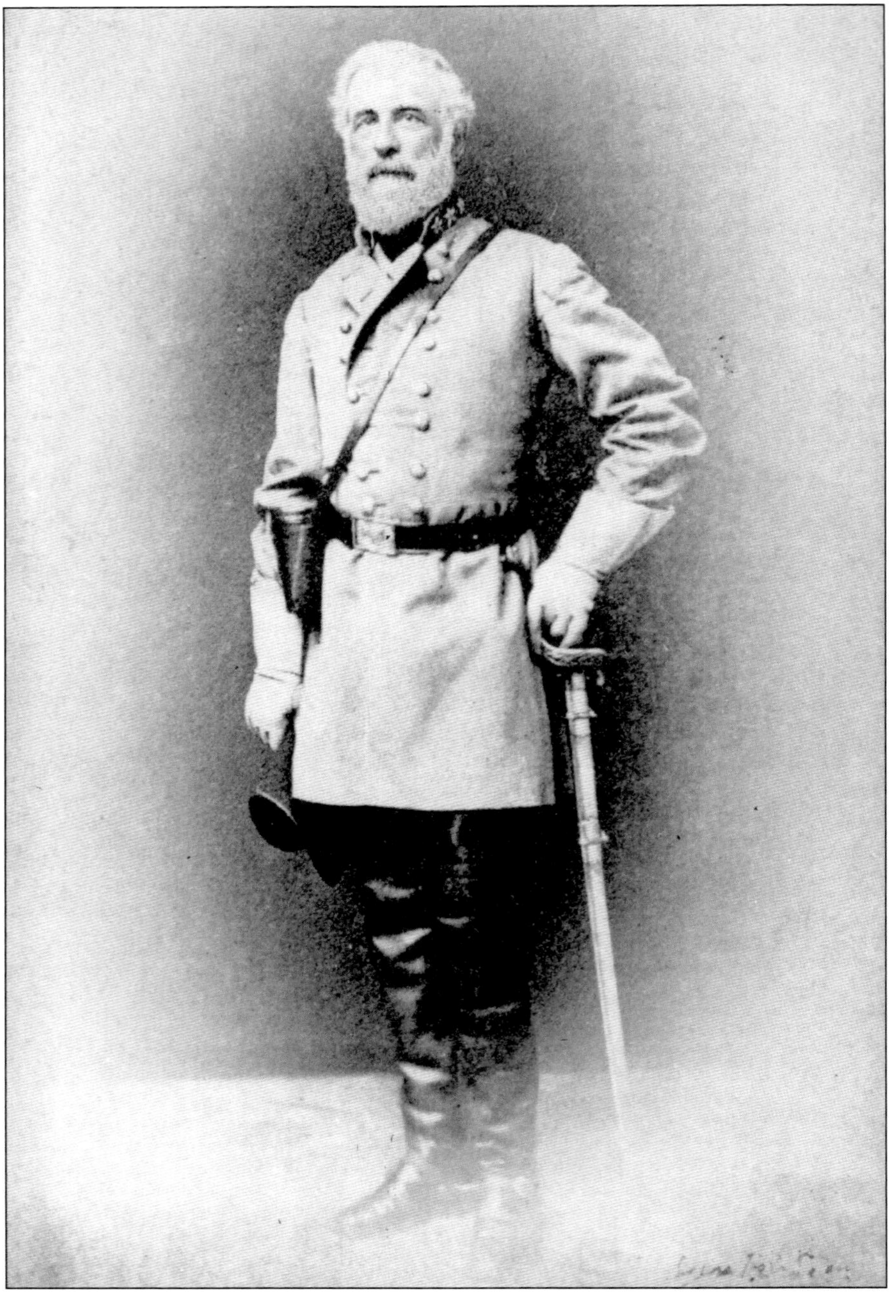

While this photograph of Robert E. Lee was not taken by Miley, it is a good example of one type of work he was doing. By the late 1860s, making duplicates of other photographs had become relatively simple and inexpensive. As a result, many professional photographers offered duplication services as a part of their work. Customers would bring older photographs that had been made with a one-off process into the photograph studio to be copied. This particular shot is a photographic portrait of Robert E. Lee taken by the noted Civil War photographers Minnis & Cowell. This photograph, one of many taken of Lee, was taken in Richmond in 1863. It was published in the *Illustrated London News* in 1864. This particular print is a copy of the original that was made by Michael Miley in Lexington sometime between 1880 and 1895.

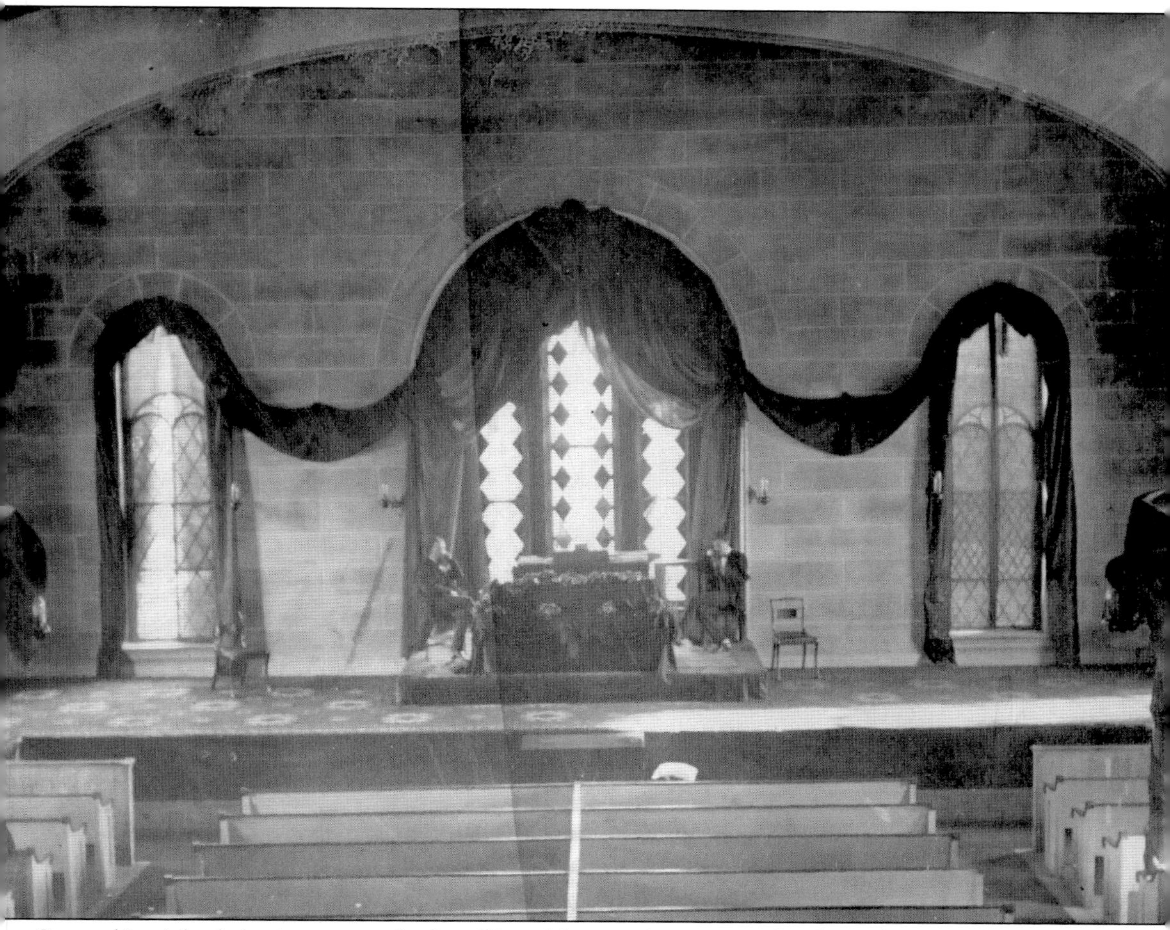

General Lee's body lay in state in the Lee Chapel for two days prior to his funeral on October 15, 1870. Work and most activity came to a standstill in Lexington and the surrounding county, and most buildings were draped to some extent in some kind of black cloth. All cadets at VMI were ordered to wear black armbands, which continued during the mandatory six-month mourning period that was declared. Five VMI cadets silently sat with the corpse while it lay in state. One of them, though it is not clear if he is seen here, was Cadet William Nalle, who wrote a detailed letter to his mother describing the events of those days. He even mentions the extraordinary rains that flooded Lexington during the preceding days, which made it difficult to procure a coffin for Lee's body. A metal casket that had been washed down the river was eventually retrieved. It had been caught in a brush pile and was lodged in the forks of a tree. It was returned to Lexington and used for the general's remains.

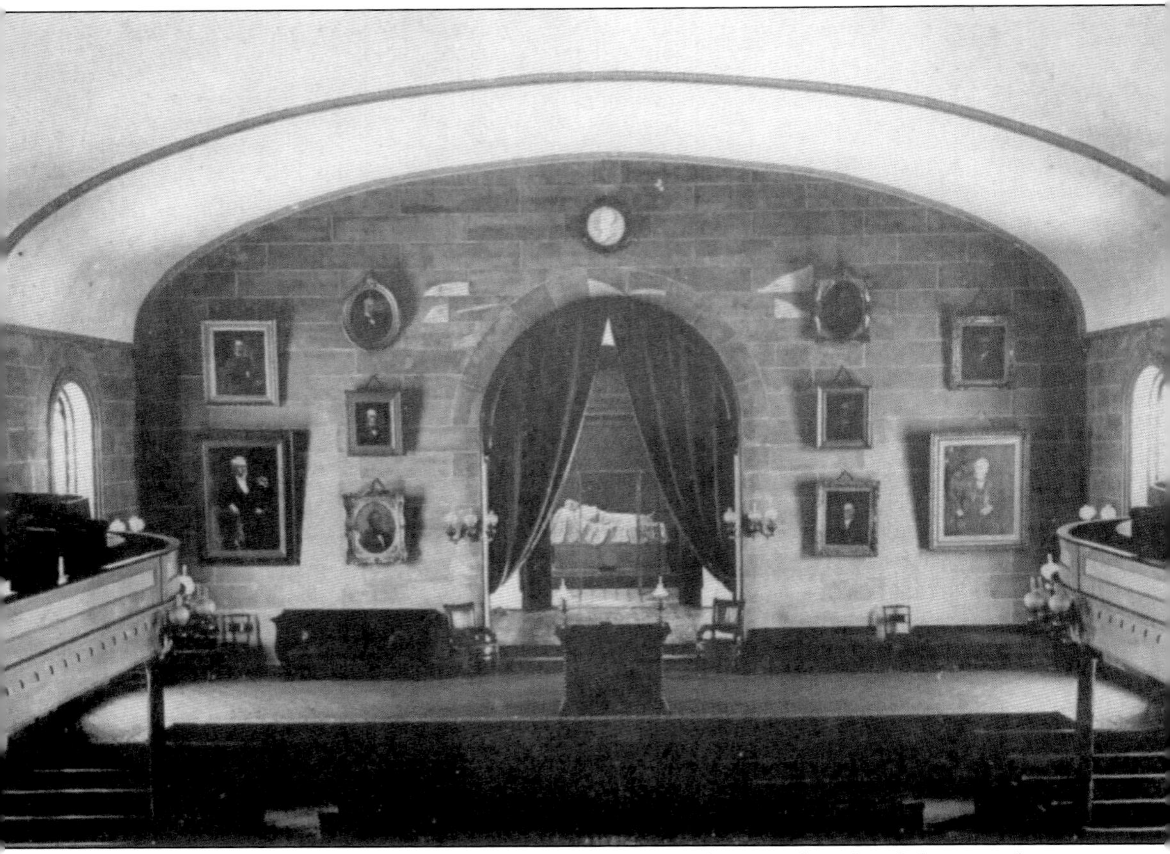

This Miley photograph from 1890 shows the interior of the Lee Chapel and the recumbent statue of Robert E. Lee created by the sculptor Edward V. Valentine in 1875. Valentine also sculpted the statue of Thomas "Stonewall" Jackson, which was dedicated in 1891 in Lexington. While the Lee statue gives the impression of a sarcophagus, it is, in fact, Valentine's representation of the general asleep on the field of battle. The statue is often also mistakenly thought of as a tomb, which it is not since Lee's actual burial site is beneath the chapel. The statue was stored for eight years until the mausoleum was completed in 1883. Sometimes referred to as the "shrine of the South," the statue became a focal point of the Lost Cause movement in the late 19th and early 20th centuries. Valentine became well known as a sculptor of historical figures in Virginia and was briefly associated with the Valentine Richmond History Center. He did one additional statue of Lee, along with ones of Thomas Jefferson, "Stonewall" Jackson, Jefferson Davis, and other historical figures. He died in 1930 in Richmond.

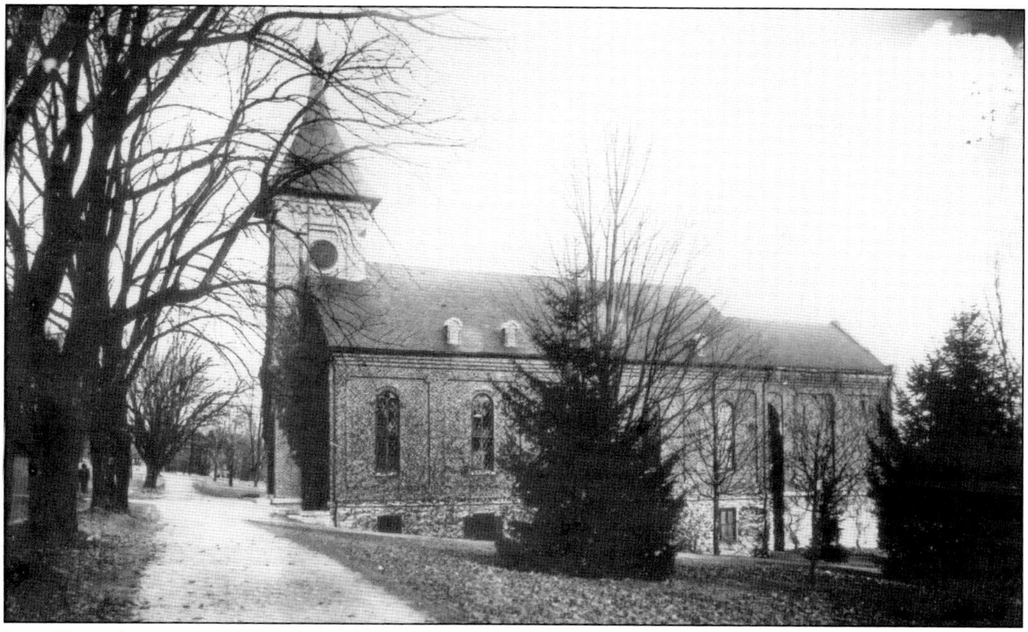

Lee Chapel was constructed in 1867 and 1868 at the request of Robert E. Lee. While Lee and his son George Washington Custis Lee were both trained engineers, the bulk of the work designing and constructing the chapel fell to Col. Thomas Williamson, an architect and professor of engineering at VMI. While it is certainly true that both Lee and his son must have consulted with Williamson, the evidence suggests that the building's design and execution were primarily Williamson's responsibility. The chapel is pleasing to the eye, as it is snuggled into a beautiful space on a campus hillside. Its architectural style is in stark contrast to the older buildings opposite it on campus, which are in a neoclassical style. There is no evidence why Lee chose the Romanesque style for his chapel. Although the chapel is a tourist attraction and museum, it continues to play a vital role in the daily life of the university. In 1926, the board voted to establish a museum in the basement for photographs of the Lee family and other relics and mementos of General Lee that are in the possession of the university.

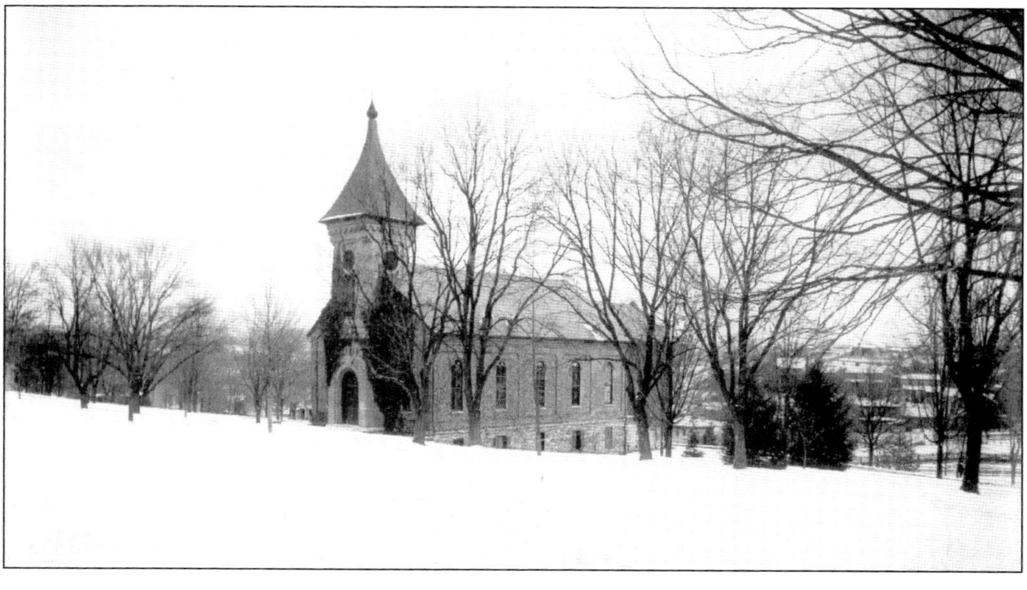

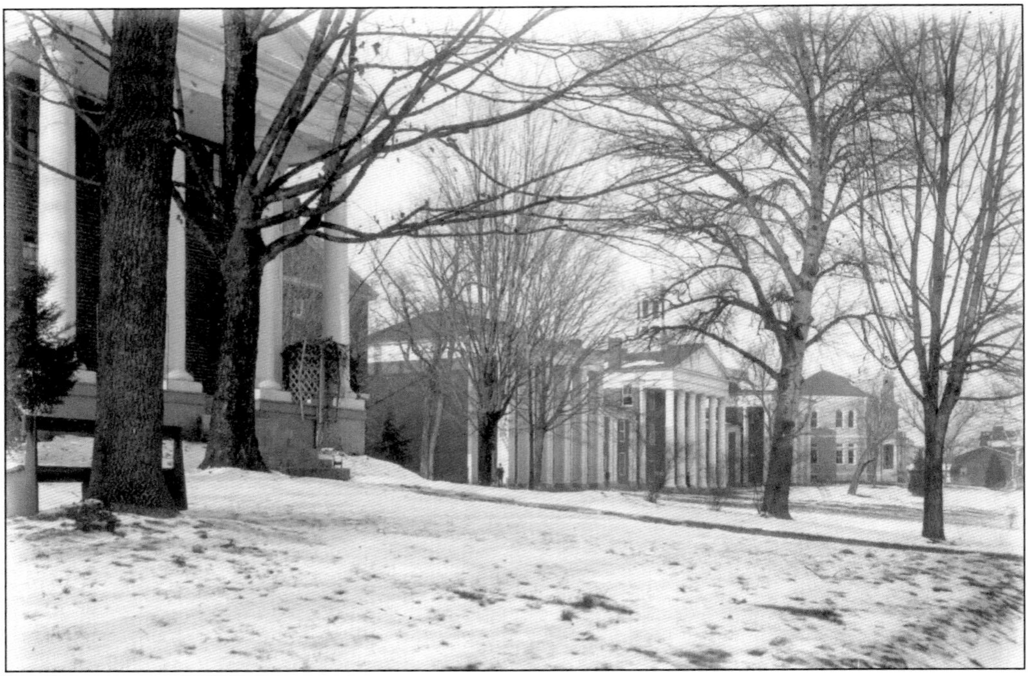

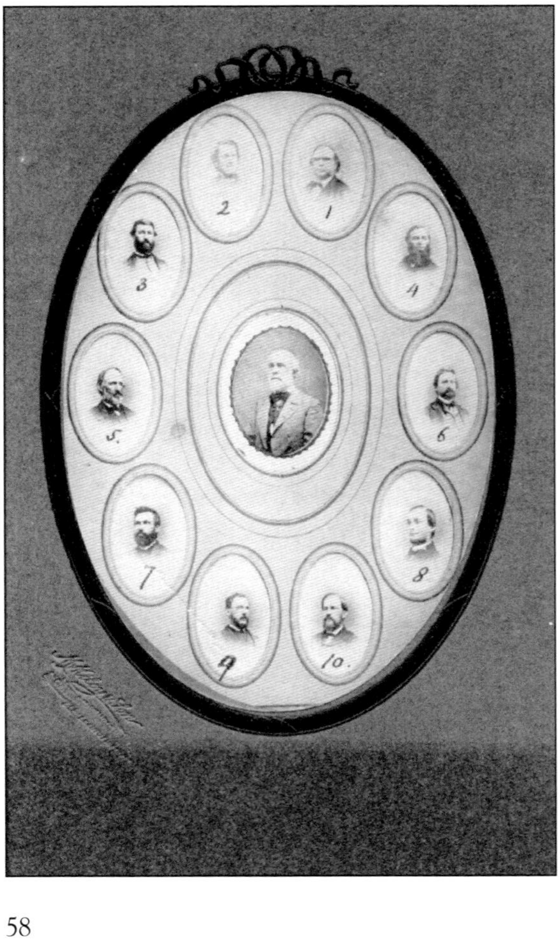

The well-balanced and perfectly composed photograph above shows the Colonnade at Washington and Lee University, as photographed by Miley about 1890. In classical architecture, a colonnade denotes a long sequence of columns joined by the superstructure of bands and moldings that are often freestanding or part of a building. Work began on the center building, originally called Washington College Building and then Washington Hall, in 1822. After Virginia seceded from the Union, students hoisted a Confederate flag on a pole attached to the statue of George Washington atop Washington Hall. School president George Junkin demanded its removal, but the students refused. When the faculty sided with the students, Junkin resigned his office and moved to Pennsylvania.

General Lee only reluctantly agreed to take on the job as president of Washington College when it was offered to him in 1865. This medallion is a copy from around 1890 of an earlier set of photographs that Miley made in 1867.

On August 4, 1865, the board of trustees of Washington College voted to offer Robert E. Lee the job of president. Lee accepted reluctantly because he was concerned that his presence could damage the school's reputation. Nevertheless, believing he might be able to do some good, he accepted and rode into town on his favorite horse, Traveller, on September 18. Under his leadership, the school was placed on solid academic footing and expanded both its curriculum and its faculty.

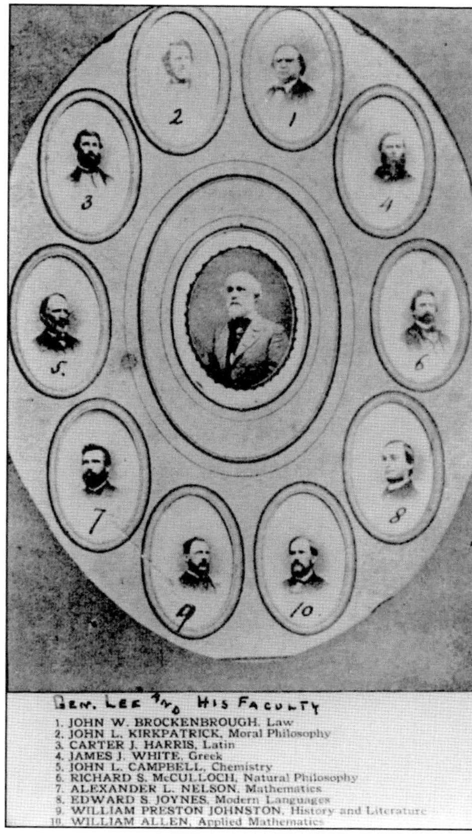

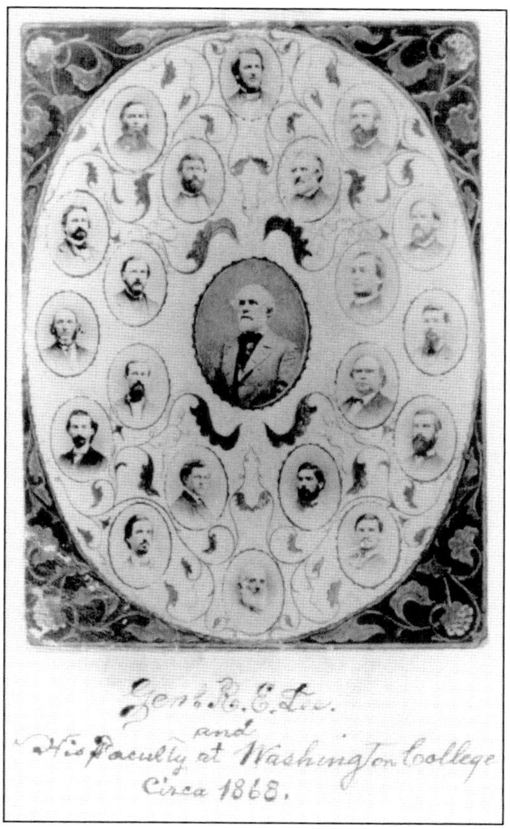

In 1866, Lexington Law School was incorporated into the college, and, in 1868, the faculty abandoned the traditional curriculum of uniform studies for all students in favor of a system of independent departments. While Lee was president, a business school was established, the departments of agriculture, commerce, and applied chemistry were created, and the engineering school was expanded. Within days of his death in 1870, the board voted to change the school's name to Washington and Lee College. These medallions are from 1867–1868.

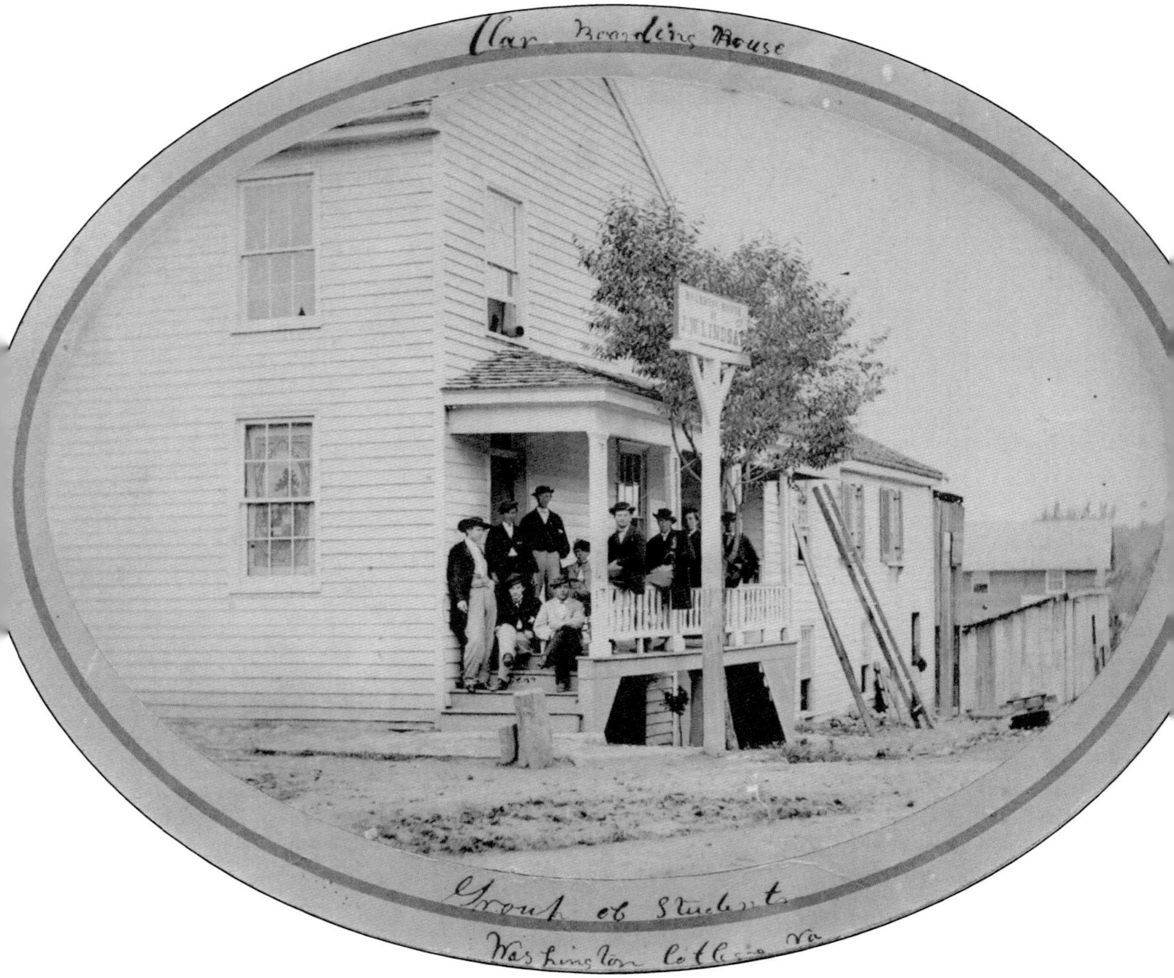

This is the full photograph that appears in detail on the cover of this book. In this beautifully engaging Boude and Miley photograph from 1869, the photographer sets an evocative mood of Washington and Lee students relaxing or posing on the front porch of the J.W. Lindsay boardinghouse. It was extremely common for young, single men to stay in boardinghouses in cities and small towns, especially before colleges and universities began providing housing. Most boardinghouses provided room, board, and sometimes extras like laundry services. Depending on the quality of the establishment and especially its reputation, the rent could be very inexpensive. Most boardinghouses had strict rules governing the behavior of the tenants, including set times for eating and going to bed. The first dormitory provided by W&L was known as the Blue Hotel, and a more modern residence hall was completed in 1904.

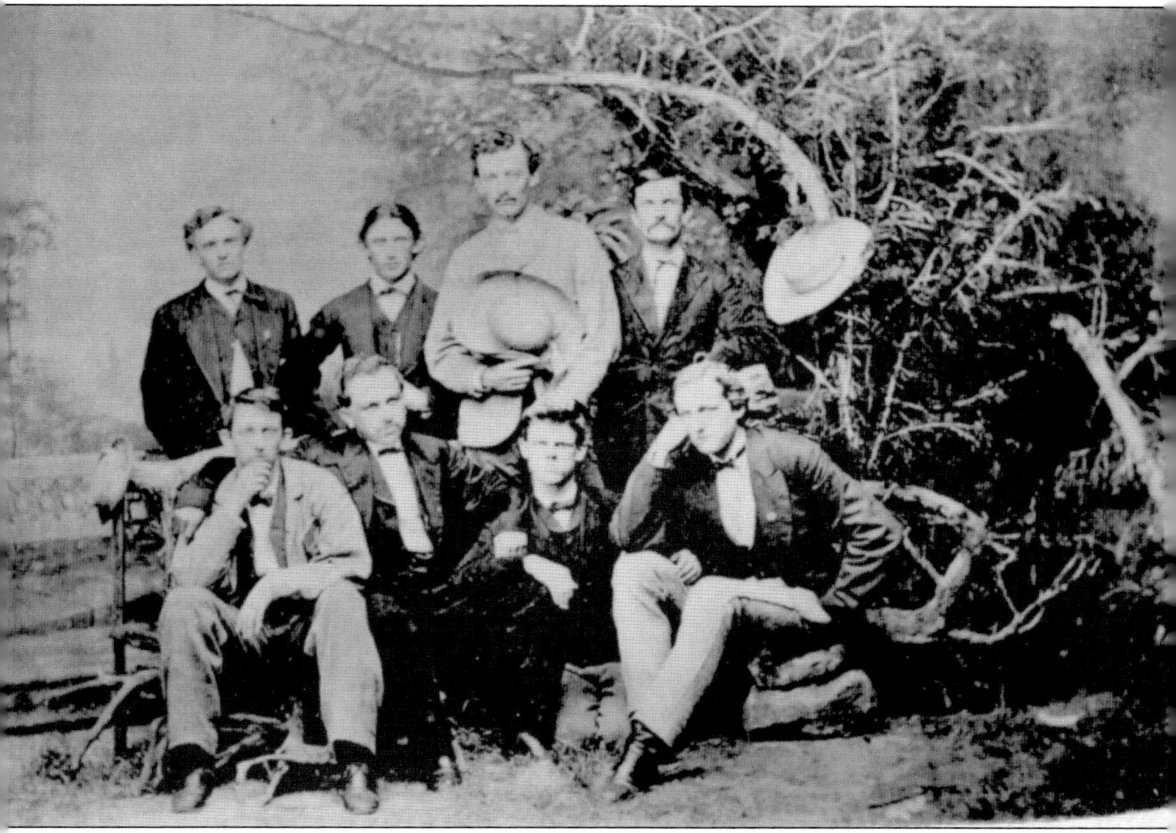

In a 1940 issue of the W&L alumni magazine, this photograph, taken in 1869 by Miley/Boude, is identified as "The Ugly Club." The club was founded in 1867 by a group of students to relieve the boredom and monotony of the five days of speech making prior to commencement. According to the alumni magazine, the group was selected "by common consent" to stage "a celebration, humorous and satirical, to relieve the more serious exercises of the Week." The speakers, or members of the club, were designated as the Ugly Man, the Pretty Man, the Vain Man, the Ladies Man, the Lazy Man, the Blow, the Little Man, the Bore, and the Critic. In one year, a member was called the Baby and was provided a stick of candy as tall as he was. He was six-feet-four and weighed 290 pounds. The celebrations were noted for their outlandish speeches and humorous antics, all designed to relieve the tension of the final week of the year. The event survived for only 10 years and died, along with many other organizations at the university, because of decreasing numbers of students. By 1881, only 96 students were enrolled at W&L.

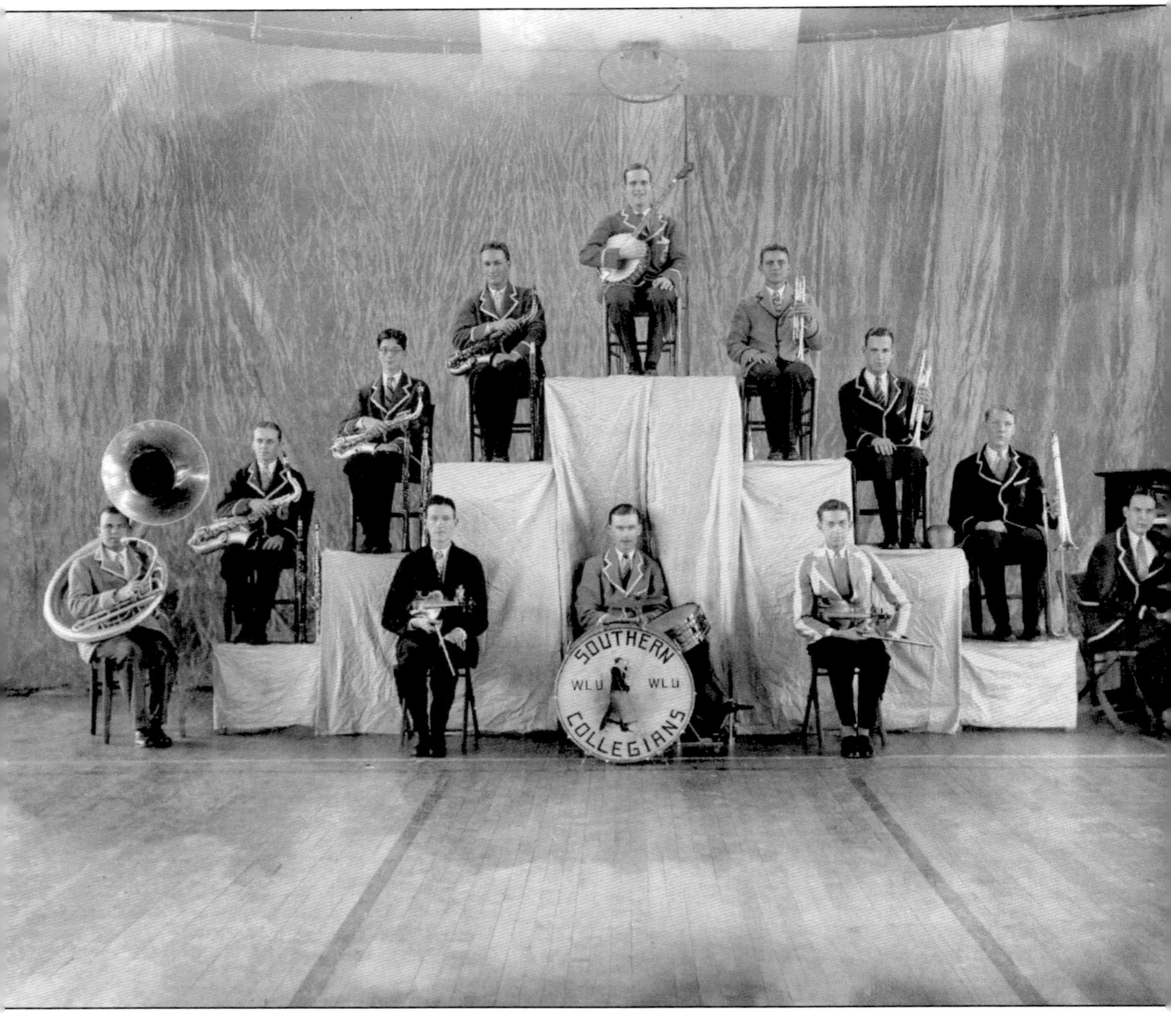

By the late 1910s and early 1920s, college dance bands and orchestras became extremely popular as a new sense of freedom swept across the country and the collegiate scene. Young people began to listen to and dance to jazz and ragtime music, and, while big name bands played on campuses, groups made up of students were also common. Sometime around 1920 at Washington and Lee, the Southern Collegians Orchestra was organized, and they became popular as college dances proliferated. The Southern Collegians were successful enough that, by 1925, they were able to book a European tour that included dates in Liverpool, Cherbourg, and Hamburg. They ended the tour with a two-week engagement in Paris. This photograph was taken by Henry Miley, as he continued to photograph W&L and VMI students and organizations for their yearbooks. This photograph dates from around 1920 and was taken in the Doremus Gymnasium on the W&L campus.

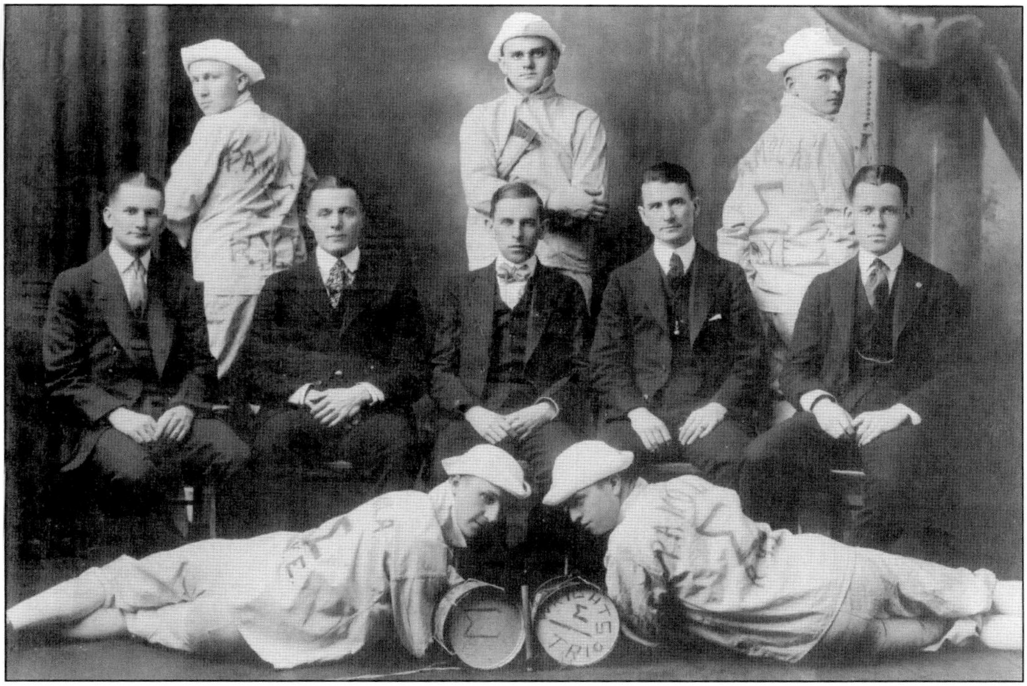

There have been many collegiate secret societies in the United States, most of which were founded in the period between 1880 and World War I. This is a photograph of the Sigma Society, founded in 1880. It is purported to be one of the older secret societies in the country and one of the oldest continuously active social organizations at W&L. Little is known about this photograph other than the fact that it was taken by Miley. The letters "P.A.M.O.L.A. R.Y.E." appear in the photograph. These letters are closely tied to the Sigma Society.

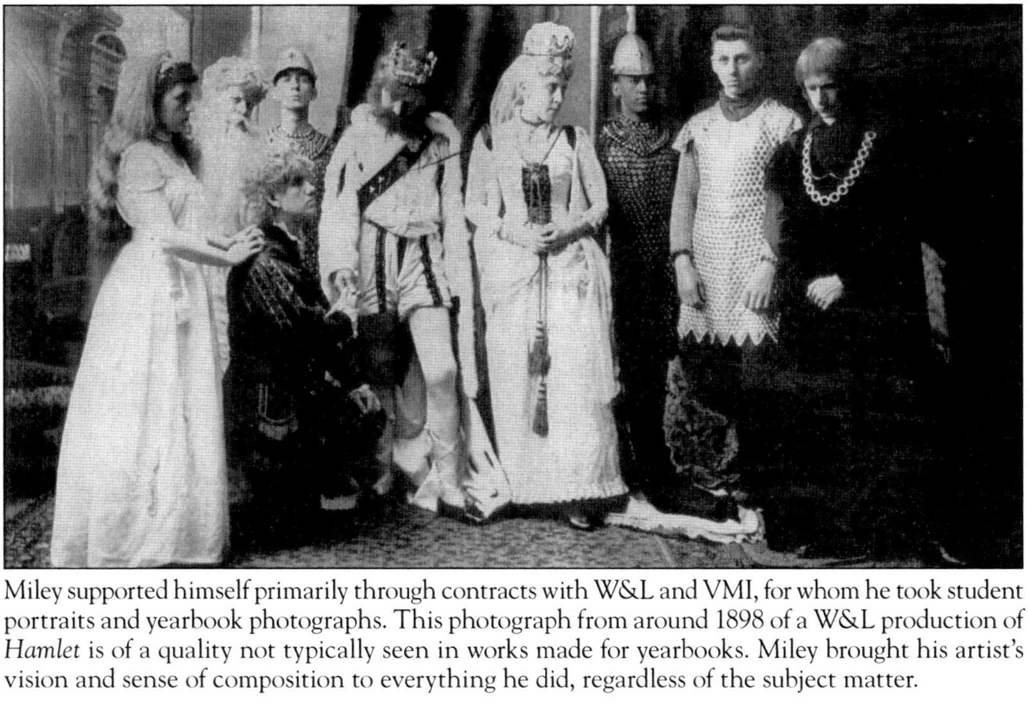

Miley supported himself primarily through contracts with W&L and VMI, for whom he took student portraits and yearbook photographs. This photograph from around 1898 of a W&L production of *Hamlet* is of a quality not typically seen in works made for yearbooks. Miley brought his artist's vision and sense of composition to everything he did, regardless of the subject matter.

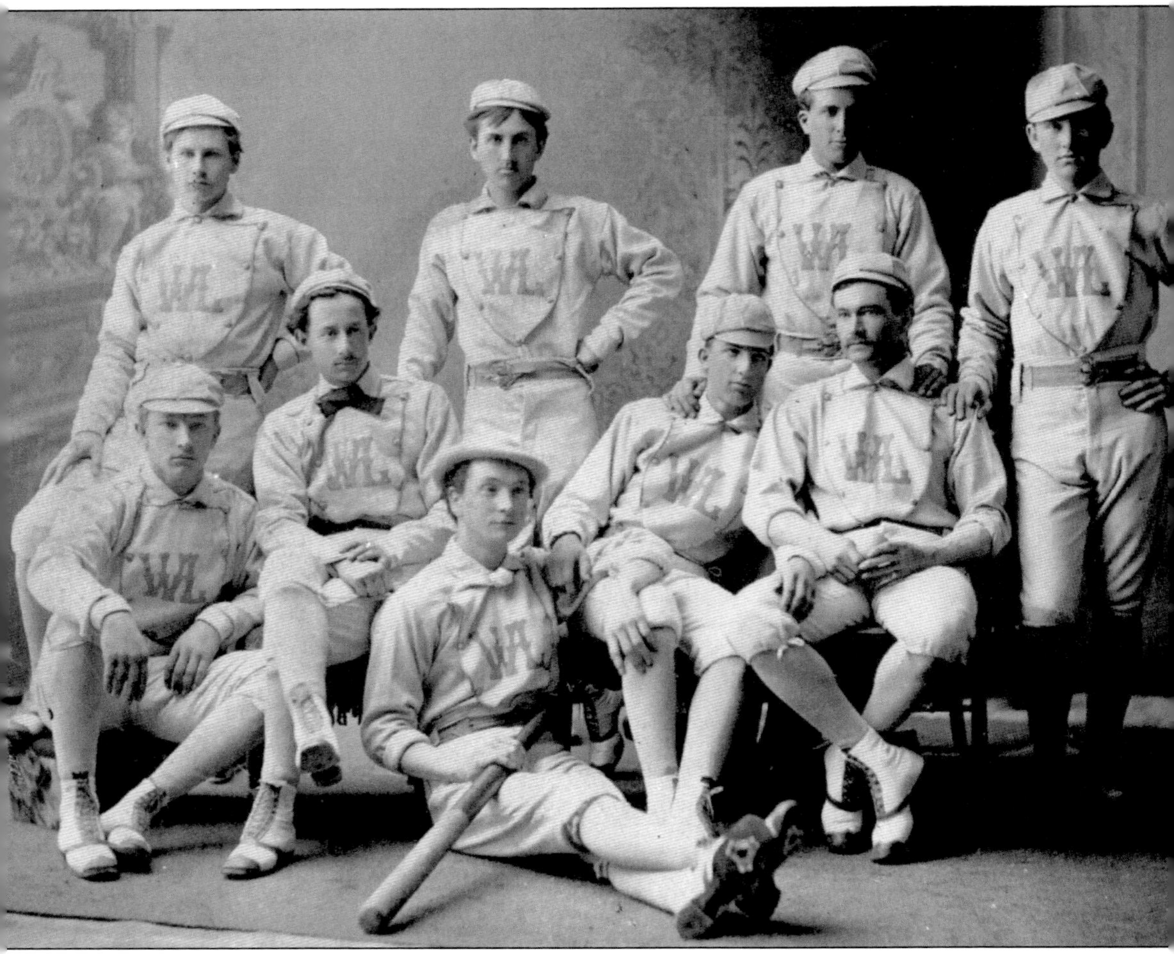

This Miley photograph of a W&L baseball team in 1872 shows a very early baseball uniform. The image illustrates how uniforms and even the attitudes of the players changed over time. The hats, bibs, shoes, and the way the players are standing, sitting, and touching each other suggests conviviality and brotherly good nature and also a certain prissiness that is absent from later team photographs, which show a tougher, more masculine appearance and demeanor. Washington and Lee claims a first in intercollegiate baseball: on May 20, 1878, George Augustus Sykes of W&L used what is claimed as the first curveball thrown in intercollegiate baseball to defeat the University of Virginia by a score of 12-0. Stunned by the new pitch, 16 Cavaliers struck out, and Virginia refused to play the Generals the next year. The series resumed in 1880. By then, Virginia had a curveball pitcher of its own. Knox College in Illinois also claims to be the first college team to have a curveball pitcher. The Baseball Hall of Fame recognizes Candy Cummings, an amateur from Brooklyn, as the inventor of the curveball in 1867. Baseball and basketball were officially recognized as college sports at W&L in 1907.

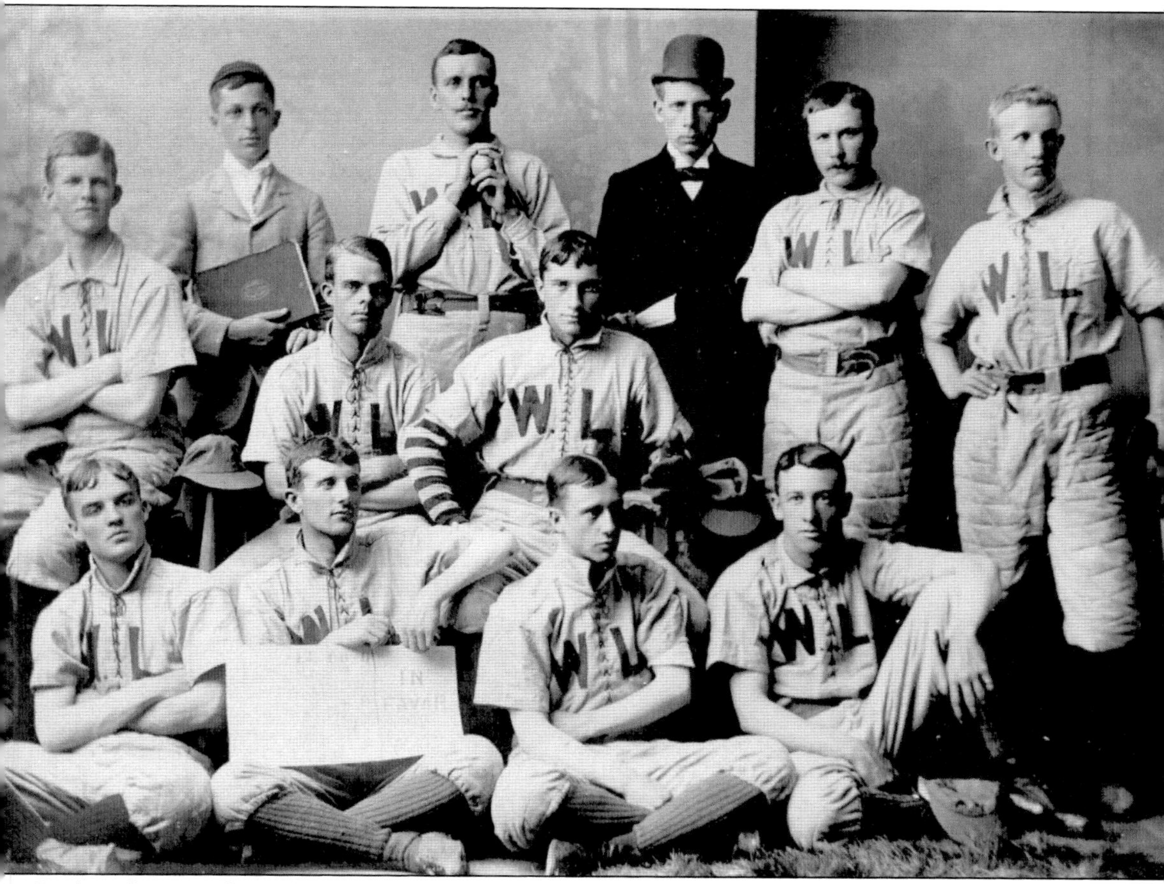

In this photograph of the 1892–1893 Washington and Lee baseball team, which was still not officially recognized as such at this time, the evolution of the game is apparent. One of the individuals is holding a book, suggestive of the importance statistics were beginning to have on the game, and there is a coach or manager in the photograph as well. There is also a seriousness to this photograph that the photograph on the opposite page lacks. The players look more like athletes, and their stances and facial expressions reflect this. One of the players is leaning on his bat while another is holding a baseball. They appear to be all about the game. In early photographs of baseball teams, there are rarely more than 10 players pictured because there were rarely more than 10 players on a team. It was not uncommon for a team to have only the required nine players. Characteristically, Miley has some of the individuals in the photograph looking away from the camera.

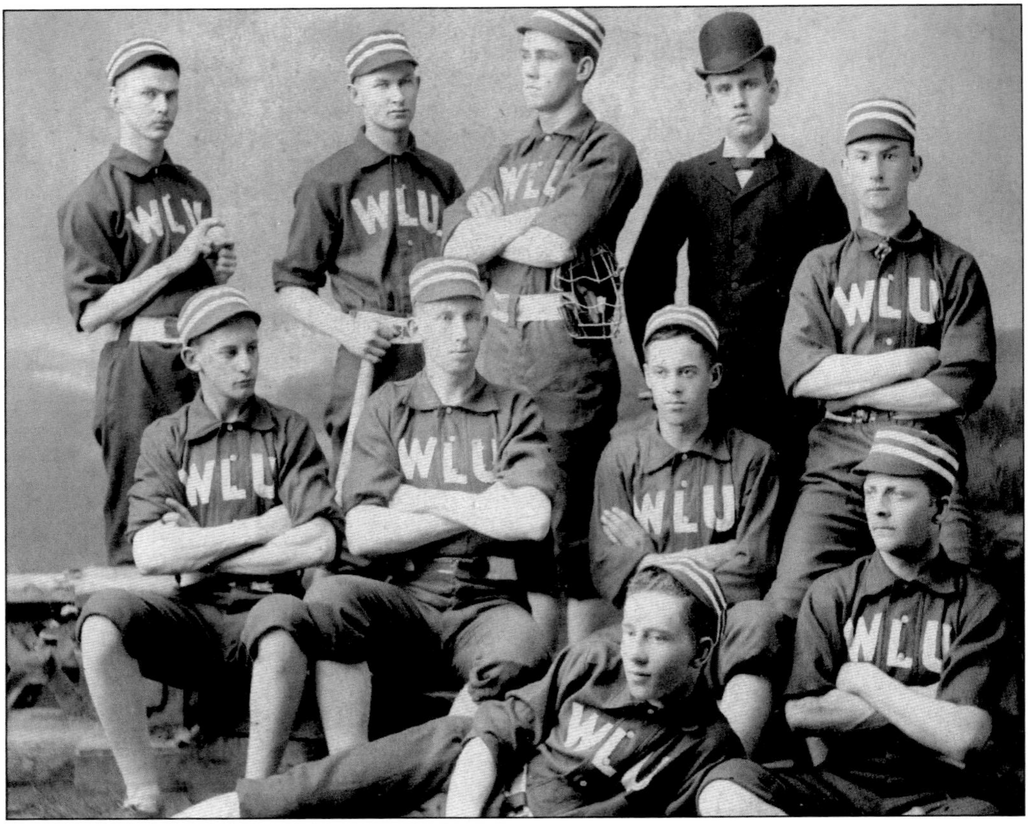

In these two photographs, from 1889–1890, Miley successfully captured the competitive masculine attitude that had permeated baseball by this time period. These young men exhibit the toughness and grit that were now part of the game but were not typical in the more genteel game that was played in the 1870s. These two photographs show these men as players ready to take the field. Visible here as well are a catcher's mask and a catcher's mitt. The role and placement of the catcher changed with the advent of the curveball as well. Before the curveball was commonplace, the catcher stood far behind the batter, but the curveball made it necessary for the catcher to hunker down directly behind the batter, a brave move that necessitated the addition of new equipment.

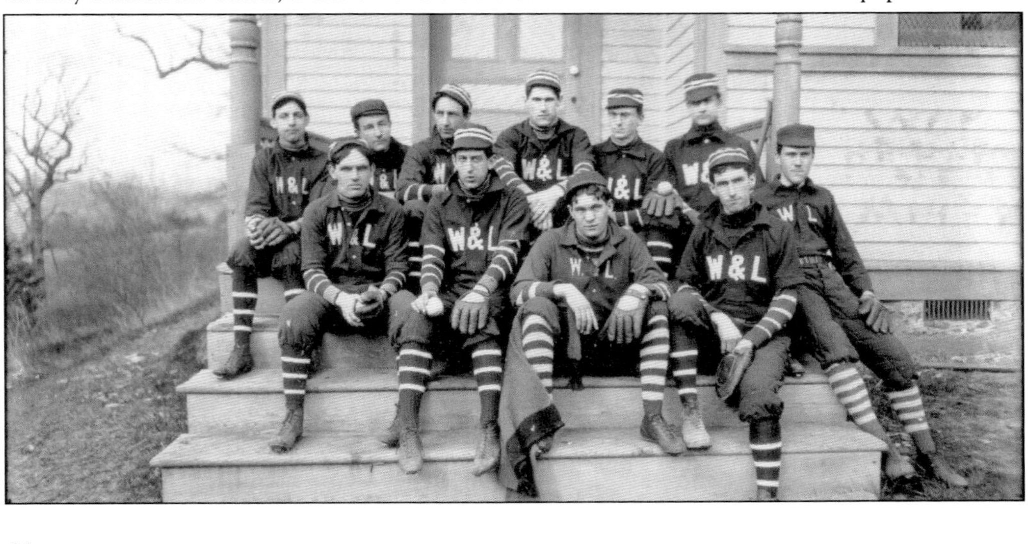

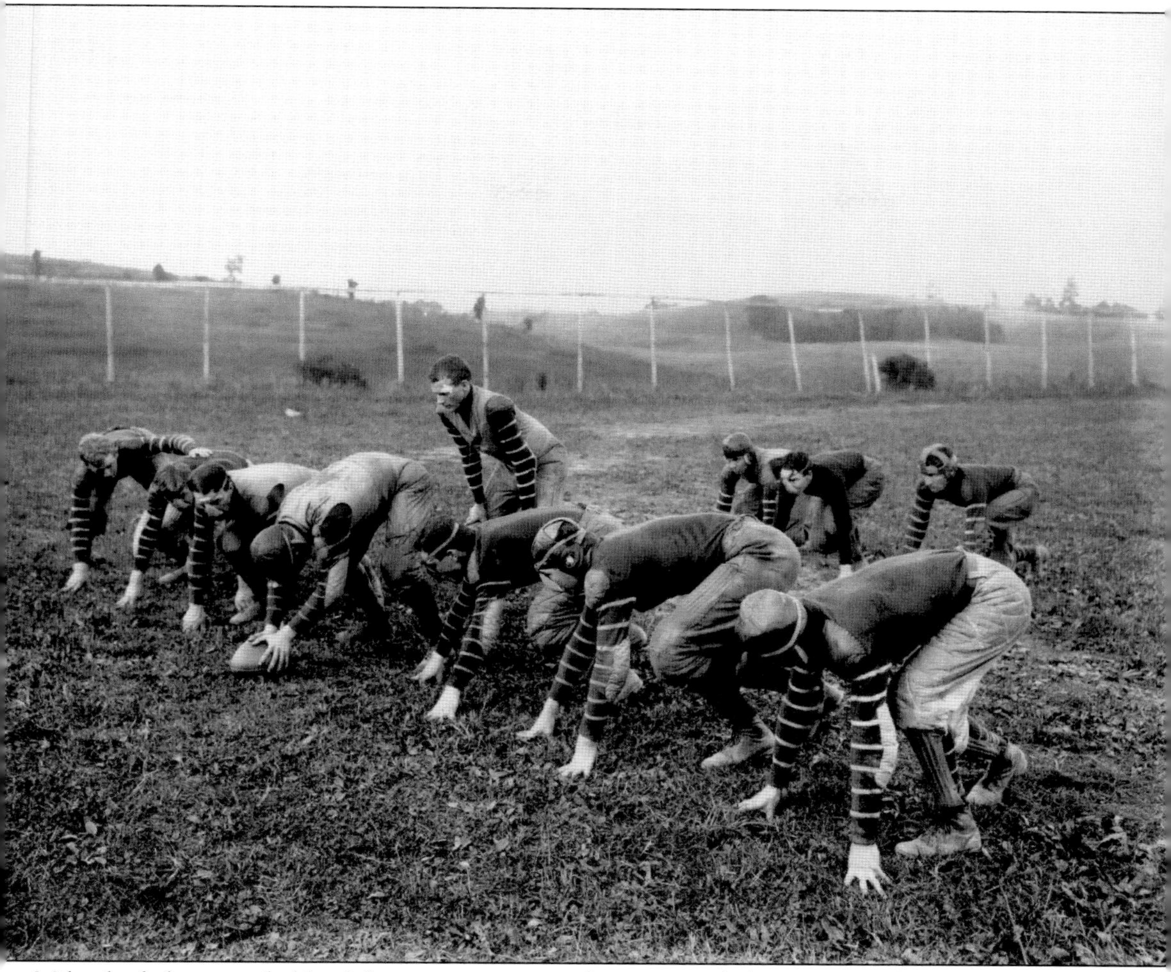

Miley had the remarkable ability to go out into the town and the countryside and capture photographs of people engaging in their normal daily activities, much in the way that photography is used today to document the ordinary. The Washington and Lee football team is seen here in the 1890s. In November 1873, Washington and Lee met neighboring Virginia Military Institute in the first intercollegiate football game in the South. The Generals emerged victorious, 4-2, on VMI's parade ground. The game is not recognized as an official athletic contest, because there were no other teams on the schedule and each team featured 25 or so players on the field. The university officially recognized football games only from 1890. In 1880, official rules were established that created the 11-man team and the snap from center, but many more innovations would come later.

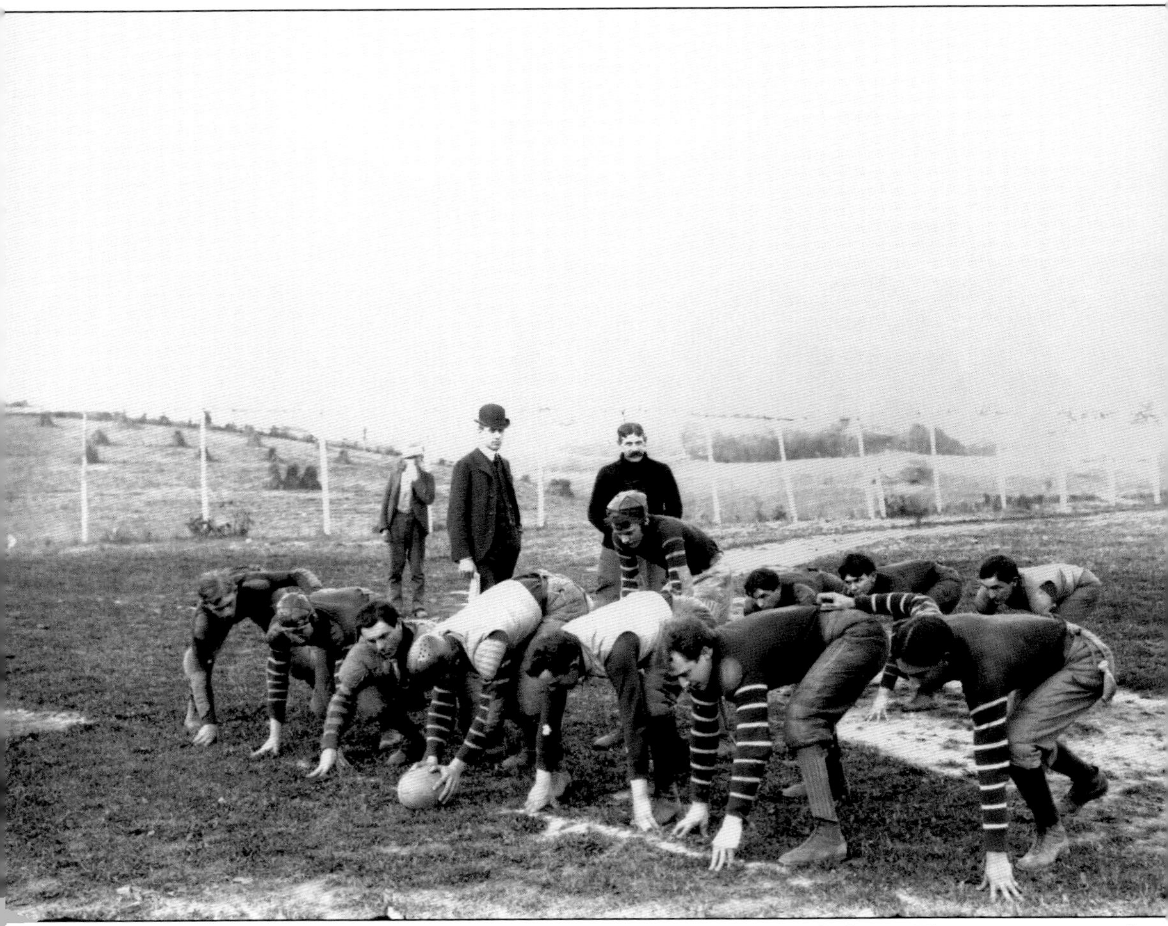

In this Miley photograph, fewer than half of the players are wearing helmets. This was not unusual at all for football teams prior to the 1920s. The actual catalyst for the creation of the football helmet was the College Football Rules Convention in 1888. That year, tackling below the waist became a legal action; as a result, pads and other protective gear, including helmets, began to be slowly introduced into the game. Two players, one from Navy and the other from Lafayette University, are credited with introducing the helmet into the game. Fashioned out of leather, there was no universal style at first. Most helmets, as seen in this photograph, were little more than leather hats that sat on top of the head. It was not until after 1900 that the leather helmet would cover the entire head. Also visible here are nose guards and earflaps, which were introduced early as protection as well. Helmets were slow to catch on; by 1920, it is estimated that only about half of the players on any given team wore them.

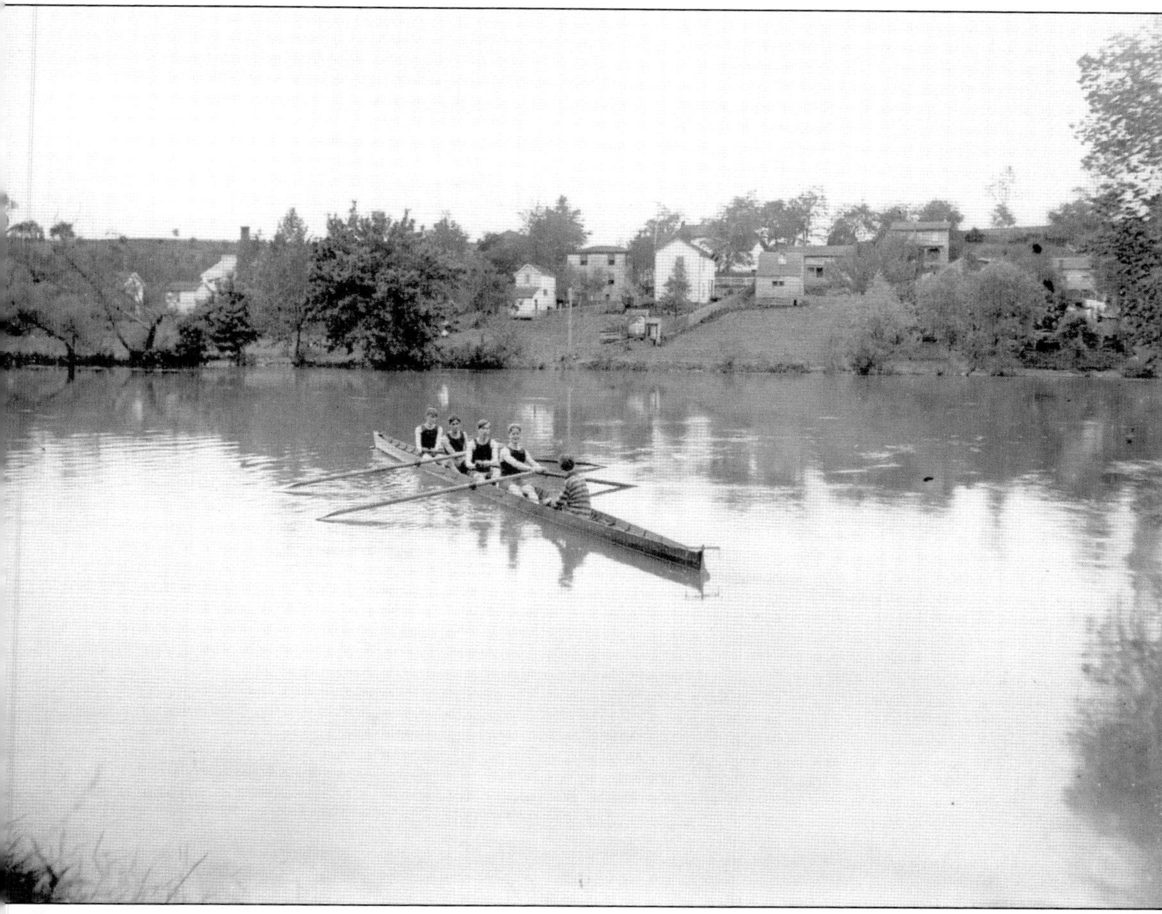

Rowing, or crew, was one of the most popular sports at both W&L and VMI in the late 19th century. This lovely photograph was taken in 1874 by Miley, no doubt during one of his trips out and about in town, on the hunt for interesting images. No one in the boat is identified, so it is impossible to know from which school they came. The sport of rowing has British origins, and the first known race held in America occurred in New York City in 1756. On the intercollegiate level, the sport has a long and renowned history, with the first documented event being the Harvard-Yale Regatta, which was held for the first time in 1852 and is purported to be the oldest intercollegiate sporting event in the United States. Though it is difficult to see, the lead rower in this photograph is beaming with delight and staring straight at Miley on the shore.

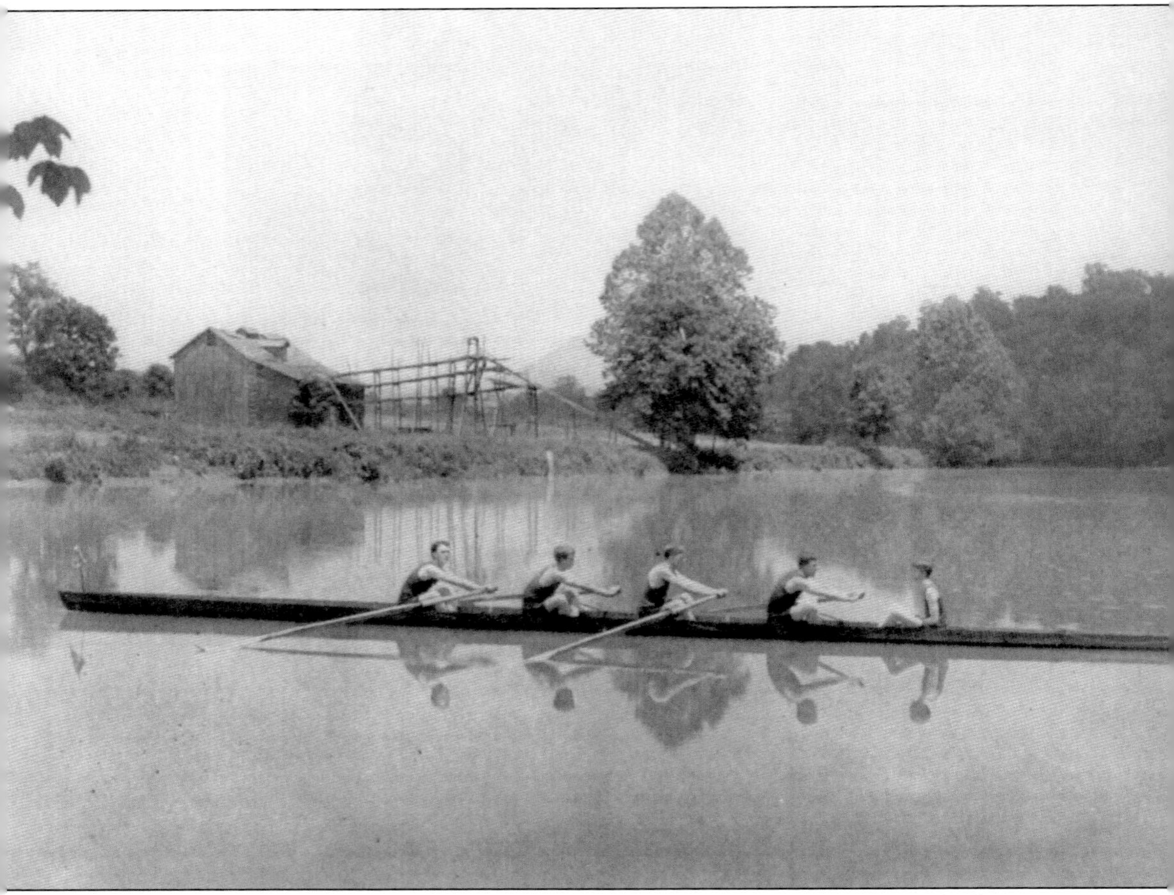

This and the rowing photograph on the previous page show how Miley was a brilliant composer of scenes that reflected not only the specific subject—in this case the rowers—but also the environment that they were in. He added the rowers to an already beautiful pastoral scene. Rowing was one of the most popular of the early competitive sports at Washington and Lee University. Races on the North River (later the Maury) are documented to have occurred as early as the late 1860s. In 1870, a group of faculty members purchased two crew boats, and intense club rivalries began to develop on campus. The sporting events drew significant crowds along the riverbanks to watch and cheer on their favorite teams. As competition from other sports intensified in the early 20th century, the popularity of crew declined, but the sport was revived and flourished in the post–World War II era.

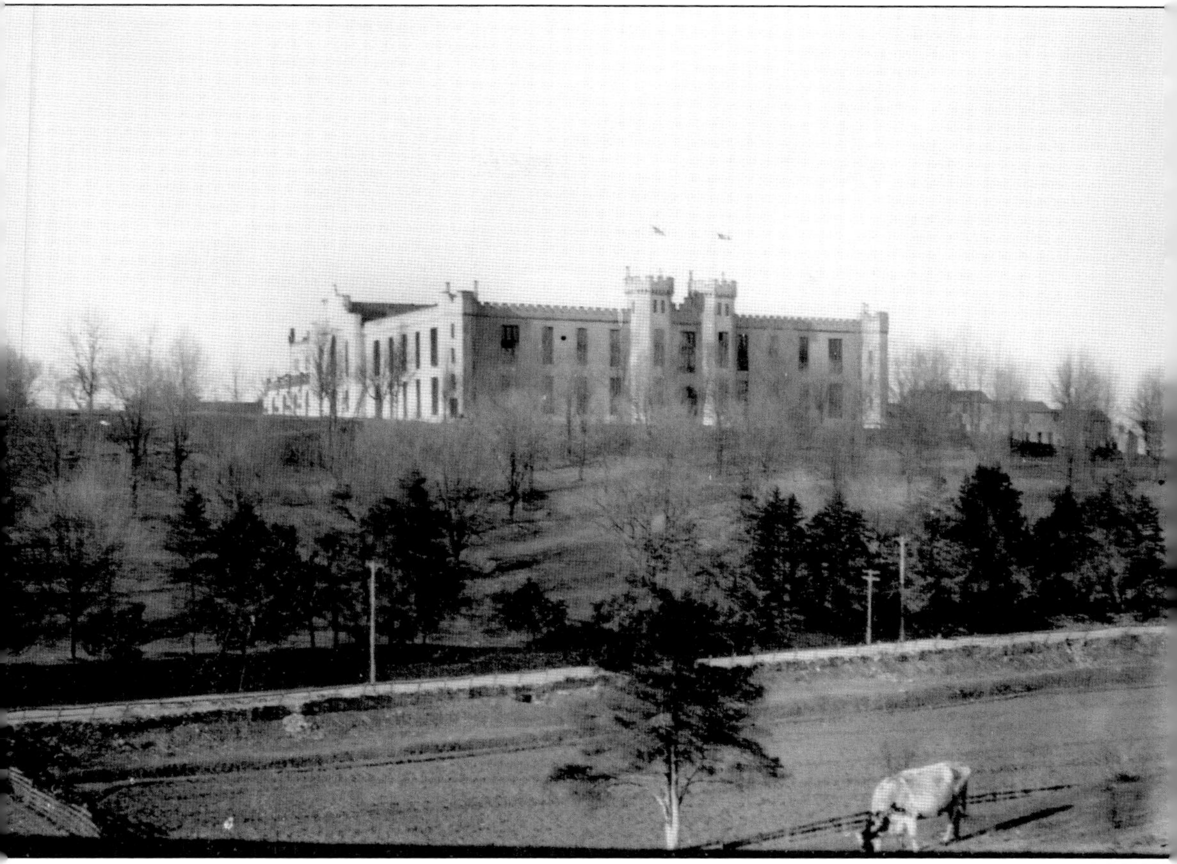

A typical Miley view, the barracks at Virginia Military Institute is seen here from Diamond Hill in Lexington. Miley's genius as a photographic artist was his ability to include so much in a scene without detracting from the central focal point. In this case, his intent is obviously to show a photograph of the barracks, but in the process, he enhances its presence on the landscape by including the hillside, the road, the utility poles, and, of course, the wonderful cow grazing in the field. The setting is almost medieval in its composition, with the castle on the hill overlooking the grasslands and grazing pastures that surround it. VMI was founded on November 11, 1839, and the cornerstone of the new barracks was laid in 1850. The following year, Thomas "Stonewall" Jackson became a member of the faculty and a professor of natural and experimental philosophy.

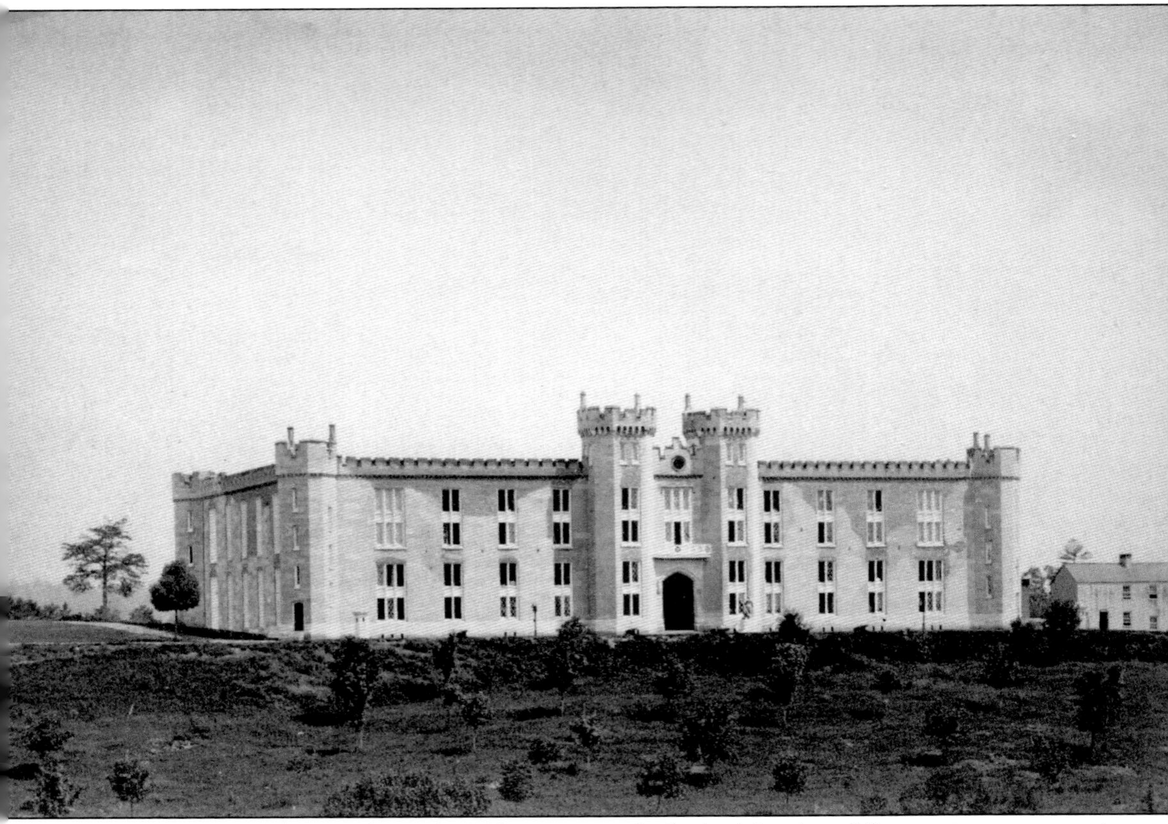

In this view of the VMI barracks, Miley captures the look of the place following its reconstruction in the wake of the Civil War. On June 12, 1864, Union forces under the command of Gen. David Hunter shelled and burned VMI as part of the Valley Campaign. The destruction was almost complete, and VMI had to temporarily hold classes in Richmond. The Lexington campus reopened for classes on October 17, 1865. It has been argued that one of the reasons that Confederate general Jubal A. Early burned the town of Chambersburg, Pennsylvania, was in retaliation for the shelling of VMI. In a strange twist of fate following the war, David Strother, the chief of staff to General Hunter and the individual who urged the destruction of VMI, served as adjutant general of the Virginia Militia and as a member of the VMI board of visitors. In that position, he promoted and worked actively for the reconstruction of the barracks. The results of that effort are seen here. The shadowy areas on the building are the new portions, left visible as a reminder of the war and its destruction.

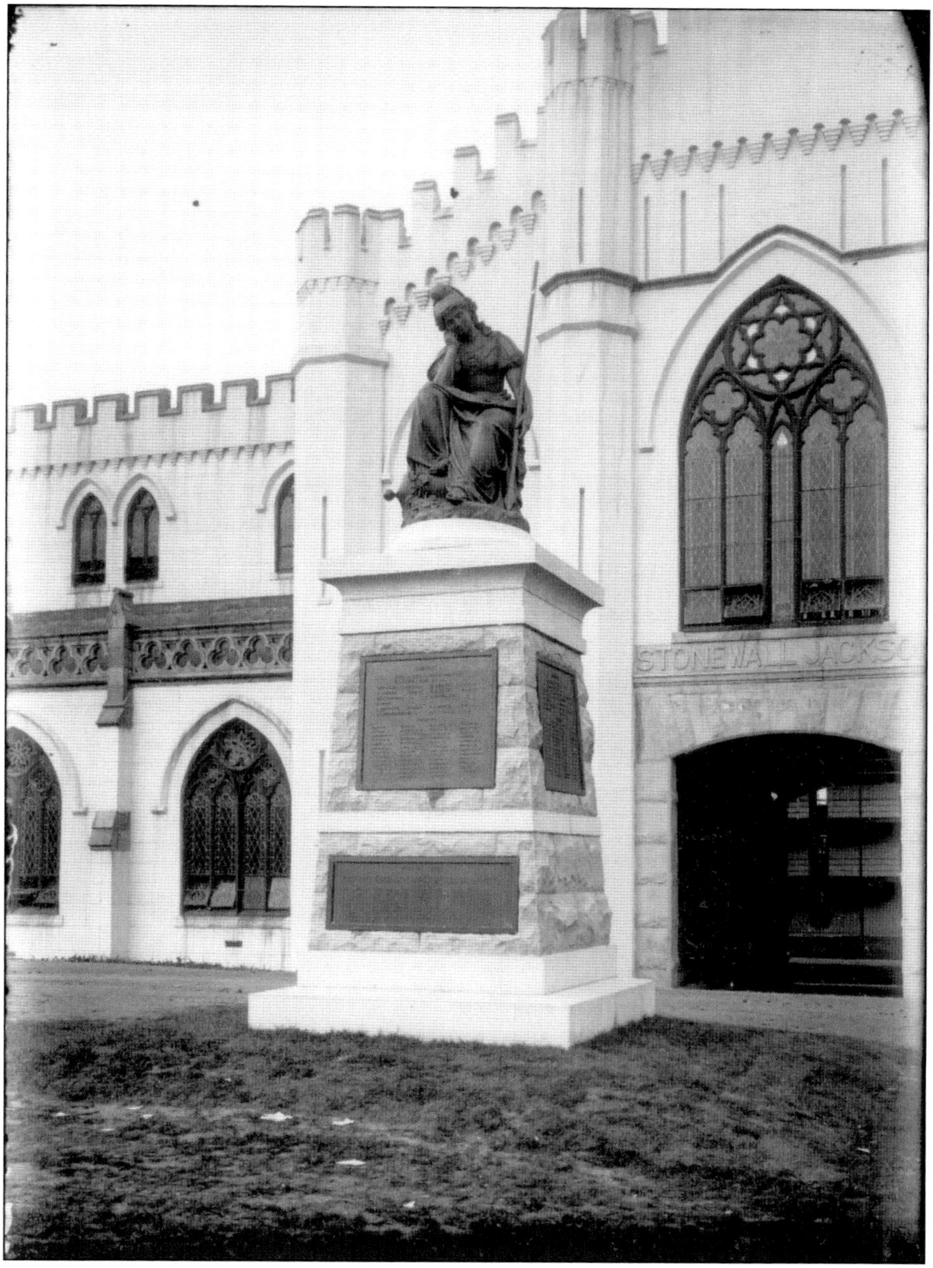

This is Miley's photograph of the statue "Virginia Mourning Her Dead," which was dedicated in 1903 and then moved to its current location in 1912. It is seen here in its original location. The statue is a memorial to the 10 VMI cadets who died at the Battle of New Market in 1864. It is a bronze statue by Moses Ezekiel, of the VMI class of 1866. Ezekiel was the first Jewish cadet to attend VMI and was present at the battle. Today, individual grave markers for the dead cadets are located behind the base of the sculpture. Remains of six of the men are set in a copper box inside the foundation of the monument. The statue itself is a complex female figure representing Virginia mourning her dead. She is seated on the ruins of a fortress with her right foot on a broken cannon. She holds a reversed lance in her left hand and wears chain mail. Her head is bowed in sadness.

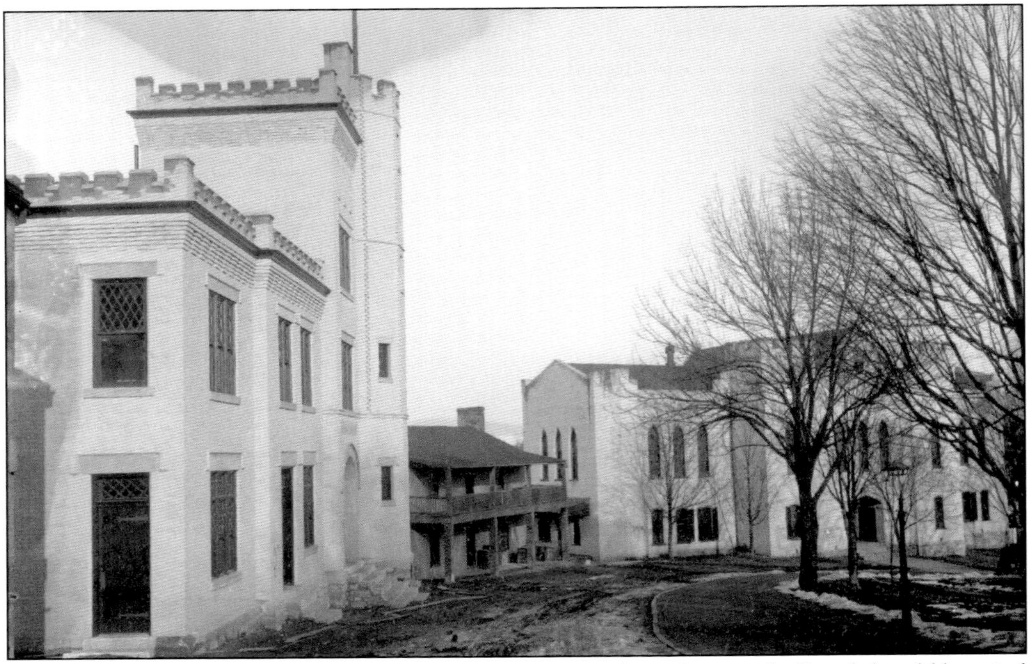

These two Miley photographs of life on the VMI campus show the mess hall and the old hospital on the VMI grounds prior to 1910 (above) and cadets on the parade grounds (below). Both photographs are undated but are probably from around 1906. Photographs of the mess hall in 1910 show that the old hospital building had been torn down by that time. Miley took a great many photographs of the grounds and buildings at VMI as part of his contract with the school. Below, a close viewing reveals that some of the cadets are in street clothing while most are in uniform. It is possible that this is a scene of young men who have just arrived at the institute being separated into their various units.

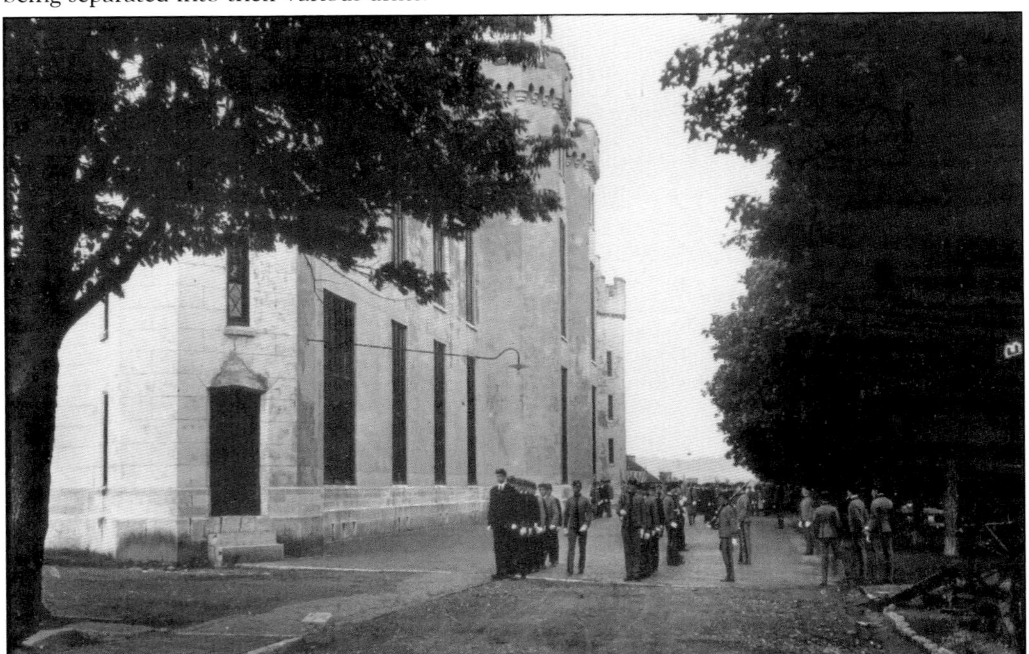

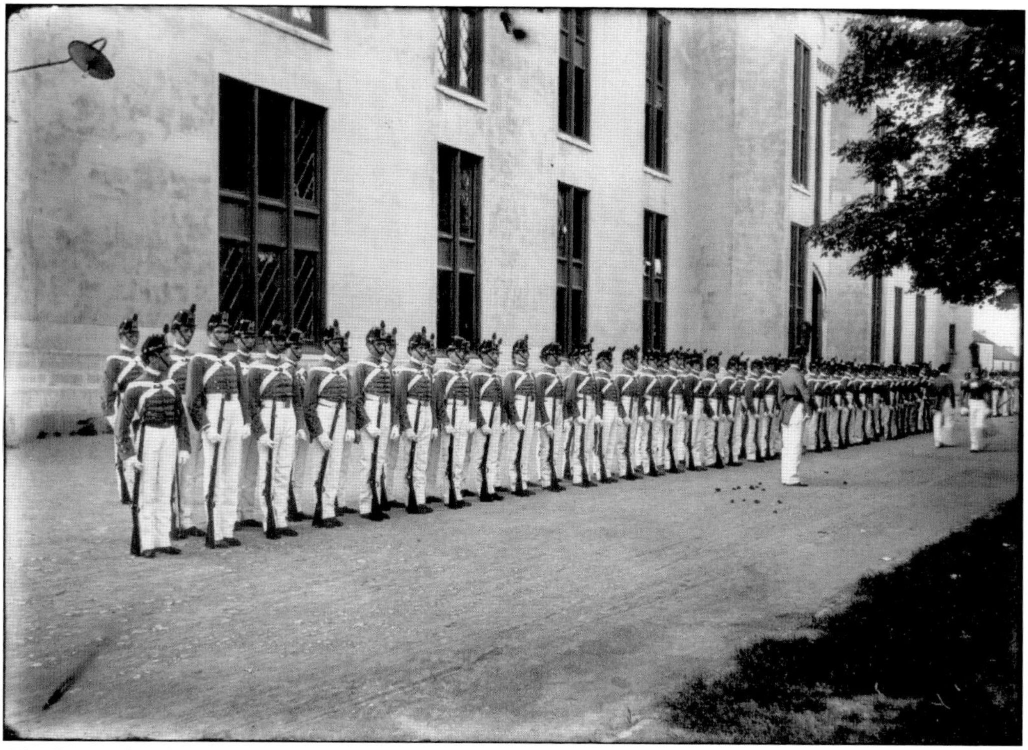

The barracks dominates the 12-acre parade ground at VMI, which is listed in the National Register of Historic Places. Parades and formations such as the New Market Day Parade and ceremony have made up an integral part of life for VMI cadets since its founding in 1839. The cadet uniform has changed little over time, and the parade uniform seen in these photographs dates back to the War of 1812.

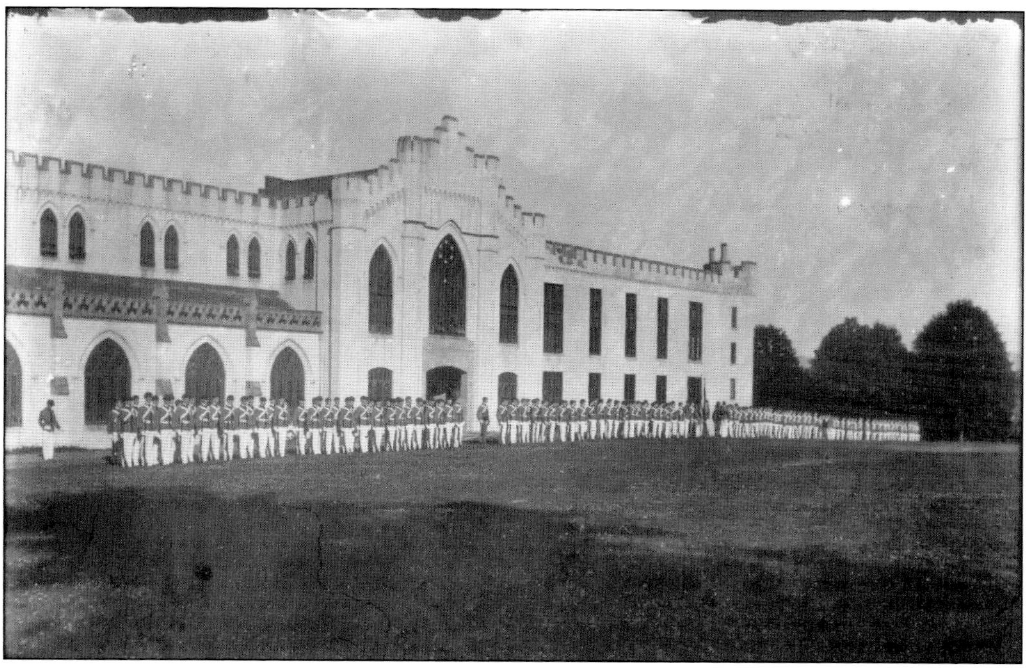

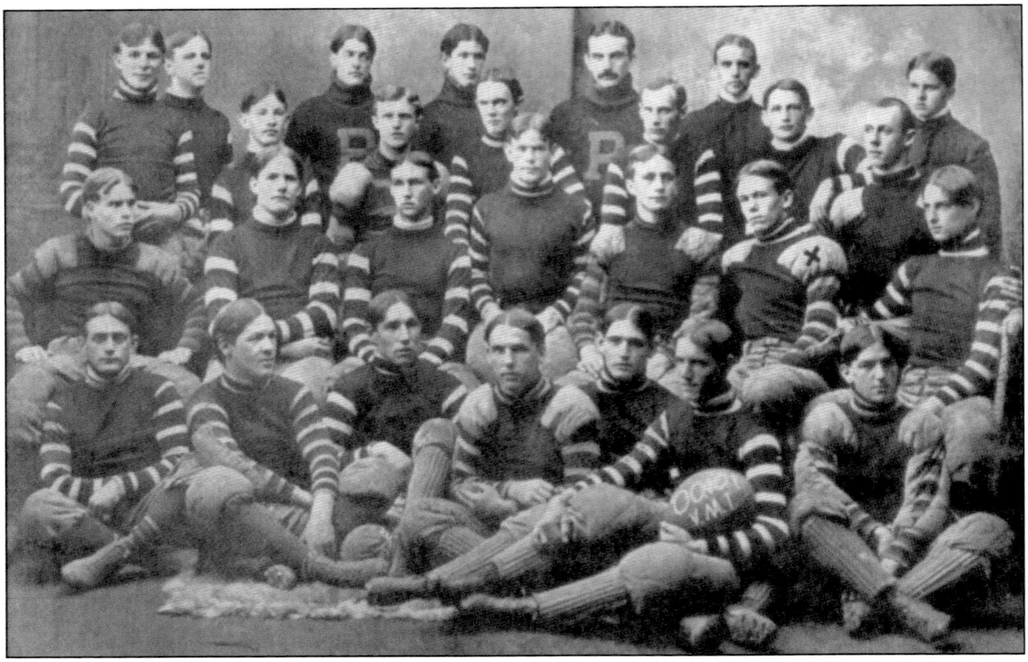

Athletics have always been an integral and important part of life for VMI cadets. This photograph of the VMI football team is easy to date, since the football being held by one cadet is marked, "00–01." Of particular interest in this photograph is the young man with the "x" on his sleeve, second from the right in the second row. He is George C. Marshall, the future Army chief of staff during World War II and arguably the most famous of the many distinguished VMI graduates.

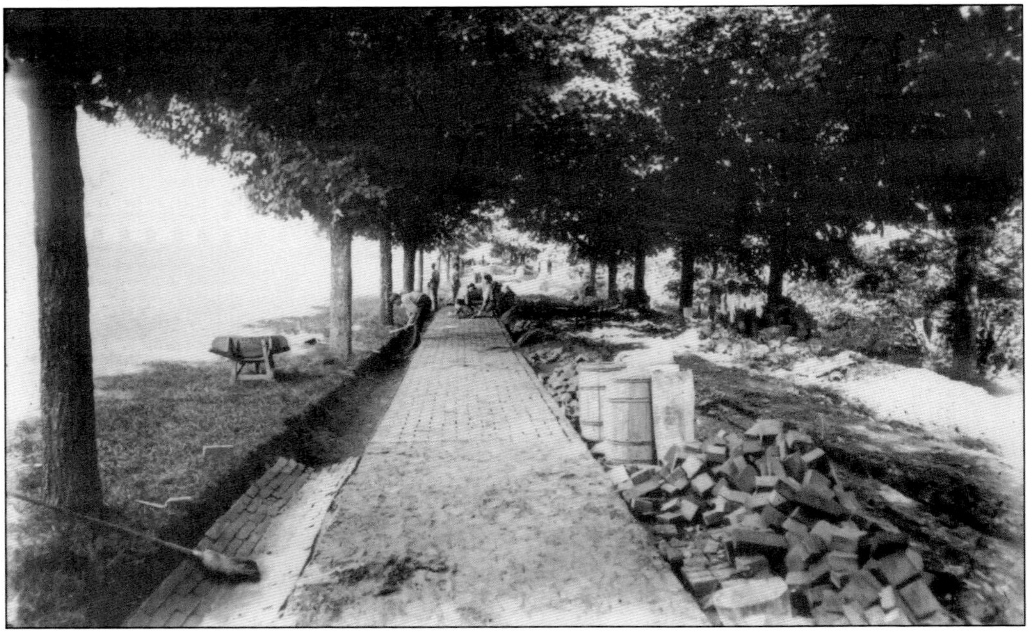

In this unusual photograph from the late 19th century, Miley has captured men at work. His camera has stopped time, yet the movement of the labor is vigorous and present in the image as the bricks are being laid and the pathway is being cut and sculpted. The work pictured is the building of the walkway into the main entrance of the VMI grounds.

Five

In the Country

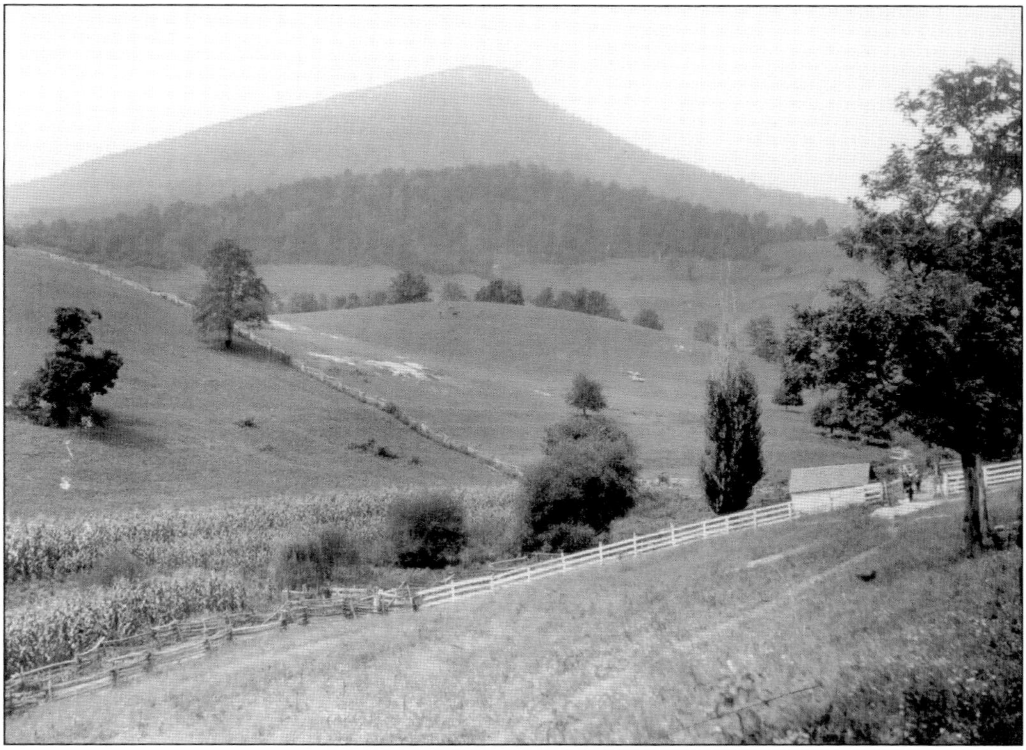

Scotch-Irish immigrants in the mid-18th century settled Rockbridge County, as they did in much of the Valley and in the mountains to the east and west. It is easy to imagine their sense of familiarity with a landscape like the one seen here, which is reminiscent of the country they left. This Miley photograph of Jump Mountain in northwest Rockbridge County serves as a fitting entry into his many photographs of the countryside he loved so much.

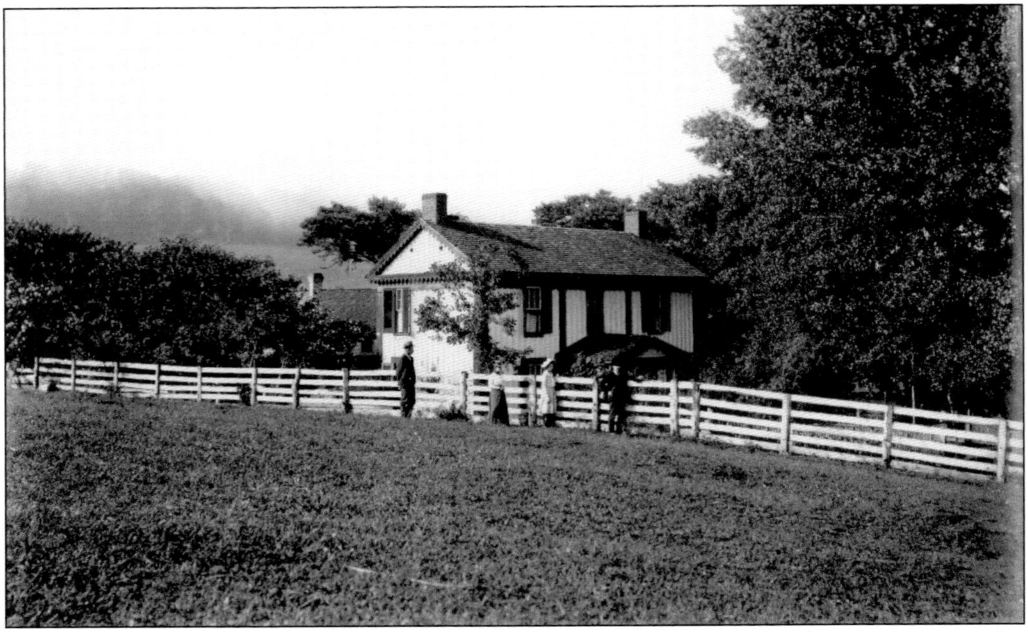

This lovely home is an example of a typical Gothic Revival–style cottage that was very popular in the rural United States in the 1850s and 1860s. Gothic details were present inside and outside the house. Books and articles by Andrew Jackson Downing, a well-known landscape architect, popularized the style, sometimes referred to as the "country cottage ideal."

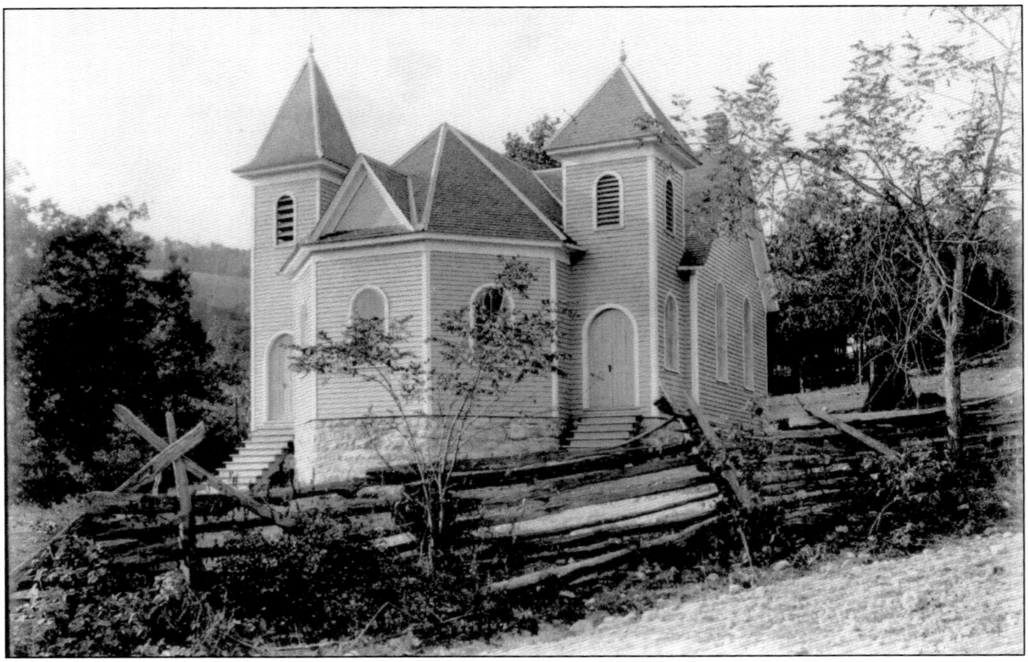

This is a Miley photograph of the Ebenezer Associate Reformed Presbyterian Church in the Kerrs Creek district of Rockbridge County. The ARP Presbyterian Church has its roots in Scotland and traveled to America with the Scotch-Irish immigrants who came out of Ulster by the thousands in the mid-18th century. Two groups were formalized as the Associate Reformed Presbyterians in 1782. Scotsman Ebenezer Erskine was important in the denomination's roots in Scotland.

Miley, always the artist, tried to capture the varied elements of natural beauty in every photograph he took, regardless of subject matter or location. The angle from which this photograph was taken highlights the rushing water and contrasts it against the stationary position of the men above it. Miley is known to have traveled a little into neighboring Augusta County looking for photographs, but not very far. This is Marl Creek in Rockbridge County. Richard Sylvester Anderson stands on the bridge, while L.R. Miller is below him.

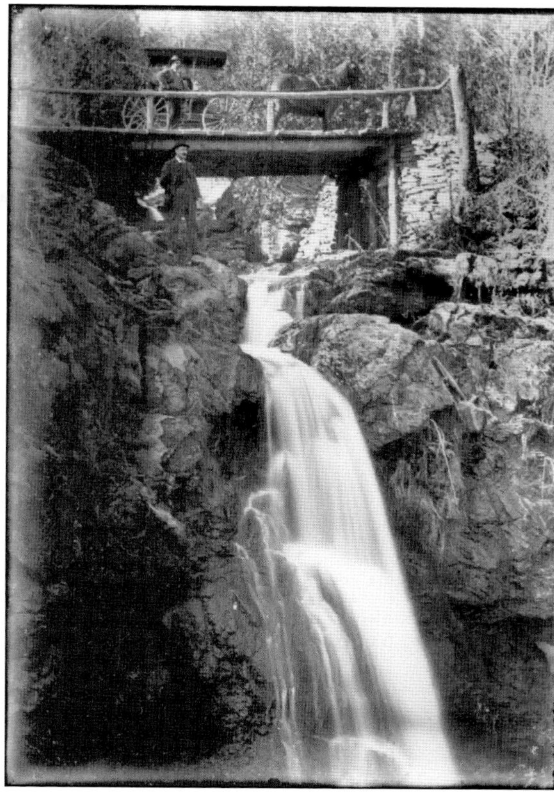

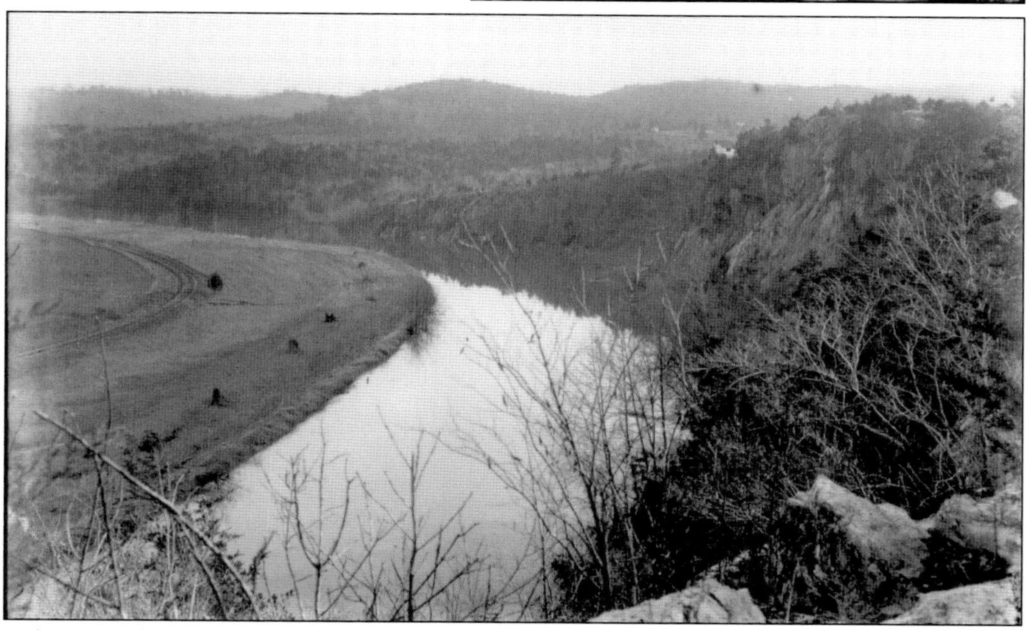

Miley was in love with the North (later the Maury) River, and he took hundreds of photographs of it from different vantage points. In this scene, between Lexington and Buena Vista in Rockbridge County, the current Chessie Trail would be on the right. In the bottomland, corn shocks and the curvature of the railroad tracks give the photograph balance and harmony. It was taken from cliffs just outside of East Lexington, upstream from Reid's (Ross's) Dam, around 1890.

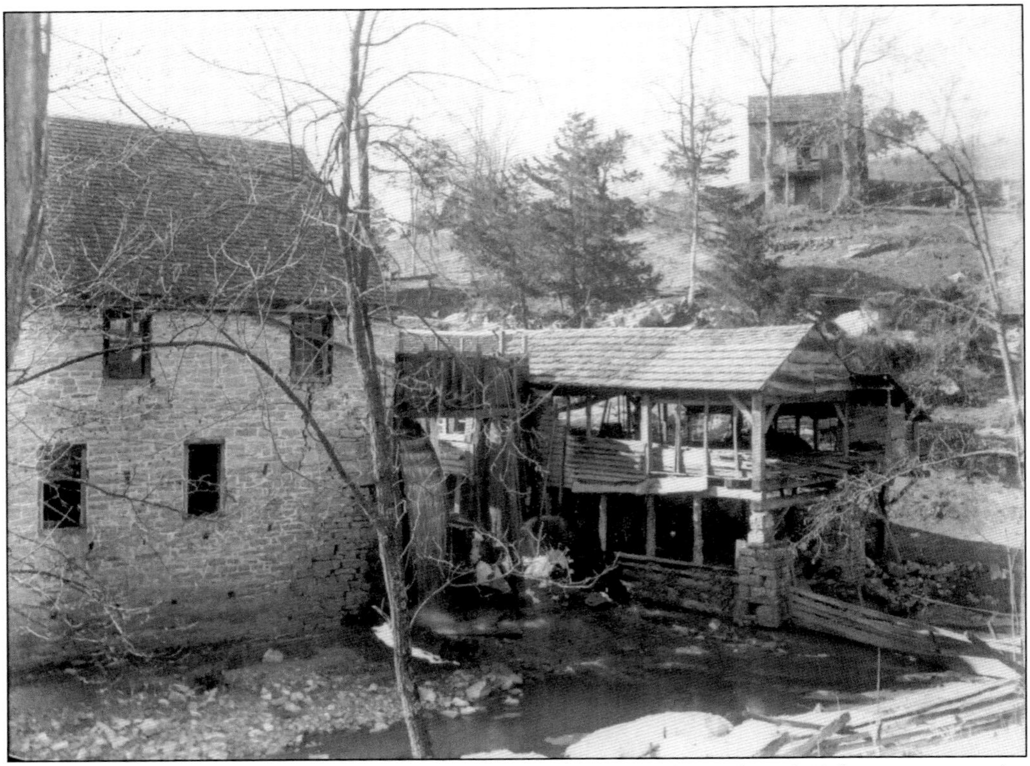

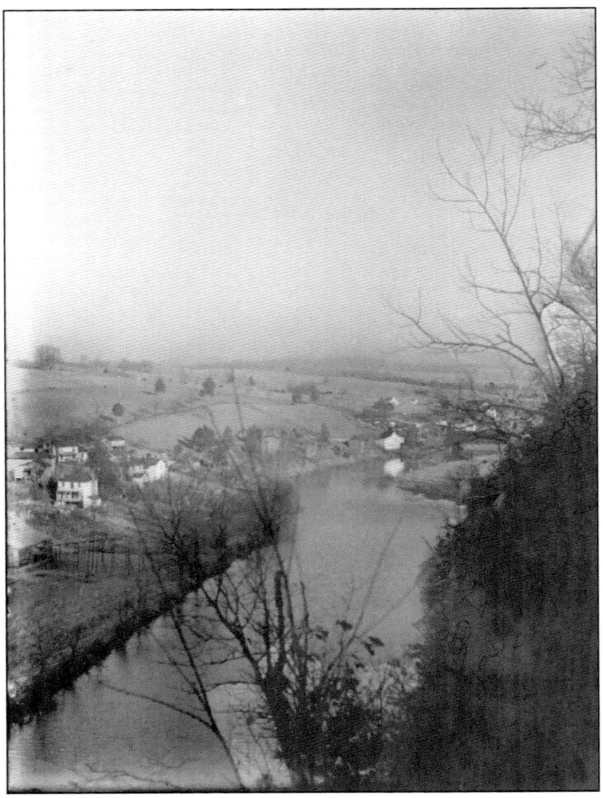

In the 18th and 19th centuries and even to some extent in the 20th, mills that ground wheat, barley, rye, and corn served as business and community centers throughout rural areas of the United States. Some mills, like the one above, could be converted to saw boards for house and barn siding as well. Miley was able to capture the actual movement of the wheel in this photograph, a feature that gives the whole scene a vibrant and lively feel.

This photograph looks from the VMI cliffs down to the Maury River and east toward Jordan's Point in Lexington. The covered bridge spanning the river is just visible behind the tree branches, and the barn in the lower left is the same barn with the ramp structure leading to the river that Miley captured in the rowing scenes on pages 69 and 70. This was and continues to be a very popular stretch of the river for recreational activities.

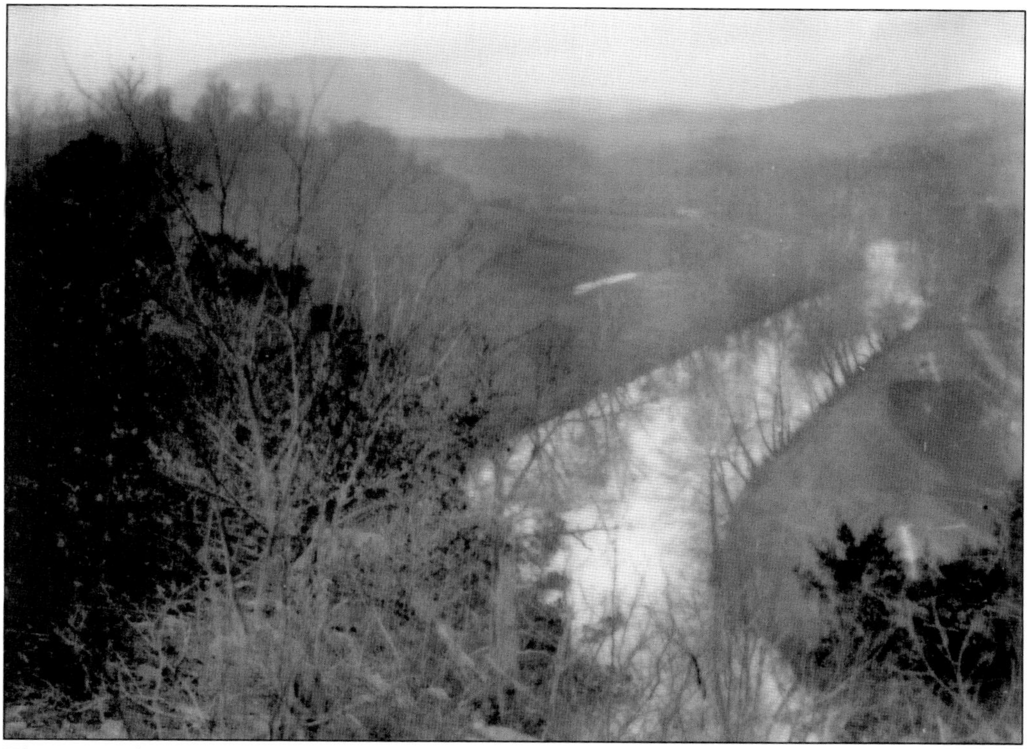

These two photographs, along with his scenes from Natural Bridge, represent work that Miley executed for his own artistic purposes and possibly for commercial purposes as well. He most likely exhibited large prints of scenes like these in his gallery, and they must have been for sale. These photographs, in addition to his large portraits, must have made his studio seem like an art gallery. He no doubt also exhibited at local and possibly regional agricultural fairs. Both of these scenes look west toward House Mountain, over the Maury River from the VMI cliffs. They are from roughly the same vantage point as the photograph on the previous page. The house at right still stands; today, the Maury Cliffs subdivision and the pole houses are directly across from it. The road on the right is Route 631.

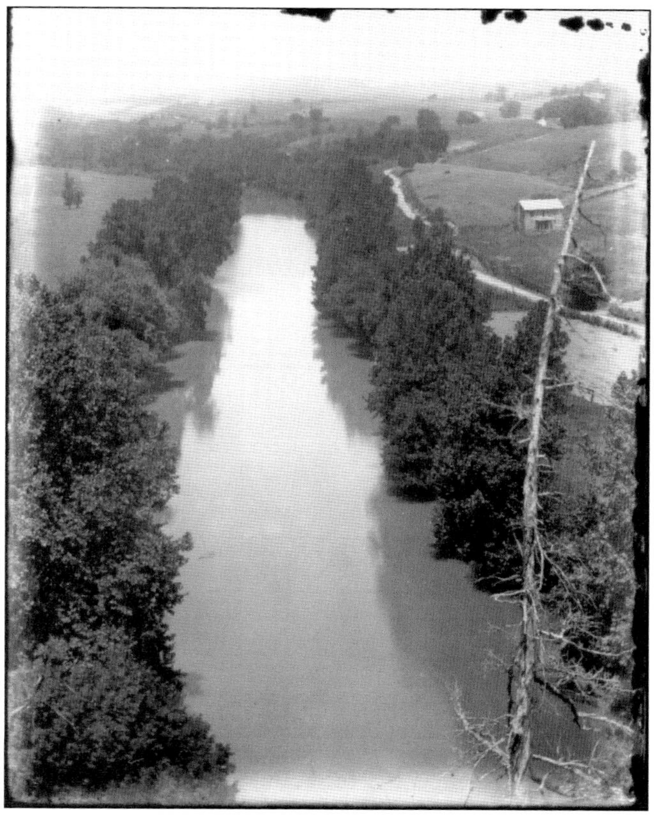

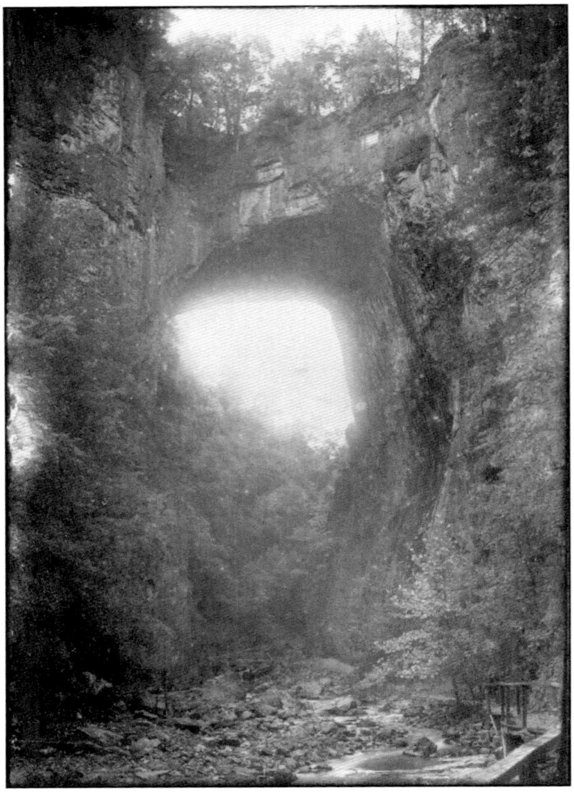

In early accounts of Rockbridge County's history, the area is sometimes referred to as Rocky Bridge, an obvious reference to the most recognizable feature of its breathtaking landscape. These two photographs introduce a series of images that Miley created of Natural Bridge. Some of them seem to emphasize the size and grandeur of the natural phenomenon, while others often reflect some commonly held artistic views of the time about depicting the relationship between man and nature. In his many photographs of Natural Bridge, Miley experimented with exposure times, camera angles, and perspective to give variety and meaning to his artistic vision. These photographs would have been exhibited in his gallery/studio in Lexington and surely would have been popular images.

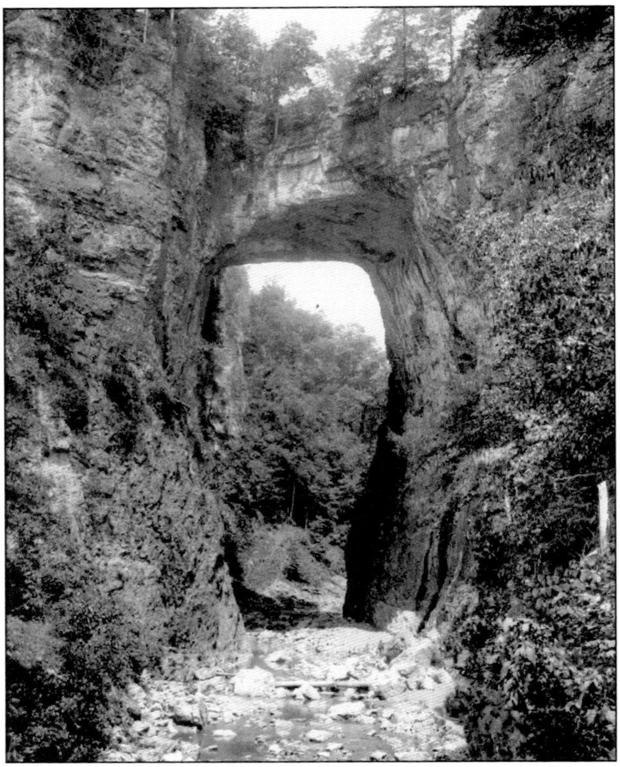

In these beautifully detailed photographs of nature, Miley expresses his strong interest in examining the relationship between man and his natural surroundings. Miley was working during a period when the country was rapidly transforming itself from a predominantly rural and agricultural society into an industrial powerhouse. This change was even evident in Rockbridge County, but in these photographs, Miley prefers to suggest a more bucolic and pastoral vision of the places he loved. It is easy to fit Miley's artistic vision into the niche created by the Hudson River School of painters, who worked with very similar subject matter. Sometimes examining the vast changes in society that dominated American life in the mid-19th century and sometimes depicting nature in an almost nostalgic manner, these artists, Miley among them, created an image of the American landscape that has left an indelible impression on America's historical consciousness.

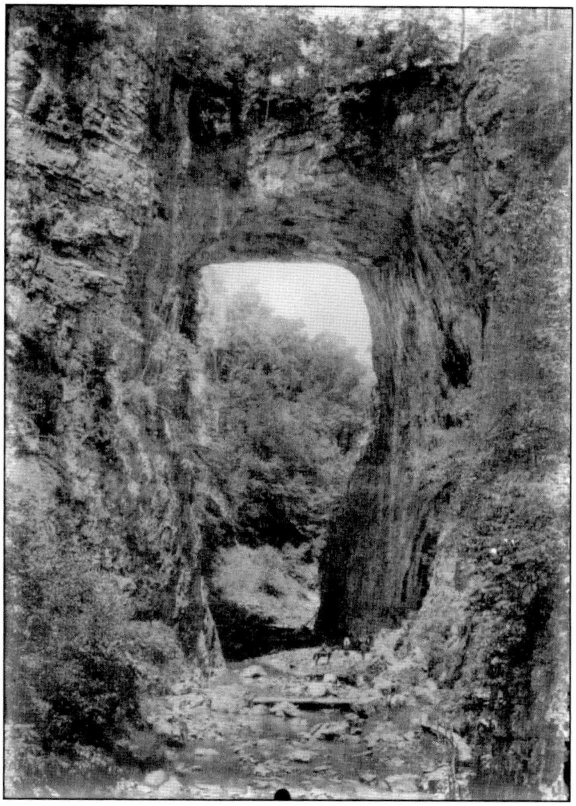

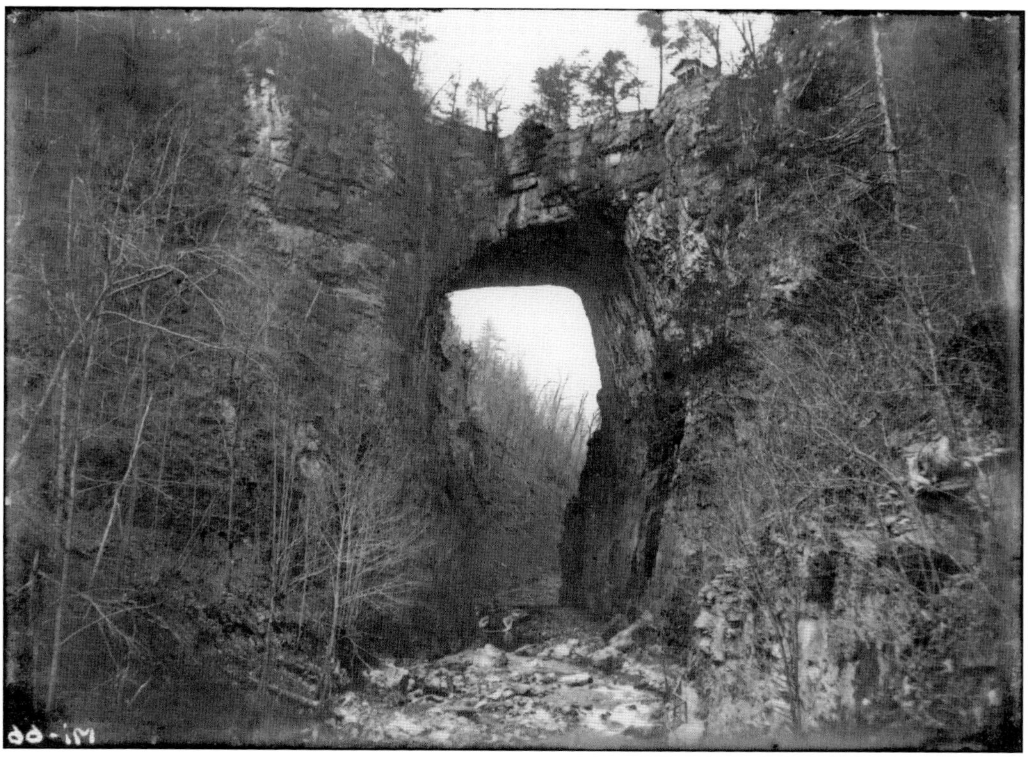

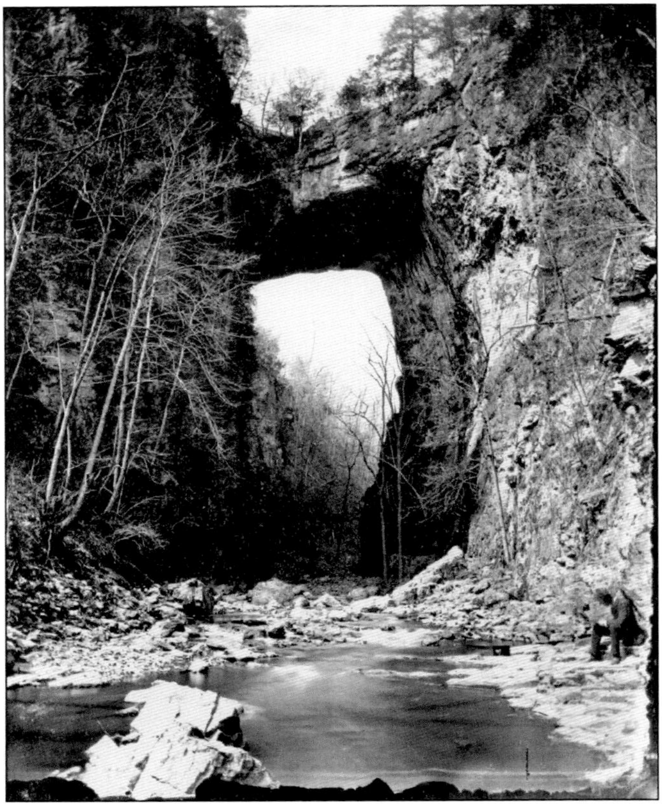

Improbable as it may seem, Thomas Jefferson purchased Natural Bridge from King George III. In 1782, he wrote in his *Notes on the State of Virginia* that "it is impossible for the emotions arising from the sublime to be felt beyond what they are here; so beautiful an arch, so elevated, so light, and springing as it were up to heaven, the rapture of the spectator is really indescribable!"

The saltpeter cave below lies along the trail to Lace Falls beyond Natural Bridge. The cave, like the bridge, is the work of natural erosion. The mineral contents of the cave became a valuable resource for making ammunition during both the War of 1812 and the Civil War. Cedar Creek flows gently along in front of the cave.

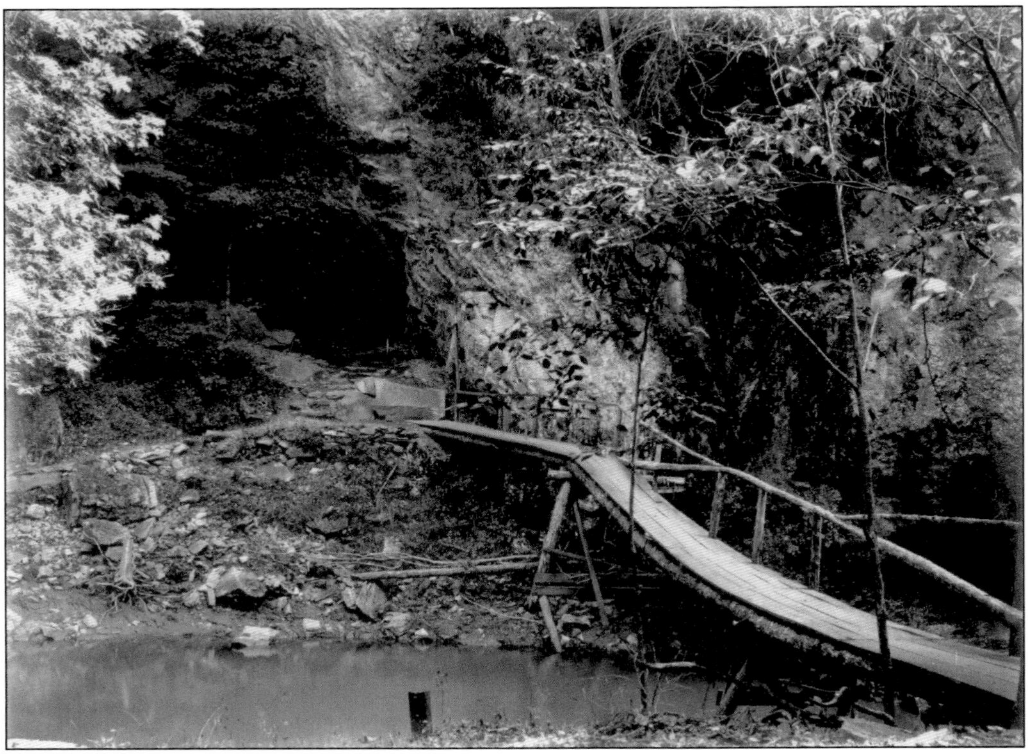

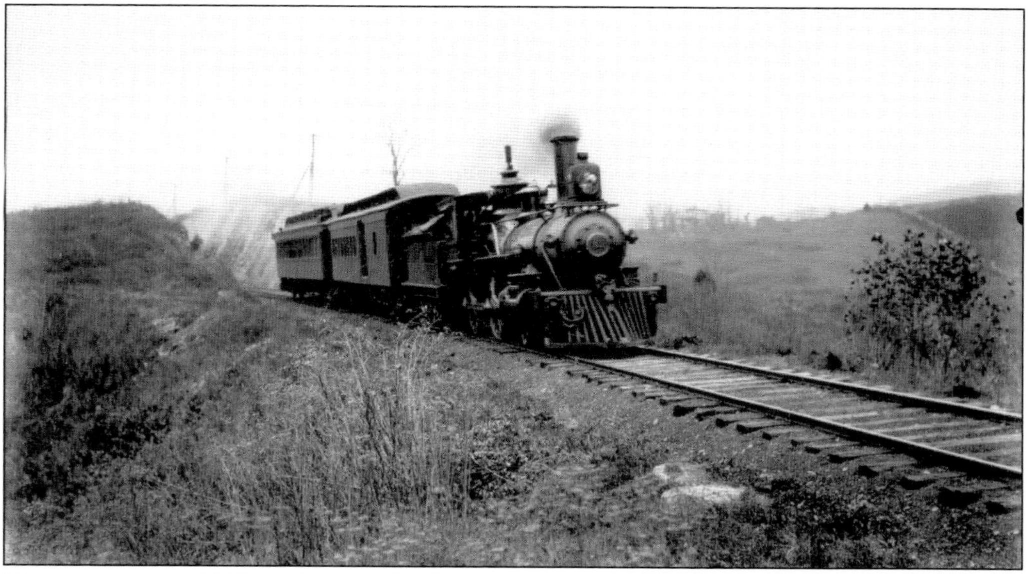

The next group of Miley photographs show various forms of transportation that coexisted in Rockbridge County in the late 19th century. The railroad, of course, came to dominate commercial transportation and alter the landscape of America, but wagons, carriages, and canal boats continued to contribute to the transportation of goods and people into the 20th century. In this dynamic image, smoke pours from the stack of the old C&O engine known as the Virginia Creeper as it makes its way out of Lexington.

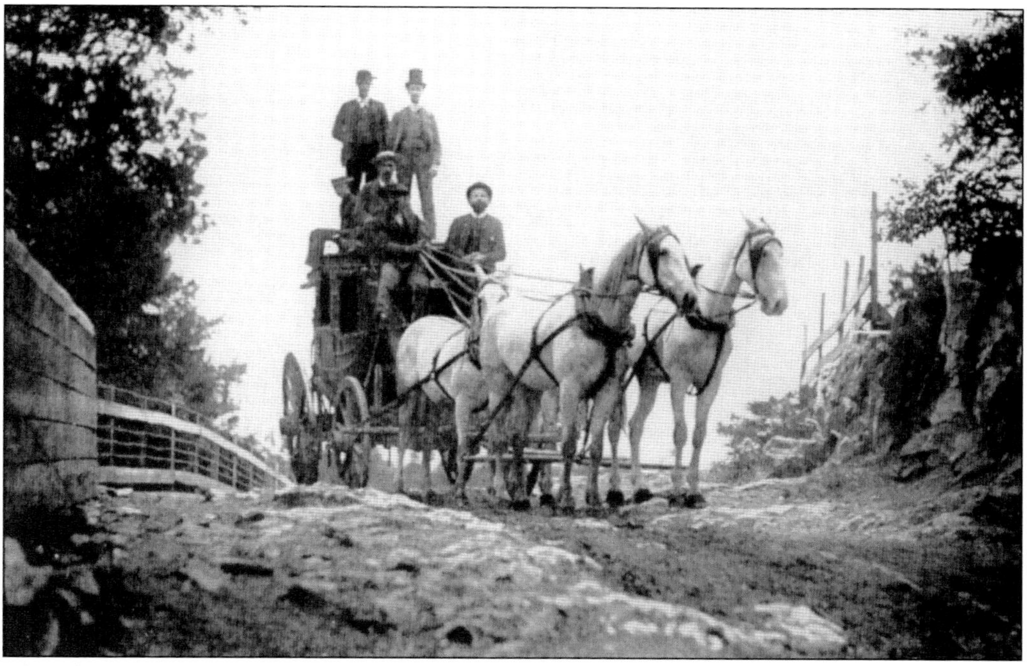

This photograph was taken by Miley around 1878. According to Marshall Fishwick, it is the "Tallyho" coming across Natural Bridge on its way from Lynchburg. It is a very intriguing image. Paired with the train photograph, it suggests both nostalgia for an earlier time and a recognition that life is changing rapidly. Technically, this would have been an extremely difficult photograph to execute because of the need to keep the horses still so a clear image could be made.

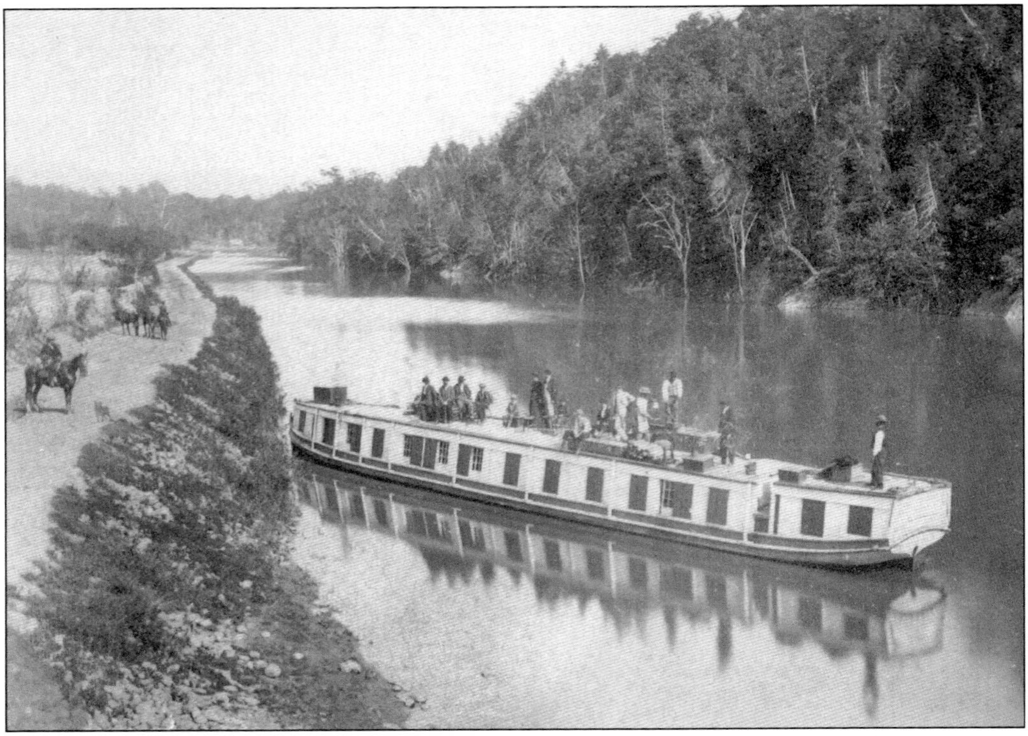

This 1868 Boude and Miley photograph shows a packet boat and the towpath at Jordan's Point. A packet boat was a craft that delivered goods, mail, and passengers along a relatively short, fixed route. Packet boats came in different sizes, but the most common size was 60 to 80 feet long and just over 14 feet wide. The average charge for traveling on packet boats was 4¢ per mile, which included meals and sleeping accommodations.

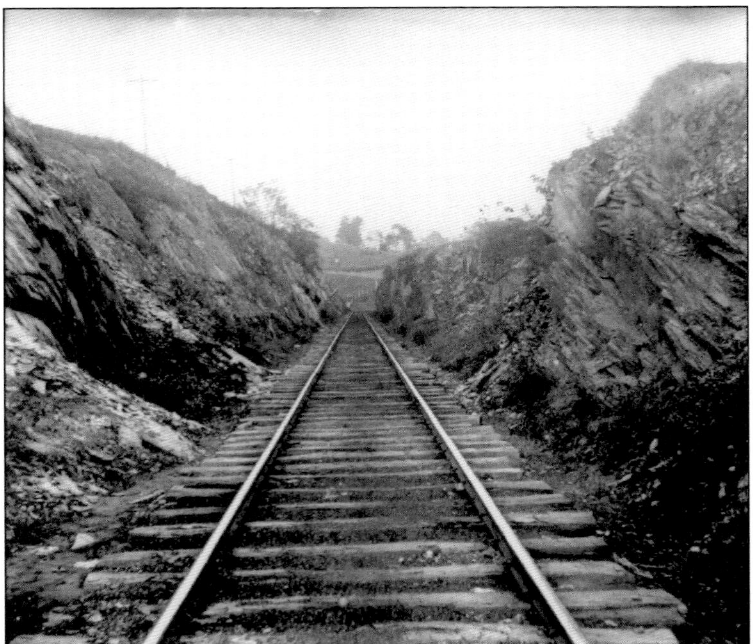

One can only assume that Miley took this photograph to confirm the primacy of the railroad, with its tracks stretching out into the future, into infinity. The cuts in the rocks and the clearing away of the earth all argue for the dominance of industry in the future, its symmetry conveying direct movement.

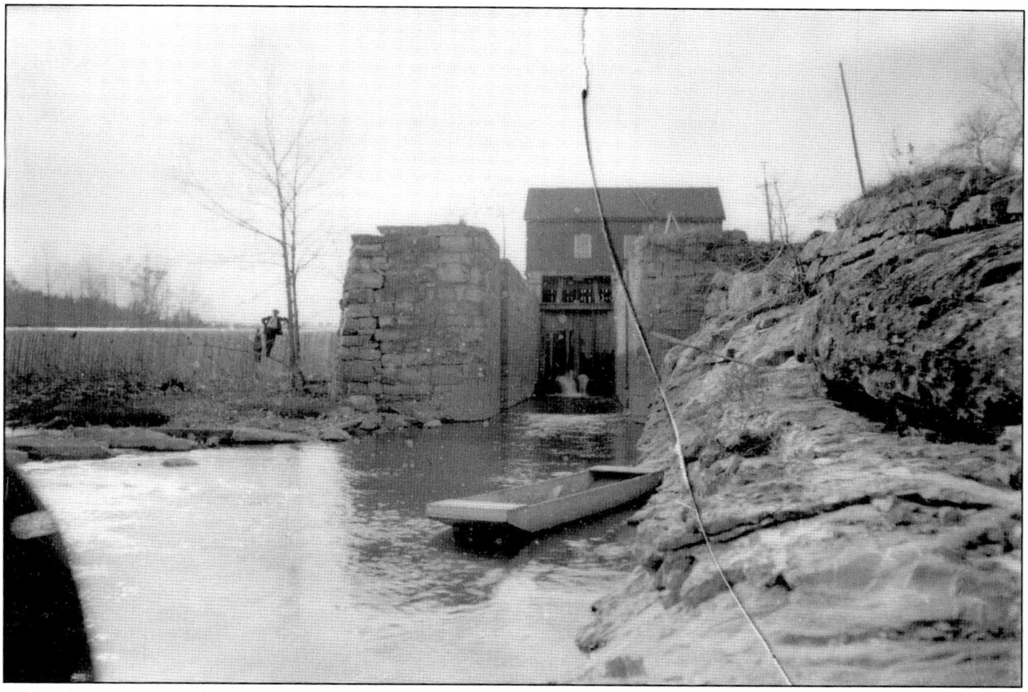

The photograph above shows a man, a boat, and a canal lock, most likely Reid's (later called Ross's) Dam on the Maury River. This is the first dam and lock below East Lexington. The ruins of the dam remain today, and this image could be recreated easily, as very little has changed in this scene. The photograph below shows the complex of structures, including the mule barn, of the canal and towpath built at the confluence of the James and Maury Rivers near Glasgow. Canal-building in America began in earnest in the 1820s and lasted even into the 20th century in some places, though canals were largely supplanted by railroads as the favored means of moving goods by the time of the Civil War. Canals played an important role in the history of Rockbridge County, and Miley took many photographs of the boats and locks.

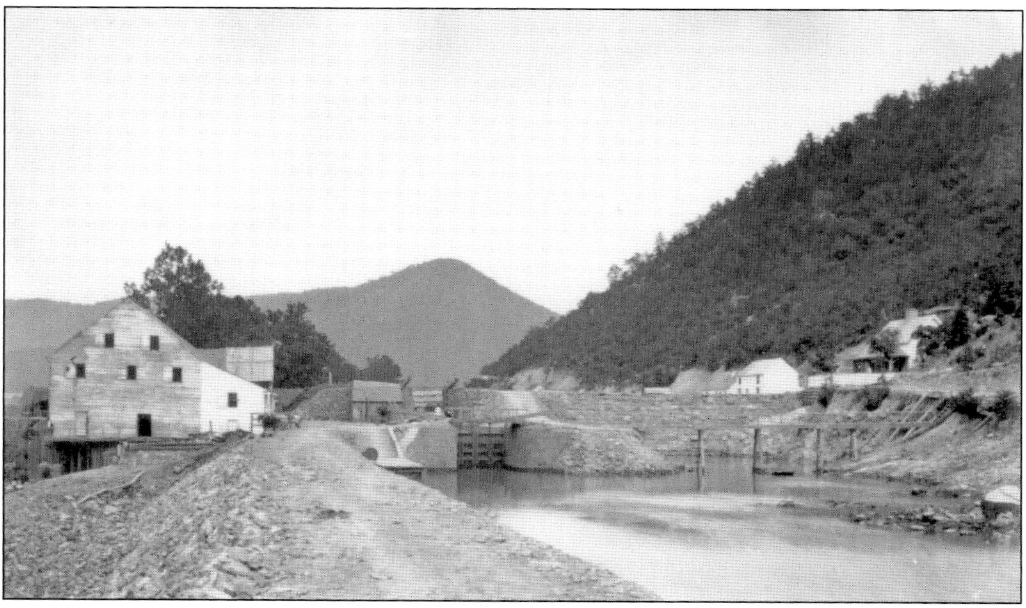

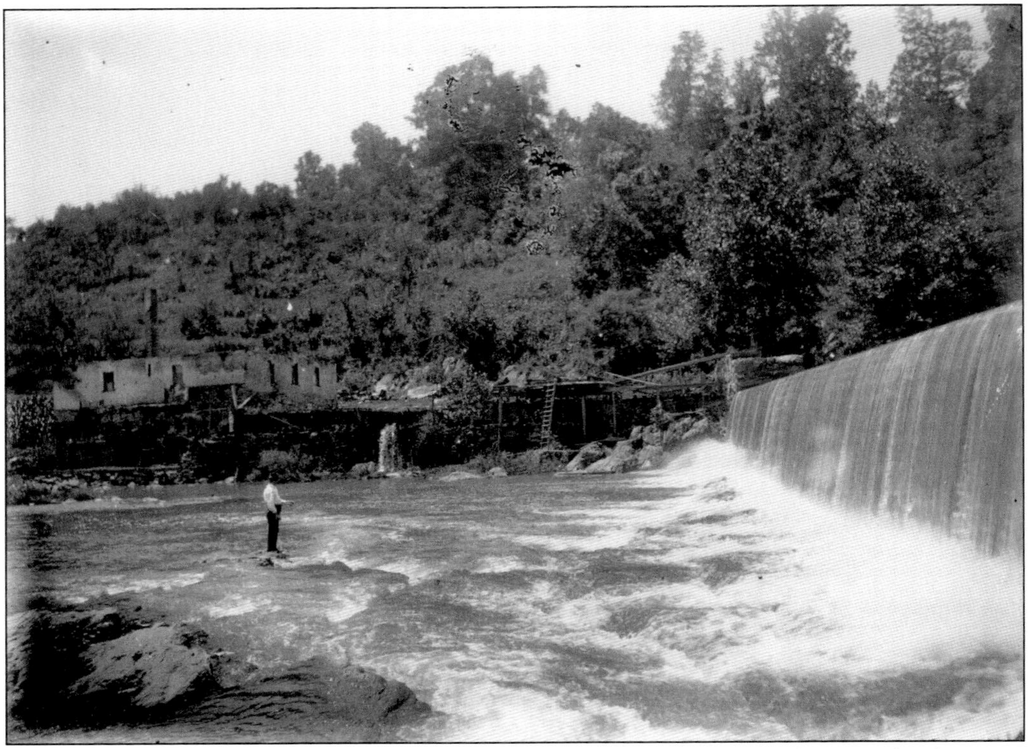

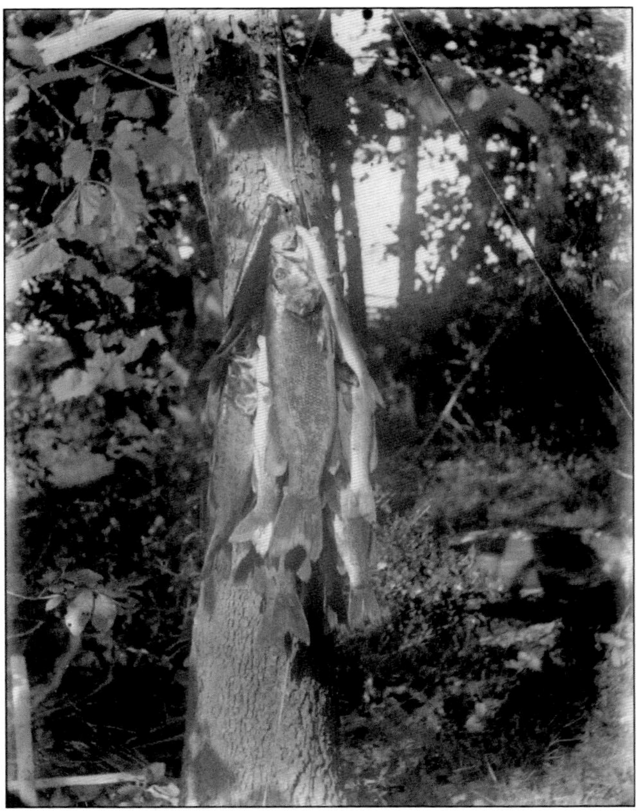

These two photographs show Miley's interest in showing the ordinary activities of his neighbors in Lexington and Rockbridge County. The man above is fishing at the dam on the Maury River, close to town. As was the case in this time period, he is not dressed in any particular way for his outing and he obviously had to get quite wet to get to his perch on the rock he is standing on. In the photograph of the stringer of fish at left, Miley is obviously playing with composition, shading, and the bending of light. It actually takes some time when first looking at this photograph to tell exactly what is pictured because the fish and the background blend together so beautifully. In Miley's hands, what could be a mundane record of a day's catch becomes a lovely work of art.

Scotch-Irish immigrants settled the Goshen Pass area of Rockbridge County, about 20 miles northwest of Lexington, around 1743. The Goshen Pass is a 3.7-mile-long gorge that was carved out by the flowing Maury River. This is possibly the only photograph Miley took of the pass; unfortunately, it was during a period of severe low water and, as a result, the whitewater effect of the river is not seen.

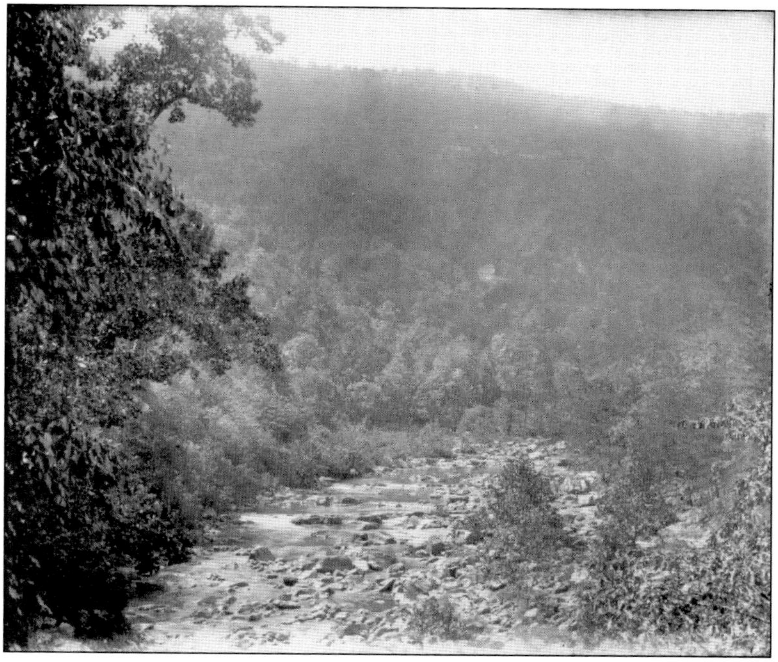

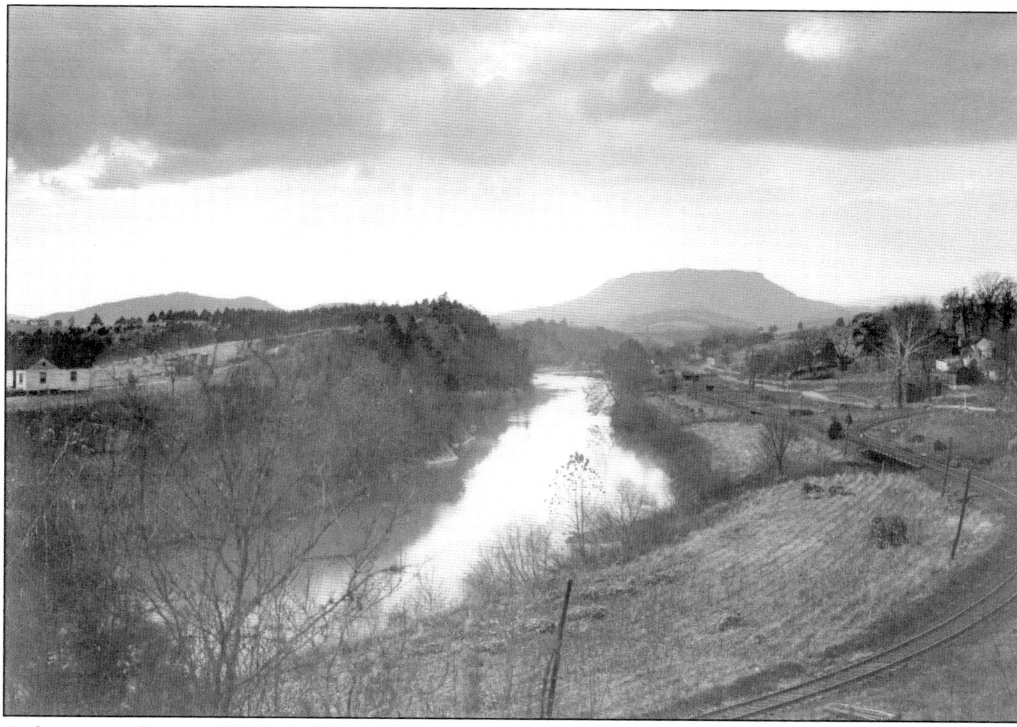

A favorite subject of Miley's, House Mountain looms in the distance, brooding over Lexington, as this photograph looks upstream from the current parking area for the Chessie Trail. This photograph is signed Miley and Son and dates from between 1885 and 1895. Looking deeper into the photograph, the acknowledgment of the railroad tracks and the telegraph poles suggests progress intruding on the pristine countryside. The dramatic appearance of the clouds was created by Miley in the printing process.

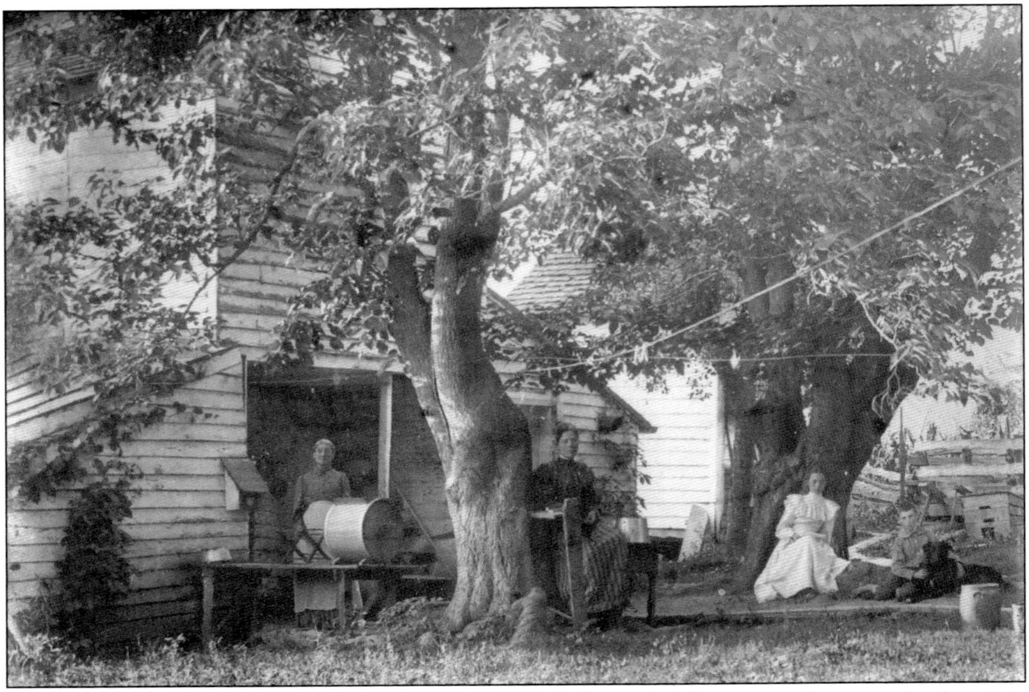

There is a slim chance that Miley was hired and paid to take these two photographs, but it is doubtful. What is more likely is that these are more examples of his interest in the lives of the ordinary people who lived in the county. According to his son Henry, Miley would take off on trips to find interesting people and scenes to photograph. There is the possibility that photographs like these would be printed and offered to the subjects, or they might be enlarged and hung in his gallery/studio. Whatever the purpose, today's viewers are the beneficiaries of Miley's curiosity and artistic vision. The fact that he may have seen himself as being on a mission to document life in the county for future generations to witness is also something to seriously consider.

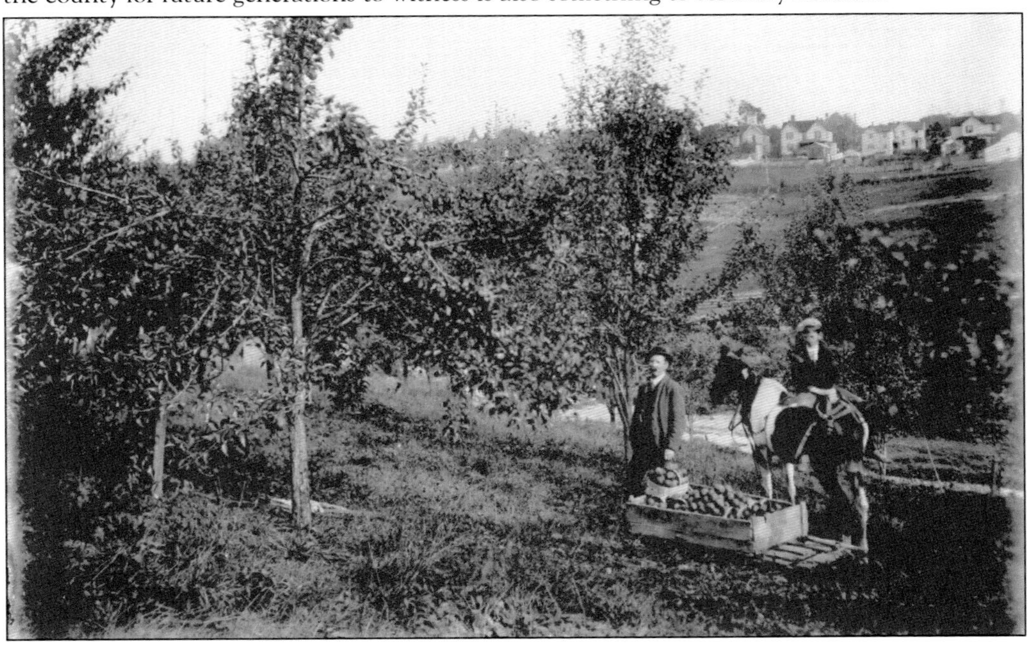

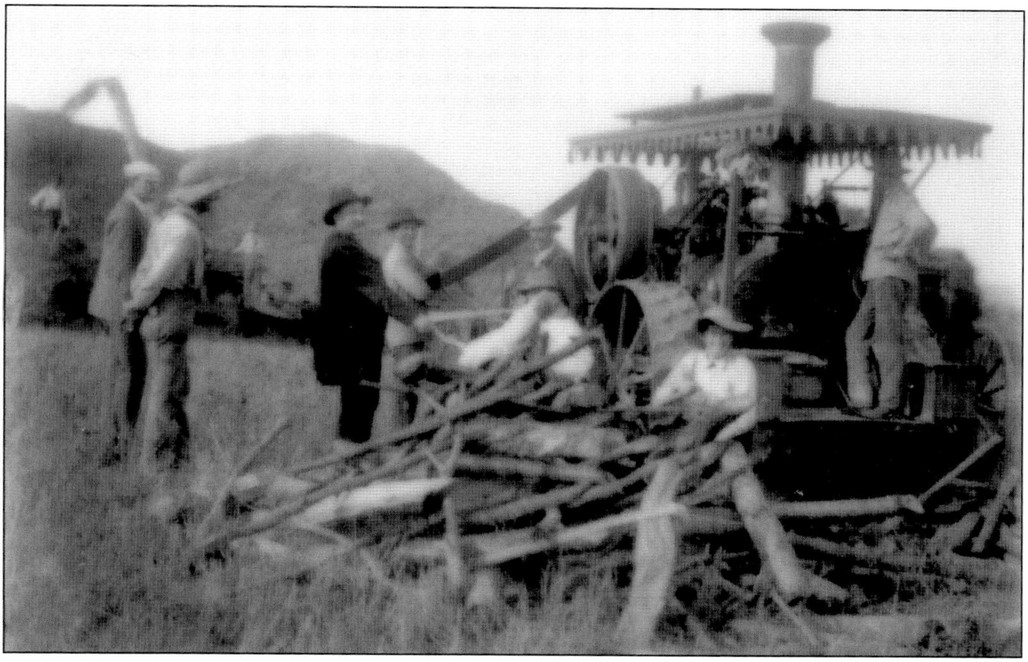

This is a Miley photograph from around 1885 of a steam-driven grain-threshing operation somewhere in Rockbridge County. The machine in the foreground is a steam engine that was fed wood to generate the steam that ran the belts that ran the threshing machine. These machines were usually moved around the county to various farms and operated by communal laborers.

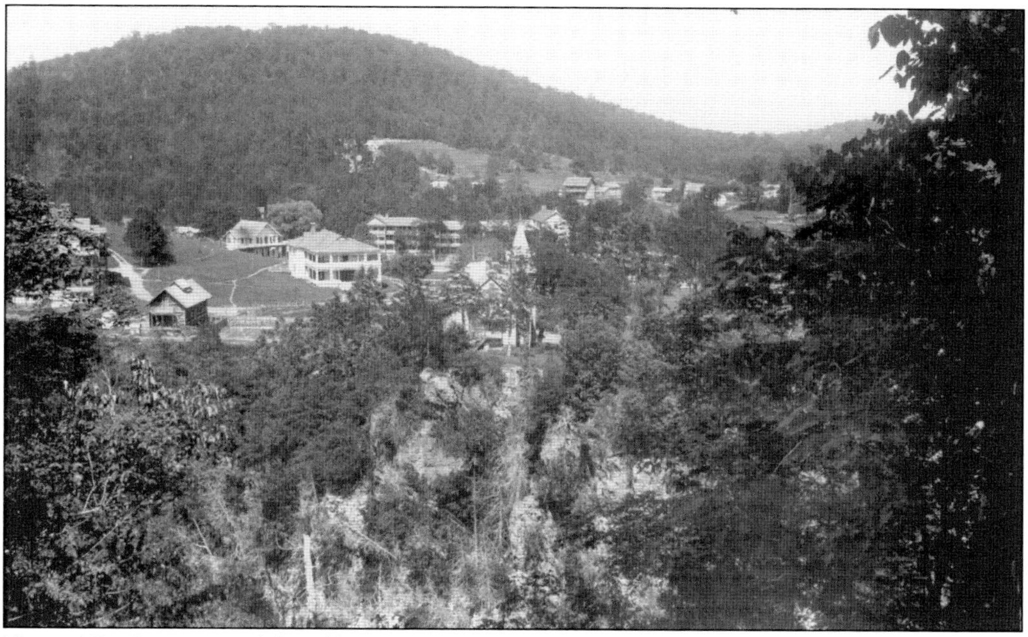

Natural Bridge is one of the oldest tourist attractions in the United States. It and Niagara Falls were places where people would take extraordinary measures to visit, even in the 18th and 19th centuries, well before railroads made the journey to see the natural wonders a little easier. This view of the complex of buildings that comprised the resort in the 1880s shows it as a thriving tourist center. Guests have been staying at Natural Bridge since 1828.

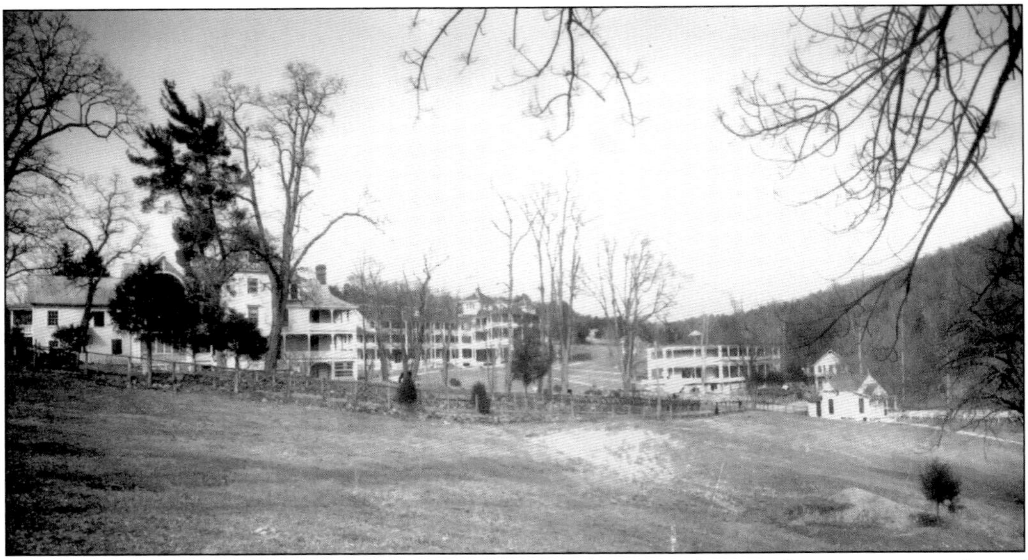

Before the main hotel was constructed at Natural Bridge around 1908, there were a number of different choices for visitors. One was the Forest Inn, built in 1833, seen below as a stagecoach approaches, no doubt filled with hearty tourists intent on seeing the great wonder of western Virginia. Though it is difficult to see in the photograph, there are actually two coaches in front of the inn, where staff are standing in front ready to welcome their guests. One of the hanging signs says "Forest Inn" and the other says "Livery Office." The photograph above shows the full array of hotel buildings and likely dates from 1906 or 1907.

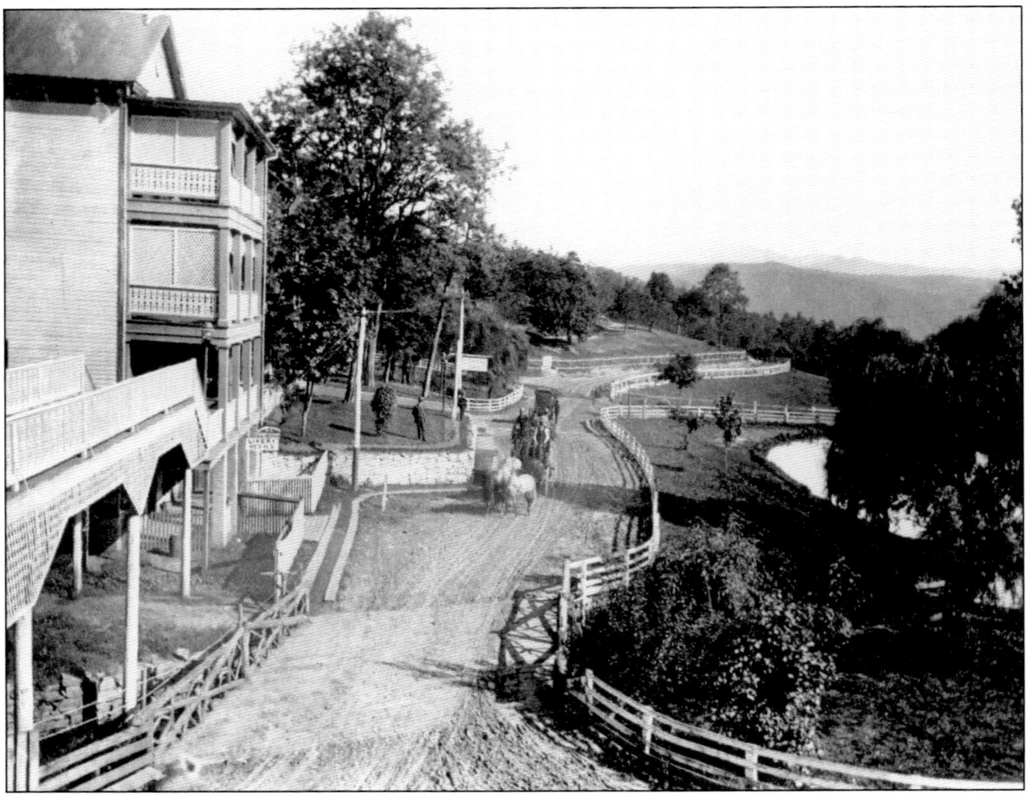

This is another view of the buildings and grounds of the village complex. The proximity of the camera to the ground in this photograph gives the viewer an excellent sense of how much dirt and mud would have affected the daily lives of everyone at this time. The building on the left in this photograph is the same as the one in the lower right of the photograph on the previous page.

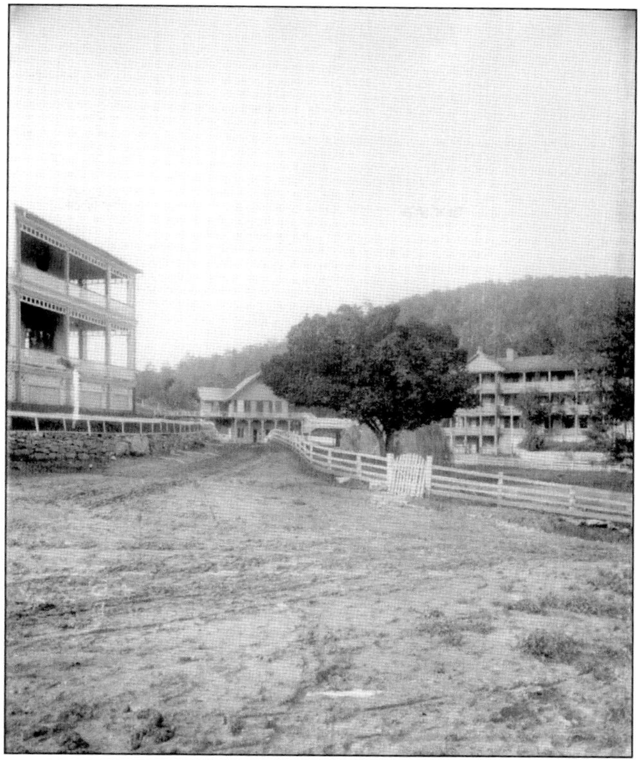

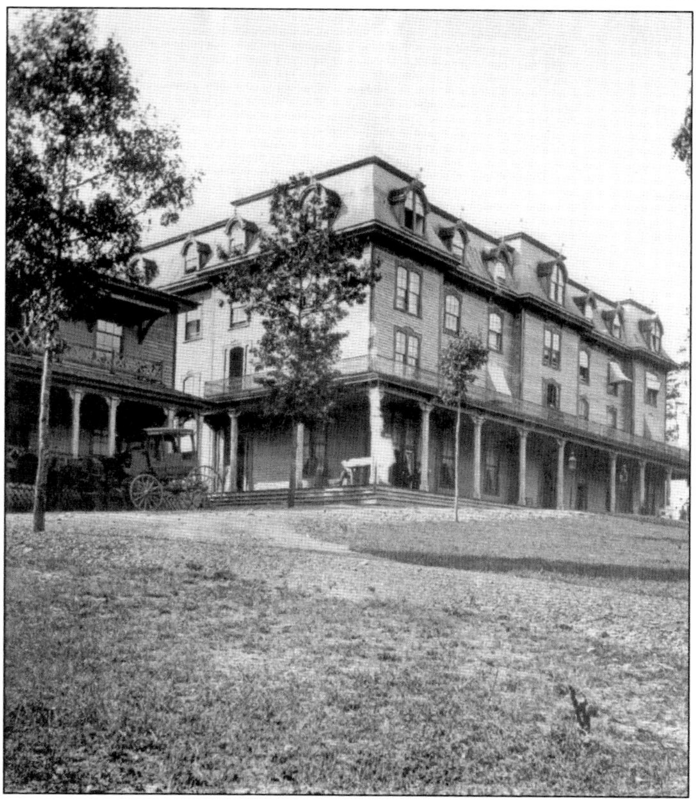

This image, definitely taken by Miley, is unfortunately of an unidentified hotel, possibly at another location in Rockbridge County.

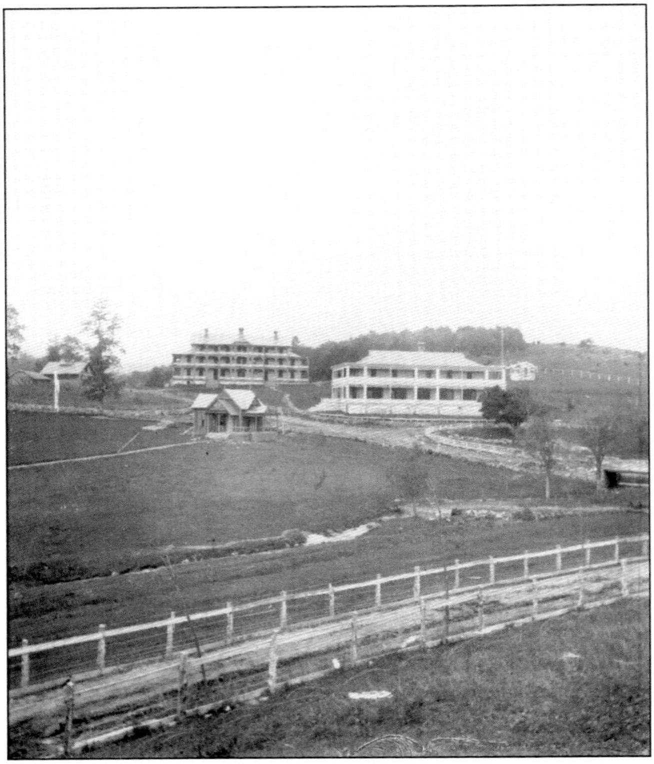

Natural Bridge attained resort status in the 1880s. Here, Miley gives a view of the Natural Bridge Hotel, including the Pavilion, the Appledore Cottage, and the smokehouse. It is probable that this photograph dates from the period before 1906. At the time this photograph was taken, the Natural Bridge hotels, including the Pavilion, the Appledore, and the Forest Inn, had a total capacity of 400 guests.

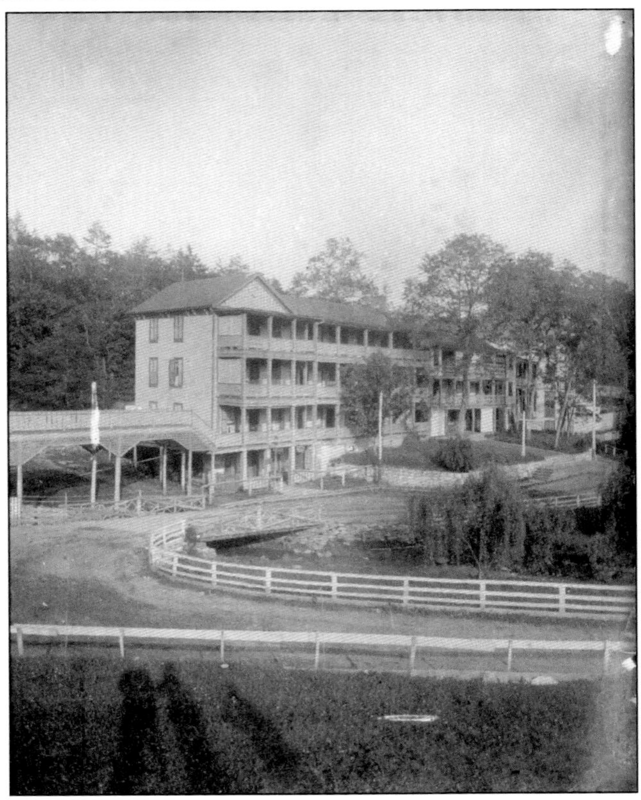

This photograph features a nice frontal view of the 1833 Forest Inn, considered to be a very fine hotel by all standards of the day.

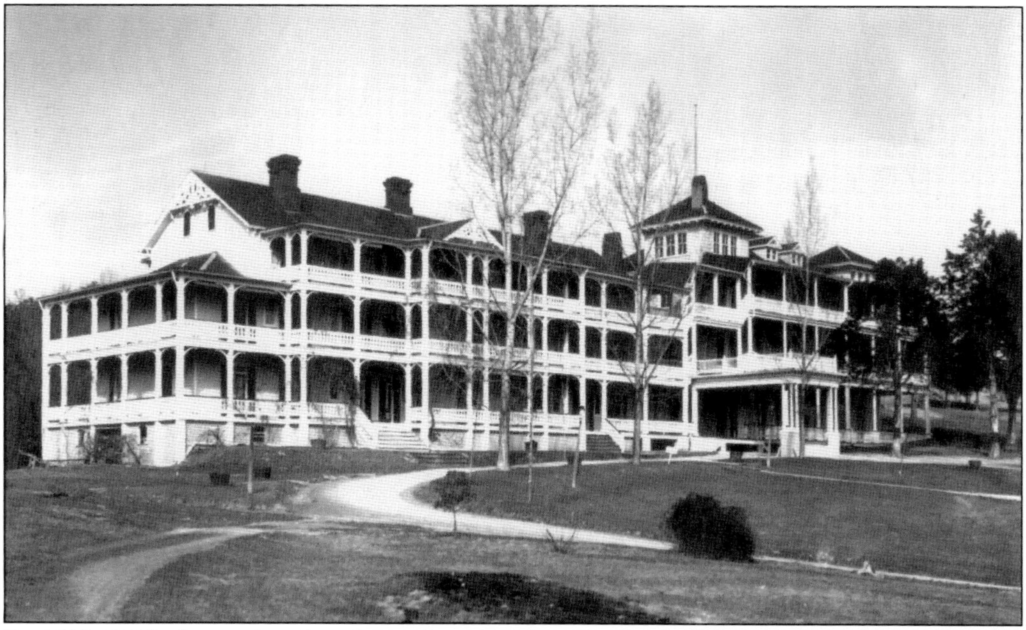

By 1908–1909, the modern hotel seen here had been built on the Natural Bridge property. In literature produced by the resort, the hotel was compared favorably to the one at The Homestead, only at a much more reasonable price. This hotel existed on the property until the current hotel was built.

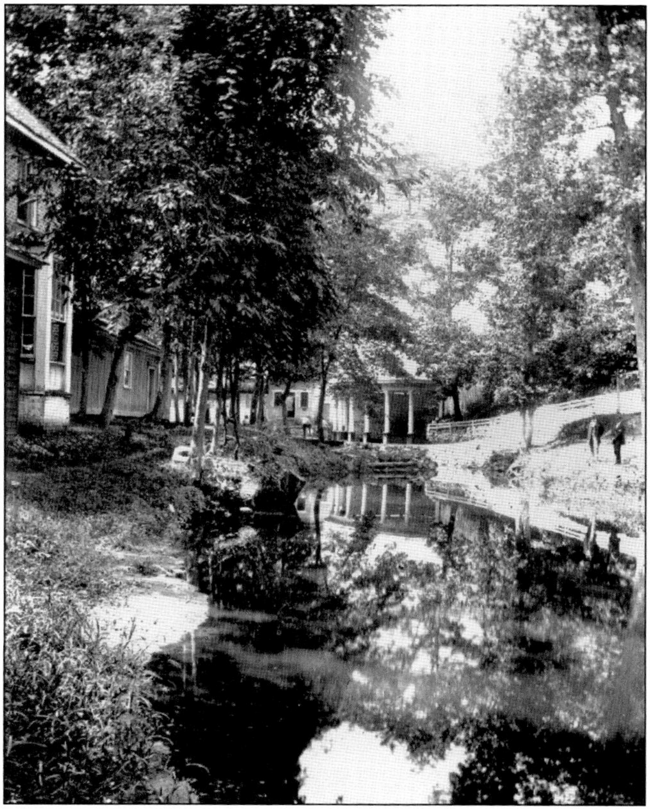

Rockbridge County abounds in natural wonders, and its sites have attracted visitors from far and near for over 200 years. Parts of the county are cut through with underground hot-water springs that have always attracted those seeking to take the water cure for their ailments. This photograph is an interesting perspective that Miley took of the Rockbridge Alum Springs Hotel. The Alum Springs Resort dates from the early 19th century and was able to accommodate 200 to 300 guests by mid-century, when it was frequented often by Thomas "Stonewall" Jackson. In this photograph, the bright, engaging effect is created by the reflections that Miley captured beautifully with his camera. He fittingly used water to enhance the viewer's appreciation of the scene.

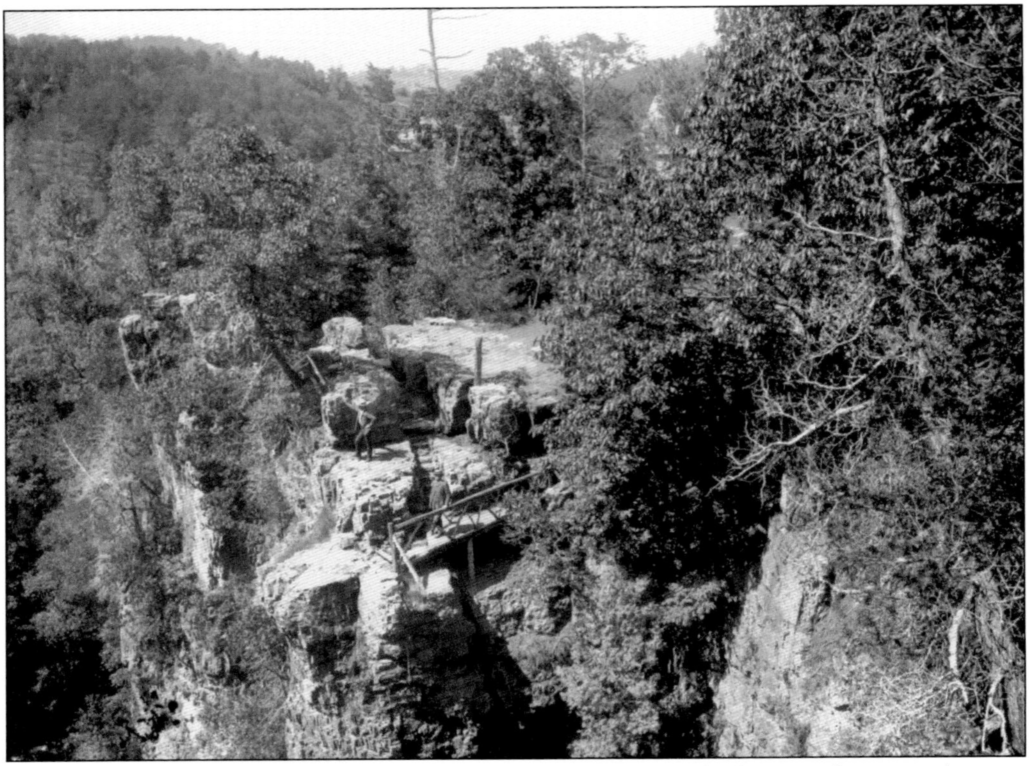

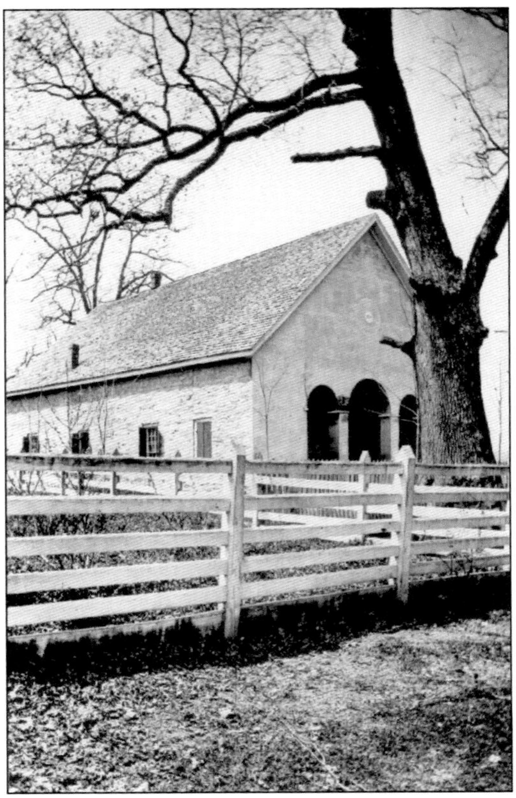

The photograph above is of a site in the Natural Bridge area known as Pulpit Rock. Close examination of the photograph shows two men standing and steps cut sharply out of the rock formation. Visitors to Natural Bridge who were so inclined could climb up this interesting rock formation said to resemble the high pulpit in a church.

Several miles north of Lexington, near the birthplace of Sam Houston, stands the Timber Ridge Stone Church, a Presbyterian church built in 1756. The first congregation to worship on this site started in 1746 and was led by John Blair, an Ulster native. In 1871, an addition was created with the three semicircular arches. The church is listed in the National Register of Historic Places.

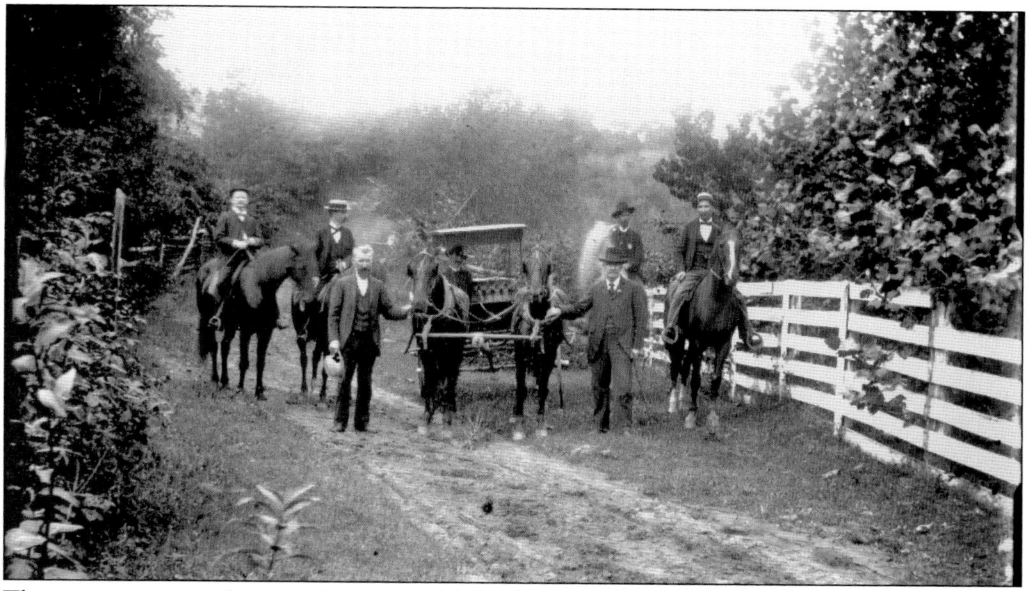

These two evocative photographs from the Michael Miley collection simply beg for some explanation, yet none is forthcoming. It is worth it to wonder if the fire that destroyed so many of Miley's records in 1907 deprived modern viewers of vital information about gems such as these. The men are the same in both. It is impossible to know which photograph was taken first, though it seems logical they were taken on the same day. Whatever the story behind them, they are beautiful and intriguing images. In the photograph below, the men are gathered at Lexington's town spring, which now lies beneath a parking lot beside Hillel House. Standing from left to right are James Eitteck, Charles Pole, John Spillaine, M.W. Paxton, and S.O. Campbell. Seated are mayor James D. Anderson (left) and G.W. Offlighter (right).

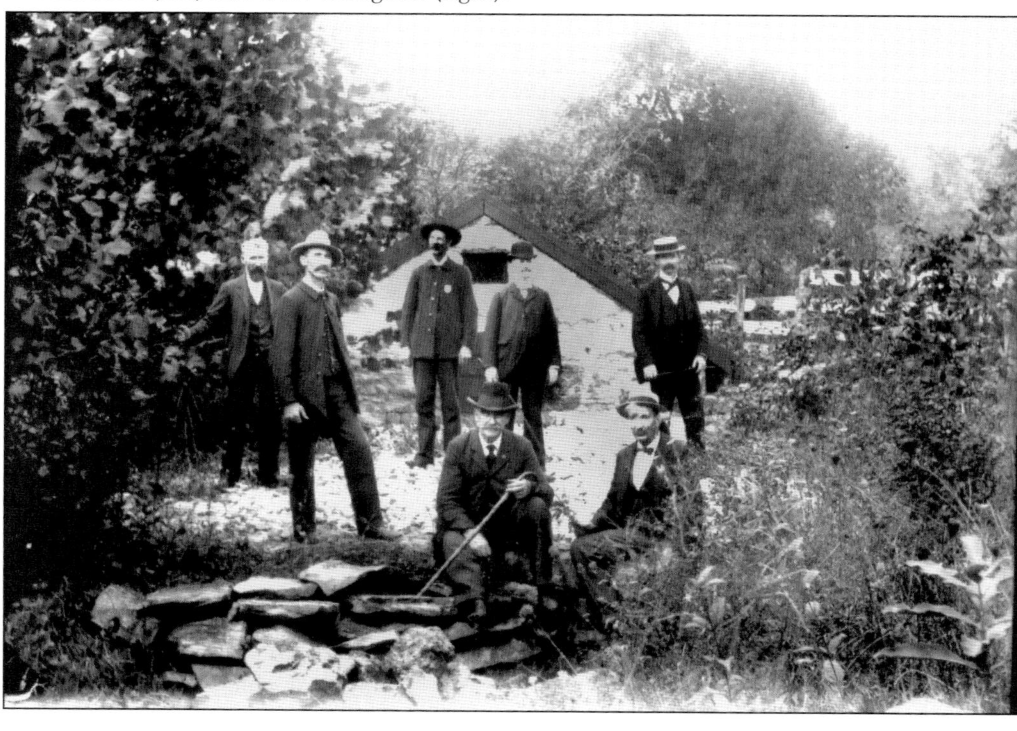

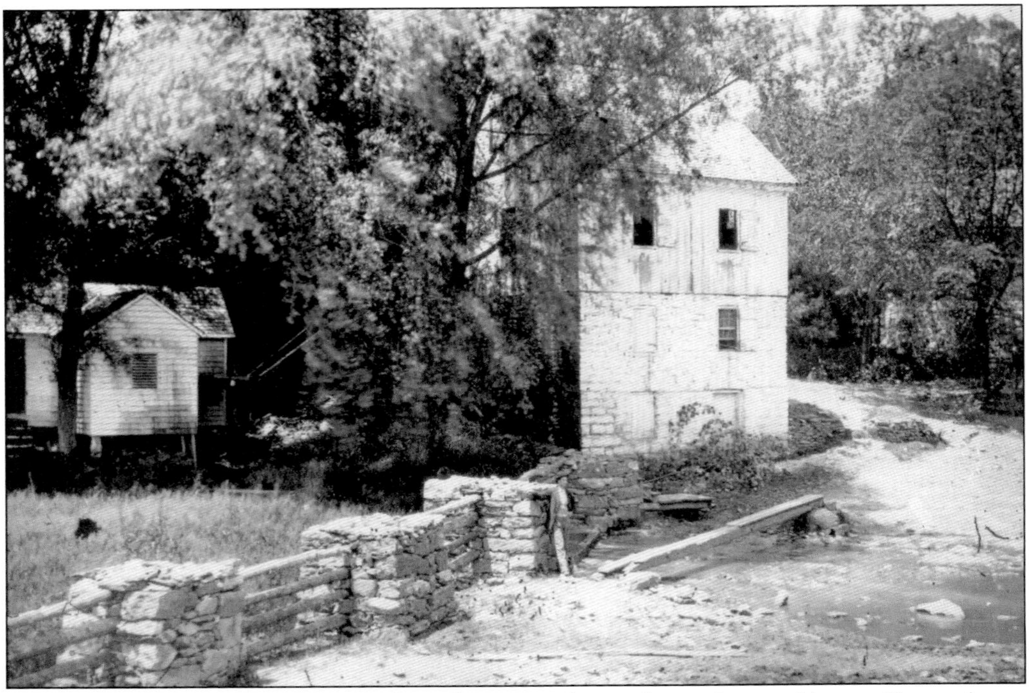

The peaceful feelings that emanate from the image above, alongside a road by a mill, are almost palpable. It is Starrett's mill, near Timber Ridge, north of Lexington. Nearly hidden details of the photograph are the young man leaning up against the stones, the wooden-beam bridge across the stream, and steps leading up and over the wall. The construction of the fence with wooden poles secured into the rock pillars is quite unusual. In most of Miley's panoramic views of Rockbridge County, he includes some water in the photograph; however, he does not in the photograph below. It shows a lovely valley, a country road meandering around a cornfield, with no sign of modernity penetrating this idyllic and exceedingly picturesque moment in rural Virginia.

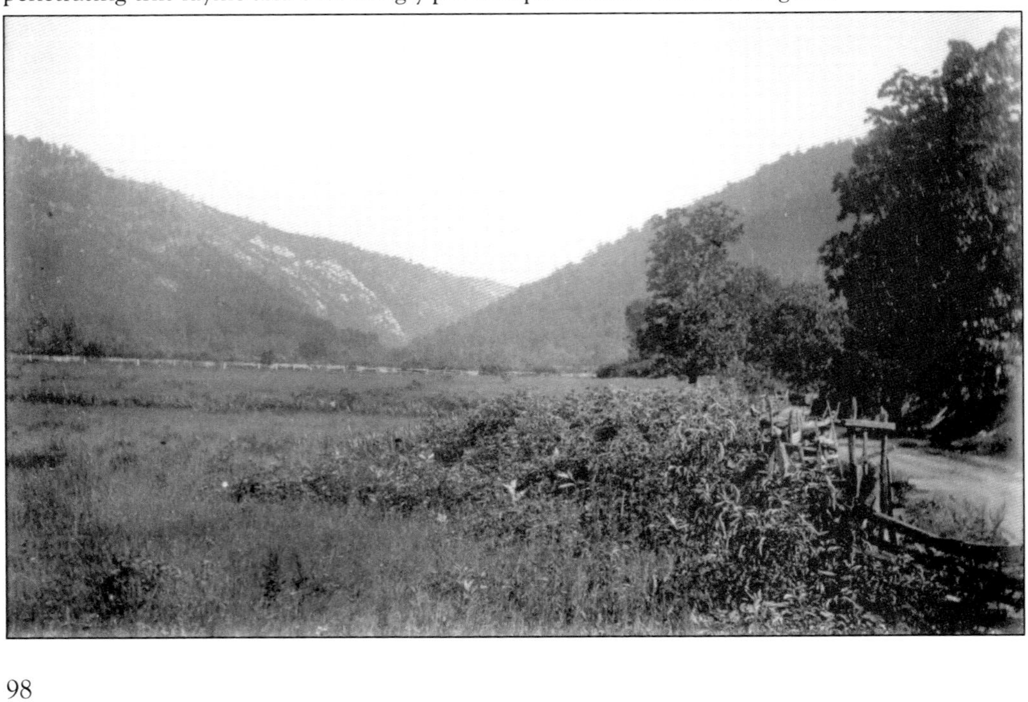

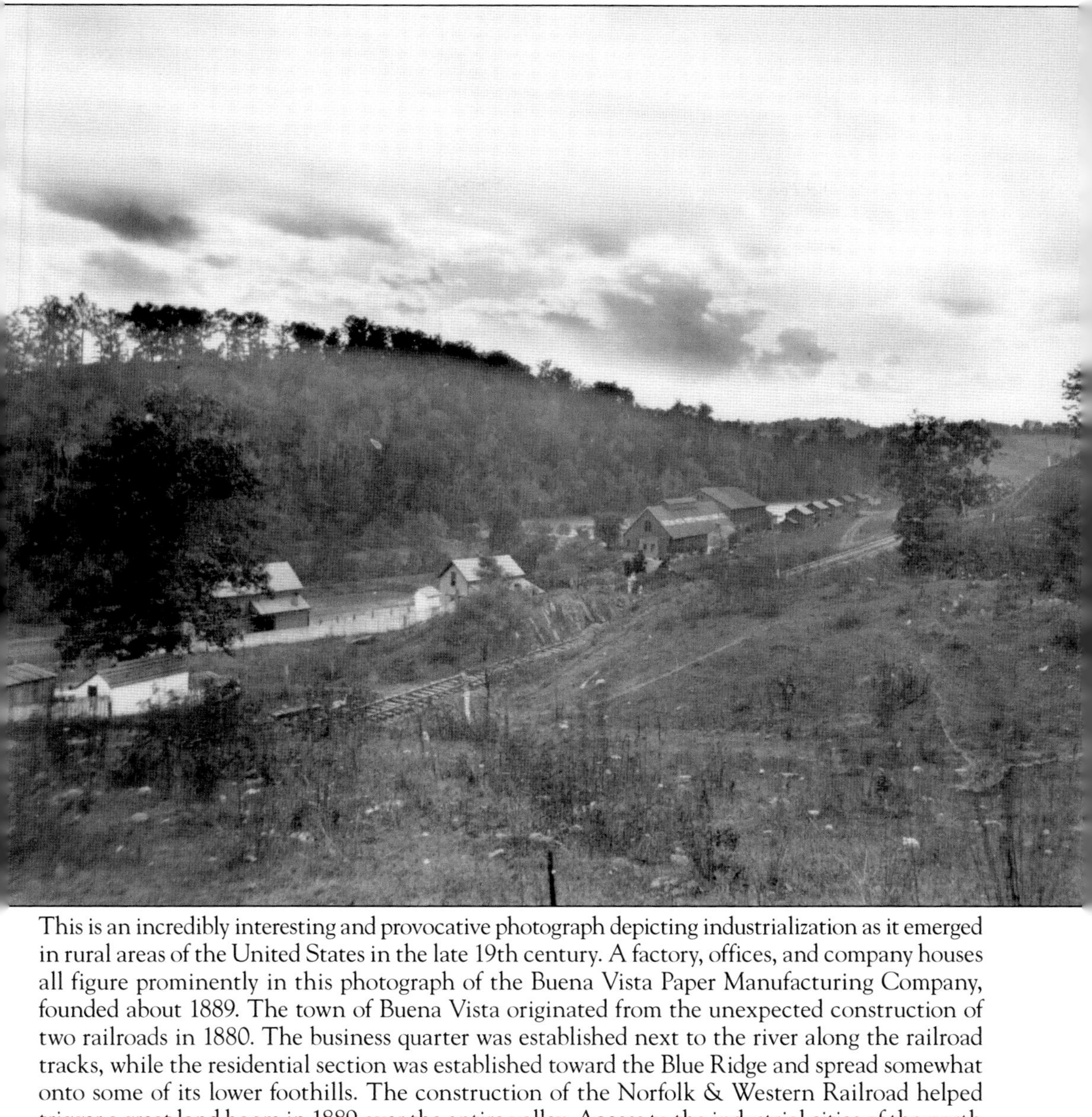

This is an incredibly interesting and provocative photograph depicting industrialization as it emerged in rural areas of the United States in the late 19th century. A factory, offices, and company houses all figure prominently in this photograph of the Buena Vista Paper Manufacturing Company, founded about 1889. The town of Buena Vista originated from the unexpected construction of two railroads in 1880. The business quarter was established next to the river along the railroad tracks, while the residential section was established toward the Blue Ridge and spread somewhat onto some of its lower foothills. The construction of the Norfolk & Western Railroad helped trigger a great land boom in 1889 over the entire valley. Access to the industrial cities of the north would now be easier and quicker. People eager to take advantage of the opportunities relocated to the town, and by February 15, 1892, it had a population of 5,240 persons. In that year, there were 19 industries, including manufacturers of iron, saddles, leather goods, woolen mills, paper, and more, employing over 1,000 workers.

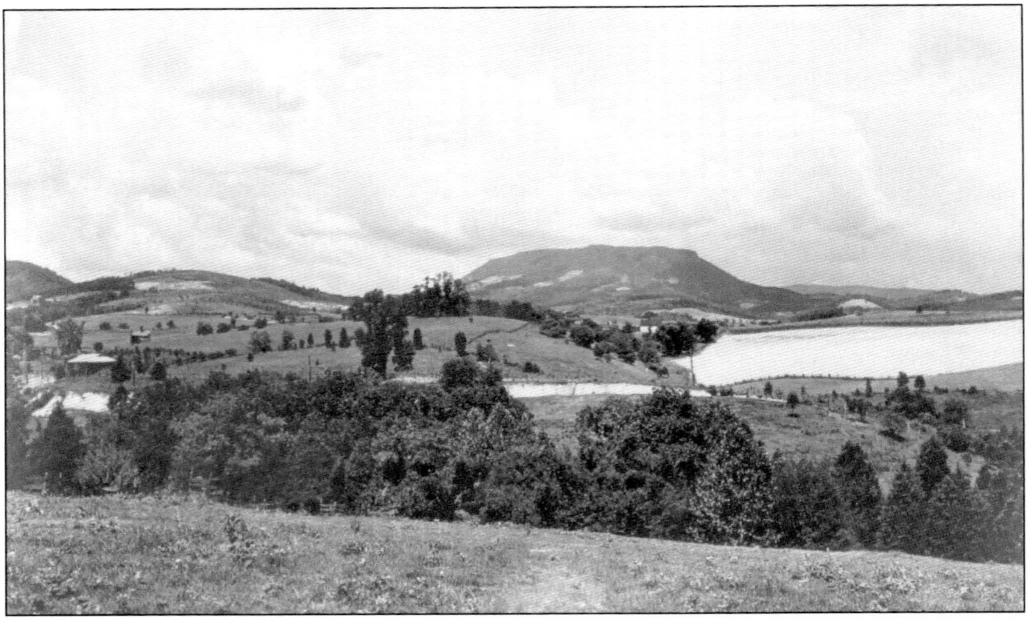

The view above, looking west toward House Mountain in the 1880s, is another peaceful and pastoral image. No wires or railroad tracks are visible to spoil the bucolic splendor of the exquisite rural scene. Only evidence of farming and timber cutting are present to suggest man's economic activities. From the early 1800s onward, prosperous men in Rockbridge County, who had made money from land speculation, farming, or in the iron trade, built fine, large houses for their families, and these still speckle the countryside today. Seen below is the home of the James Alexander family. If Miley were not hired by a family to photograph their home, he would have offered them the opportunity to purchase prints of his work in his gallery.

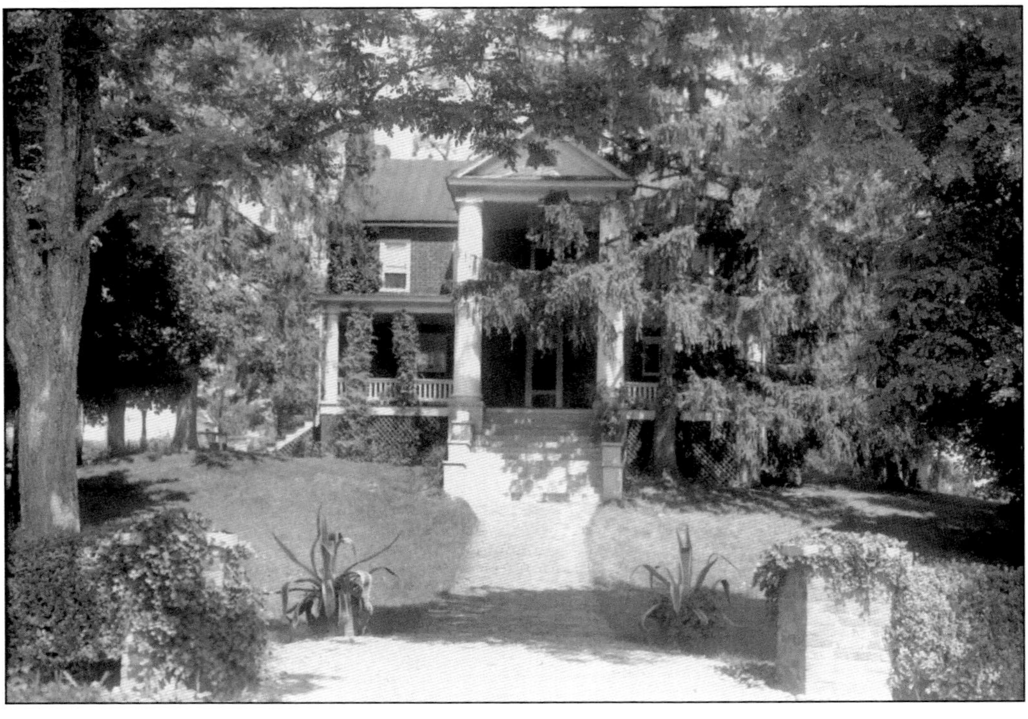

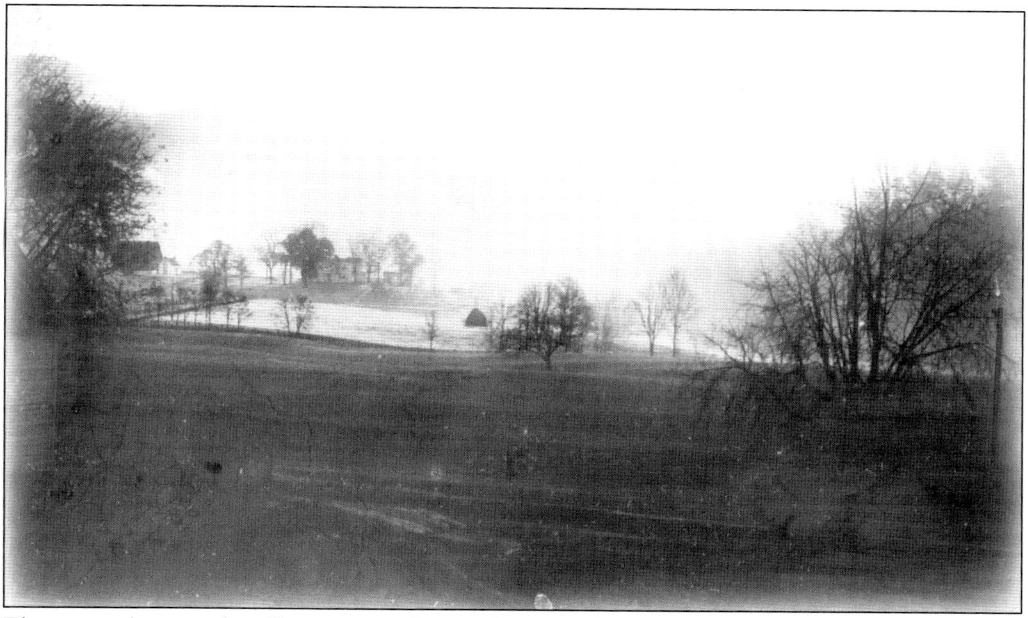

These two photographs offer very appealing and even enchanting views of two farms in Rockbridge County. Both afford insights into how closely connected the farm or plantation houses were to the working activities of the farm. Barns and other outbuildings are within easy walking distance of the main residence, which created wholeness and suggests the nexus between life and work in preindustrial rural America. The photograph above is one of several that Miley made of this scene, each showing a different use of light and shadow that he manipulated in the printing process. The photograph below, more straightforward, is of the Hickory Hill House, going toward Natural Bridge.

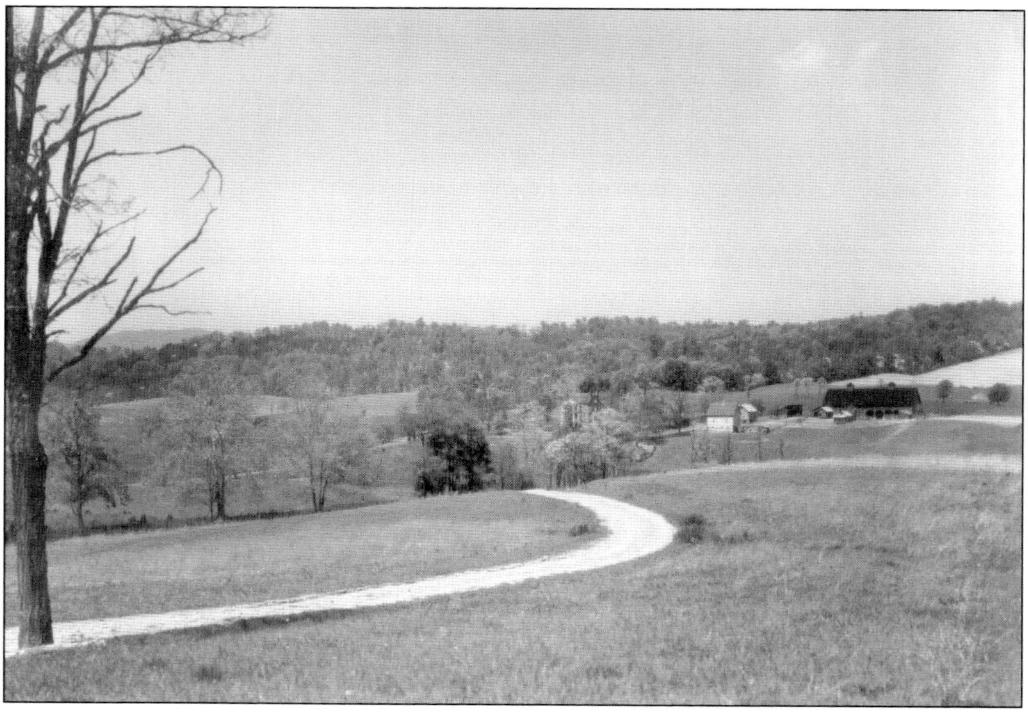

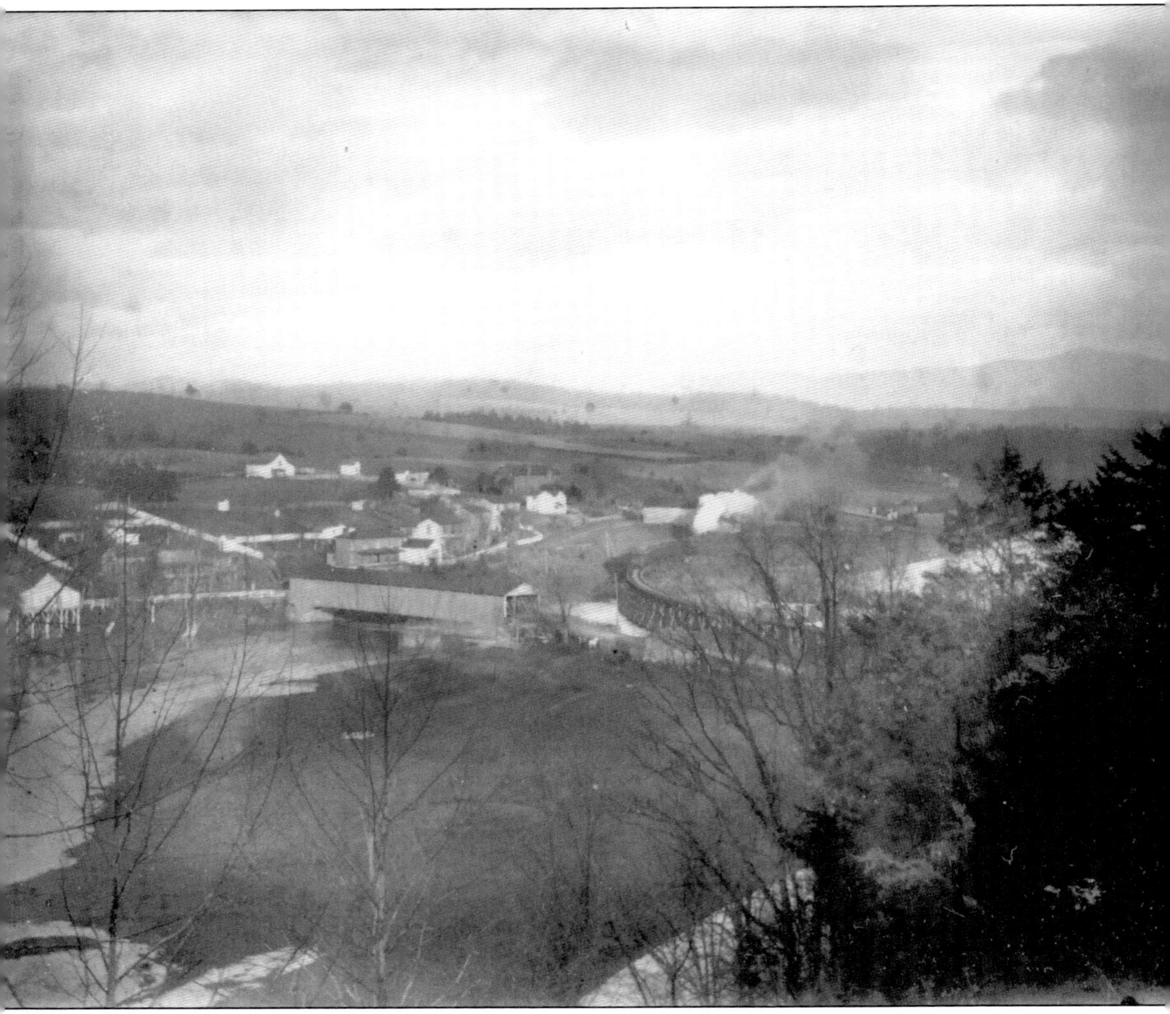

This is an exquisite photograph from Miley, probably taken in 1900, which shows the full flavor of life in a small Virginia town that is changing and adjusting to the modern world. From his vantage point from the VMI cliffs overlooking Jordan's Point, Miley points his camera at East Lexington. This image is all smoke and light, rolling clouds, and rolling thunder from the iron horse that dominates the center of the scene. The modern trestle gracefully turns away from the older wooden covered bridge, leaving it behind in the clouds of smoke puffing from the engine of progress. It is likely, however, that in this scene, the engine has slowed down considerably and is backing into Lexington, which was required at the time.

Six

In the Town

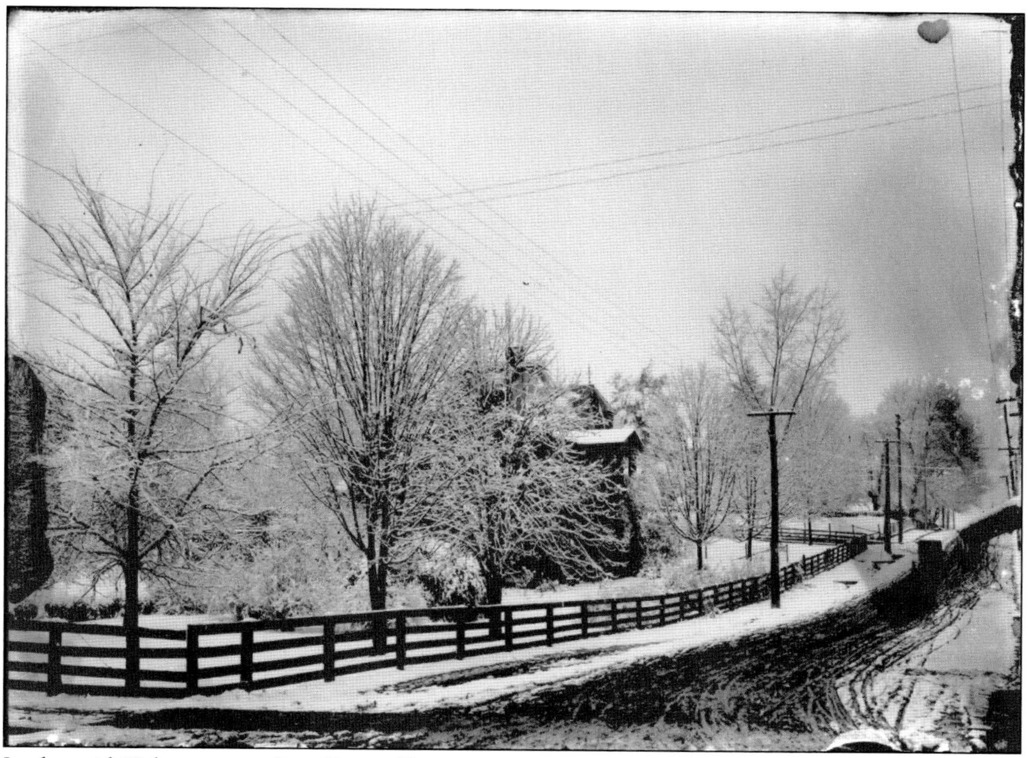

In the mid-19th century, the village of Lexington was witnessing an economic boom that spurred a great deal of building, most of it occurring along Main Street. The Presbyterian church went up in 1845, as did many other prominent commercial structures in the center of town. Many of the town's prominent citizens were engaged in some type of commercial trade, and small-scale manufacturing was on the rise. In this snowy scene of the Hopkins house on Nelson Street, a carriage is just barely visible, but the telegraph wires overhead show that the modern world had arrived.

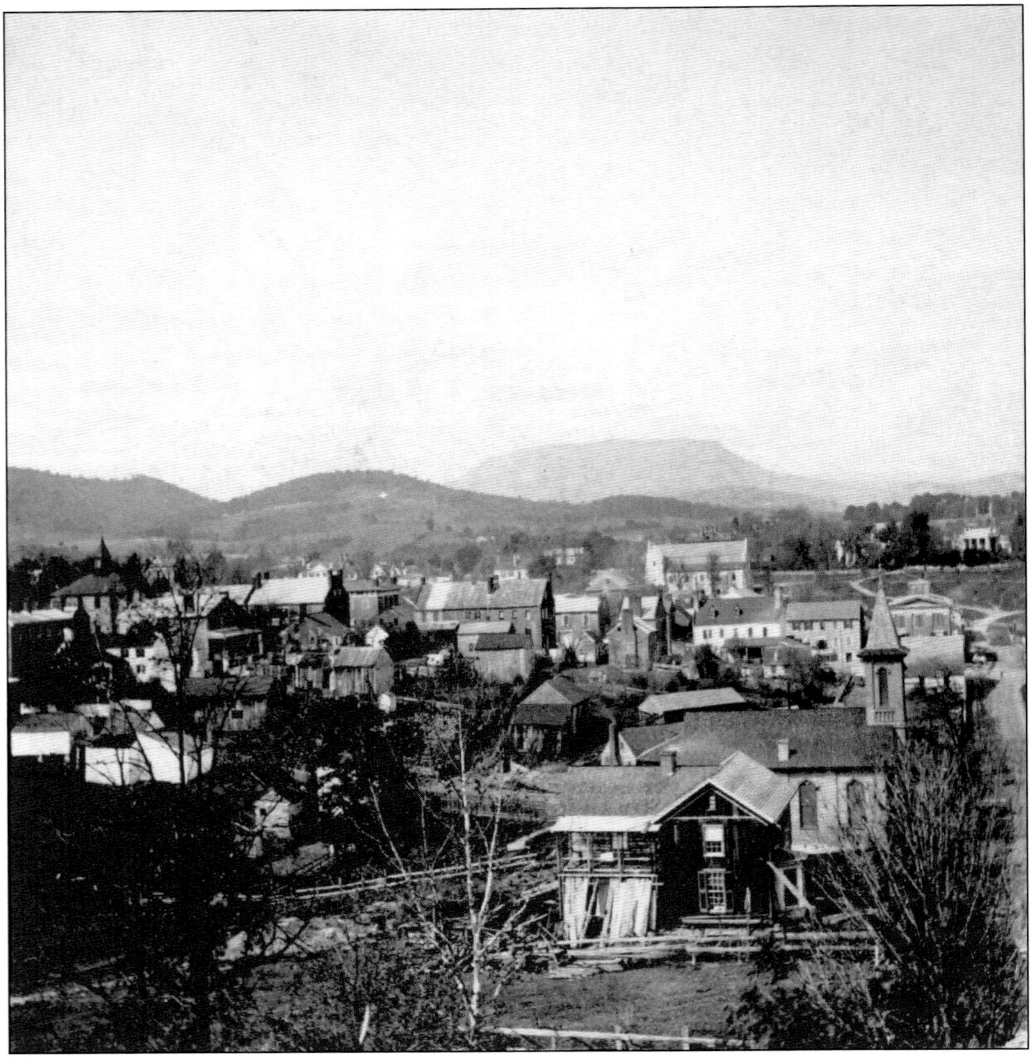

This is a view of the town of Lexington looking west. Taken by Miley from one of his favorite vantage points, the roof of Blandome, the Italianate villa on Tucker Street at the top of Henry Street, many details of the growing village can be discerned. The Lee-Jackson House is on the right in the background. The photograph was taken during the construction of the Robert E. Lee Episcopal Church, completed in 1883, but, in this photograph, the church steeple has not yet been added. The original county courthouse, with its cupola, is visible on the far left of the photograph. The church in the foreground with the steeple is the first St. Patrick's Catholic Church, which was finished just at the time this photograph was taken. The street on the right of the photograph is Henry Street.

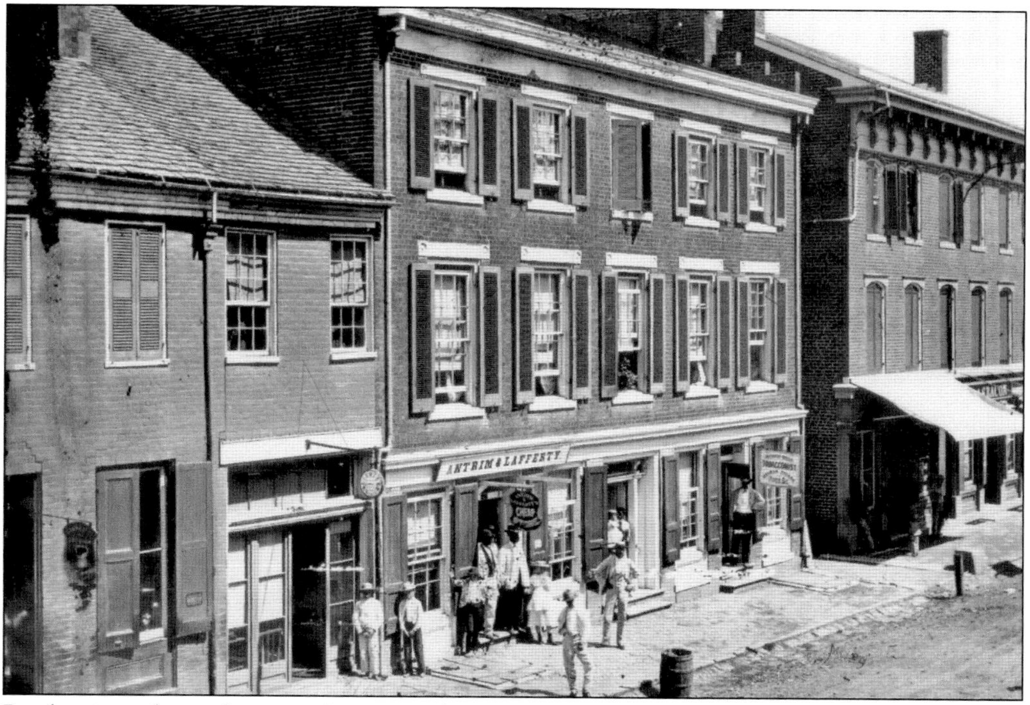

By the time these photographs were taken, commercial development along Main Street in Lexington had been proceeding with vigor for at least 20 years. The canal from Richmond had reached the southern end of the county in 1851, an event that stimulated commercial and manufacturing activity of all kinds. In that same year, the project to lower the street levels in the center of town was also begun. In the photograph above, the camera's perspective indicates that Miley was on an upper floor of a building across the street, and the poses of the individuals in the photograph suggest their awareness of the photographer's intentions. The photograph below shows Main Street looking south. There is no indication why there is a line of men stretching across the street. It is a Boude and Miley print from around 1867.

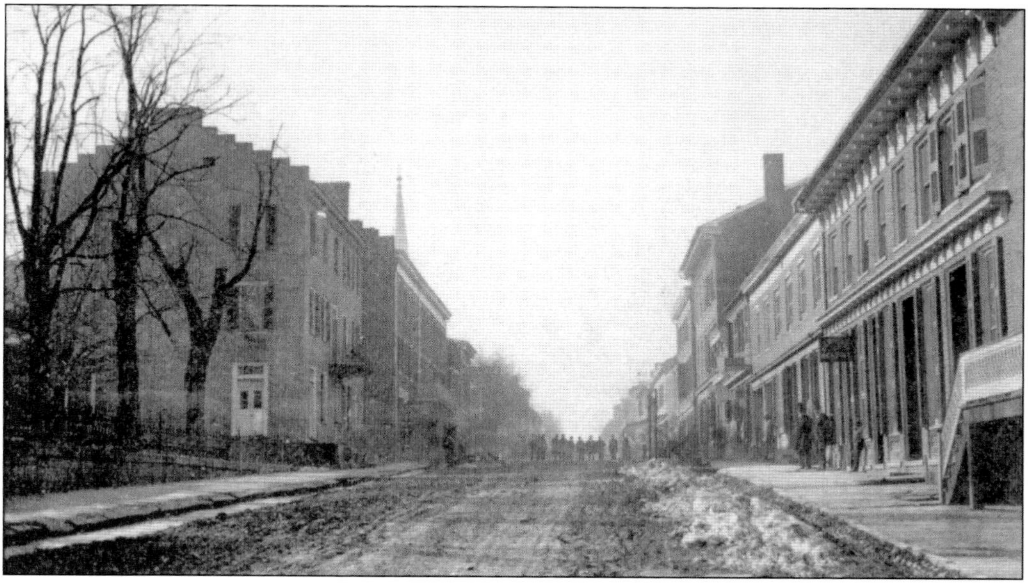

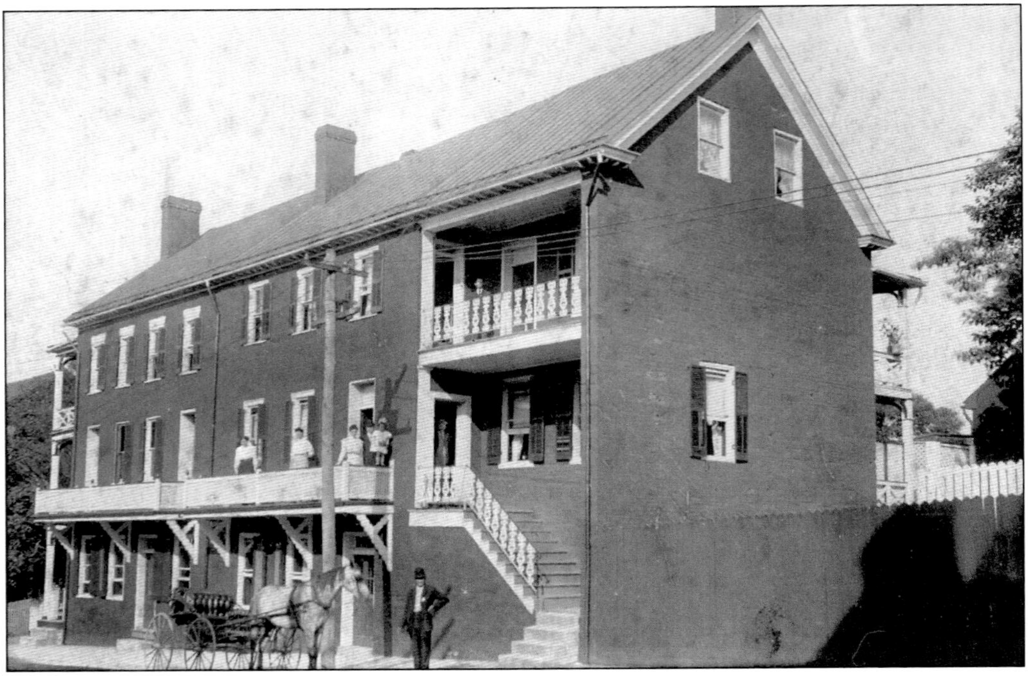

The intentionality of photographs like these creates a charm and immediacy that is sometimes lacking in historical photographs with no human subjects in them. These people, dressed up, posing for the camera, are real and alive. They are posing in front of and in the Central Hotel on Main Street in Lexington about 1895. The building is now the McCampbell Inn. The photograph above has the back stamp of J.L. McCown on it. McCown worked as a photographic printer for Miley for many years, where he learned the trade. McCown later opened his own photographic studio in Lexington. The photograph below is a superb example of Miley's ability to capture a moment in time. This is a Memorial Day parade in Lexington around 1907 or 1908. The view is looking north, and the Trinity Methodist Church and the Lexington City Hall and Fire Department, with its bell tower, are visible in the background.

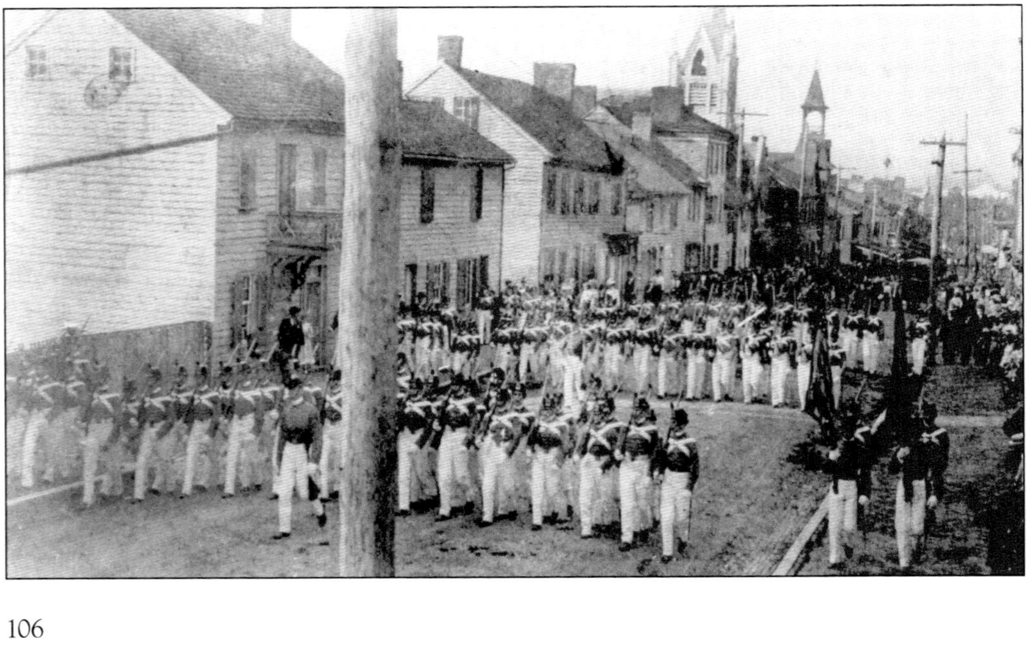

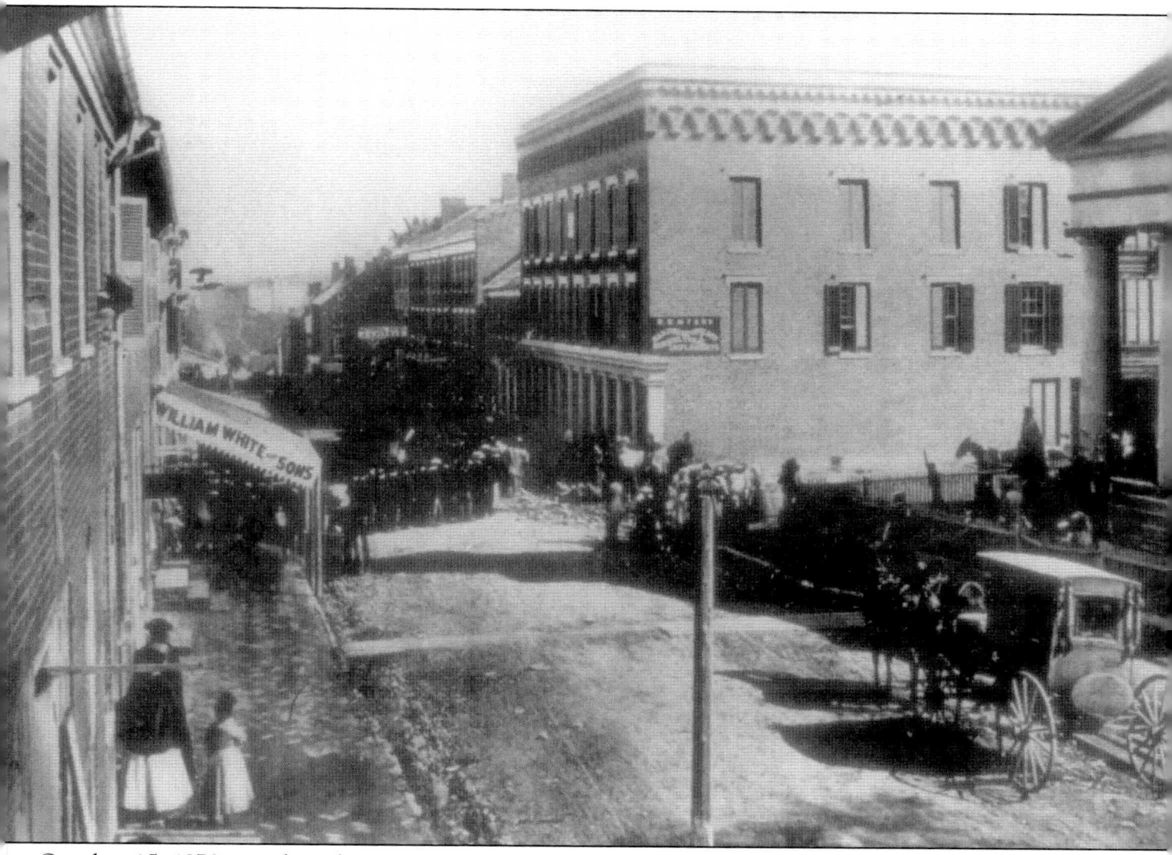

October 15, 1870, is a date that generations in Lexington would never forget. Miley is following the funeral procession of Robert E. Lee through the streets of Lexington. The general's body had lain in state in the chapel for two days; at 10:00 a.m. on October 15, the funeral procession began from his home on the W&L campus and wound its way through the town. In this photograph, the procession is turning left on Main Street, heading north. The columns of the Lexington Presbyterian Church are on the right, as is the Henry H. Myers dry goods store.

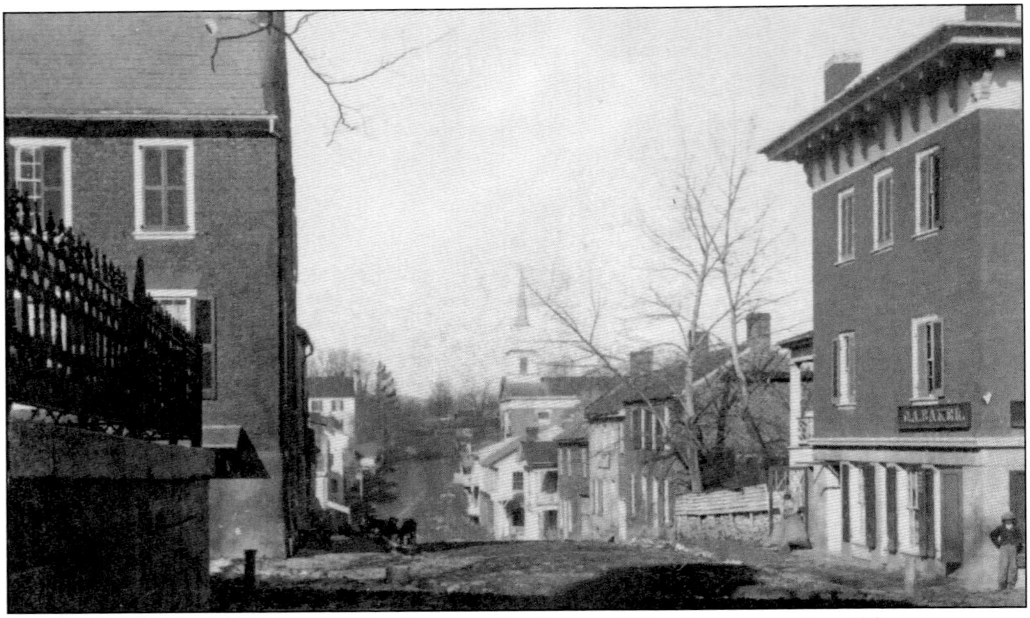

The street in the foreground of the photograph above is full of water, mud, and horse manure. The dirt and grime that was an ever-present aspect of life in this era is gone for most people today, and it is hard to imagine the extent to which everyday life was influenced by dirt and mud and how the smells of this day would have differed from today. The 1867 Miley-Boude image above shows Washington Street looking west at the Main Street intersection. The Alexander-Withrow House is on the opposite corner. The sign on the building on the right, where the woman is sweeping, says "R.A. Baker." The photograph below is from much later, probably around 1928, and was taken by Henry Miley. It shows a prominent building in Lexington, both then and today. At the time the photograph was taken, it was the Harper and Agnor store; today, it houses The Palms Restaurant.

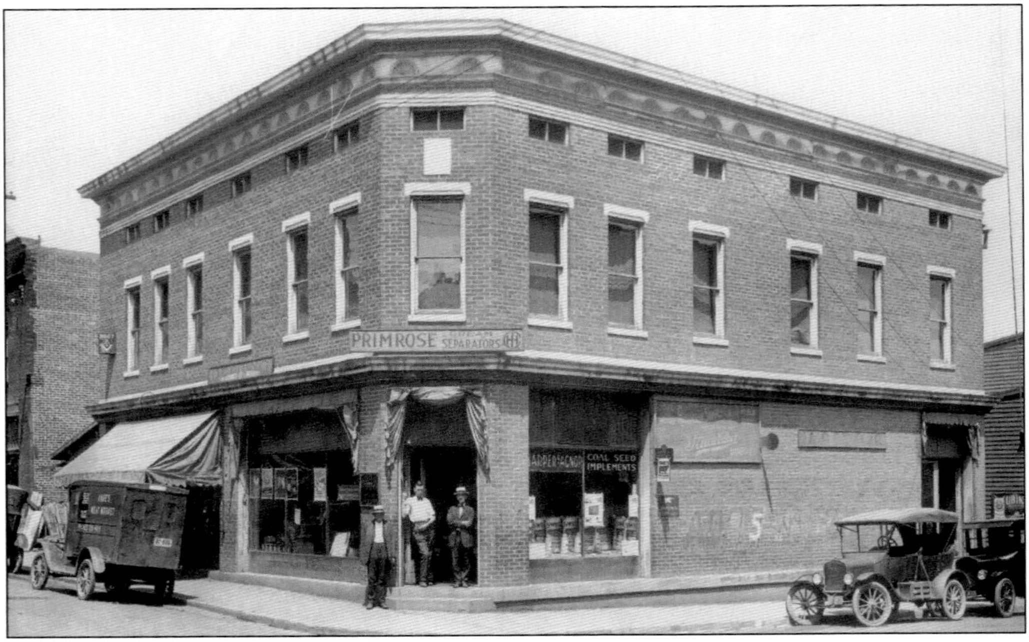

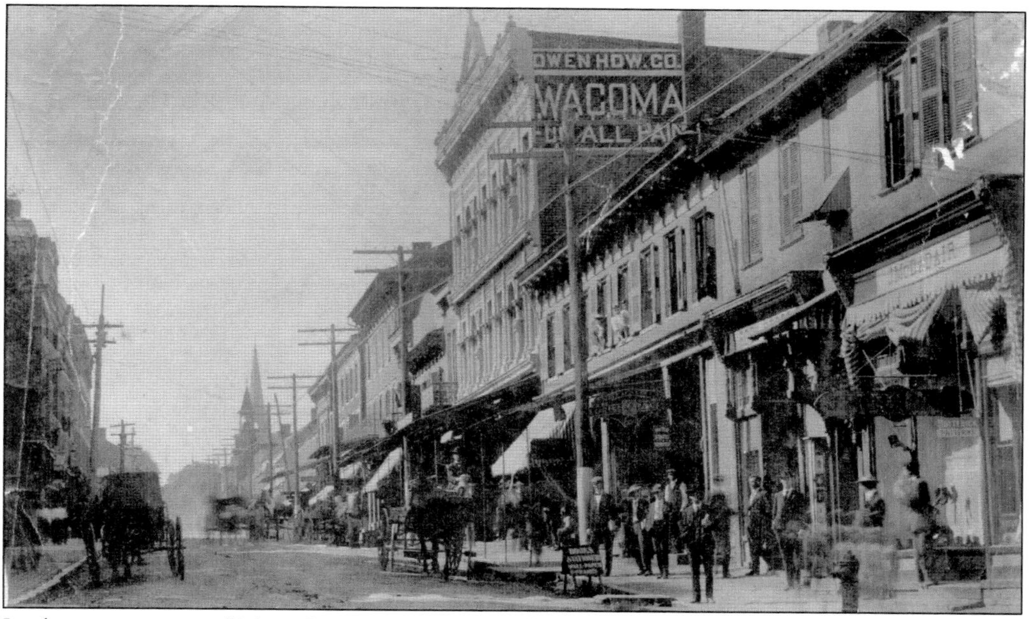

In these two views of Main Street in Lexington, looking toward the south, there is a great deal of evidence suggesting a thriving economy and the hustle and bustle of town life. Above, many men and boys are gathered in front of the bookstore. Several boys are hanging out the second-floor windows, looking toward the camera. In fact, the men on the street appear to be posing for, or at least turning to look at the photographer. The name on the building, Wacoma, refers to a patent medicine. The photograph below, taken at an earlier time, probably around 1890, shows the same scene. An incredible commotion of some kind is taking place in the street, and it is easy to see from this scene how even in the horse-and-buggy era, people complained regularly of traffic congestion. An interesting sign on the building on the right says, "Millers Photographic Art Studio of Enterprise and Push."

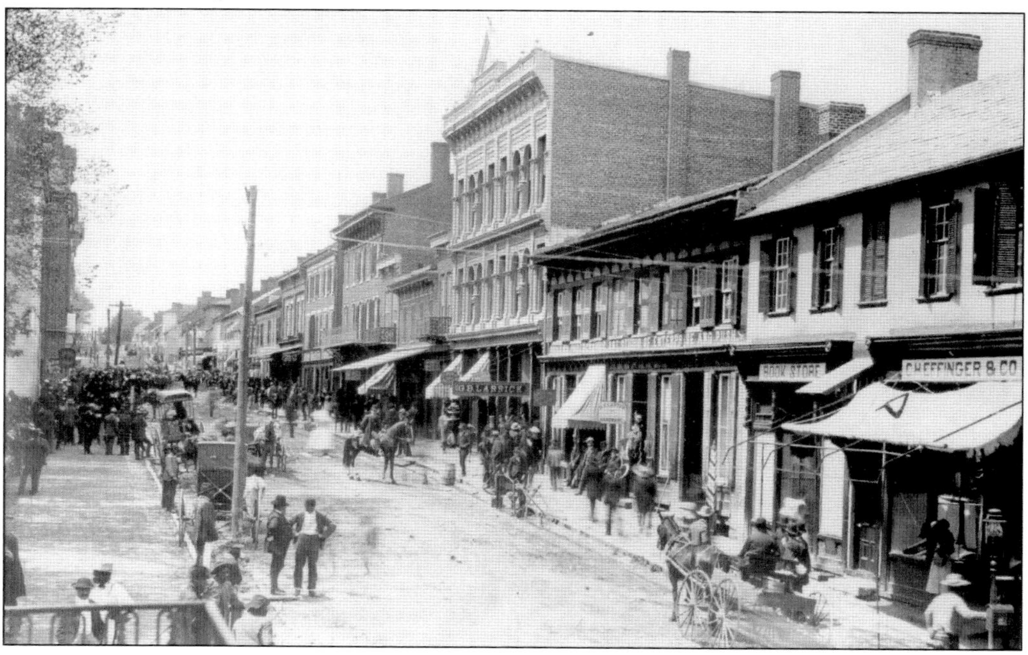

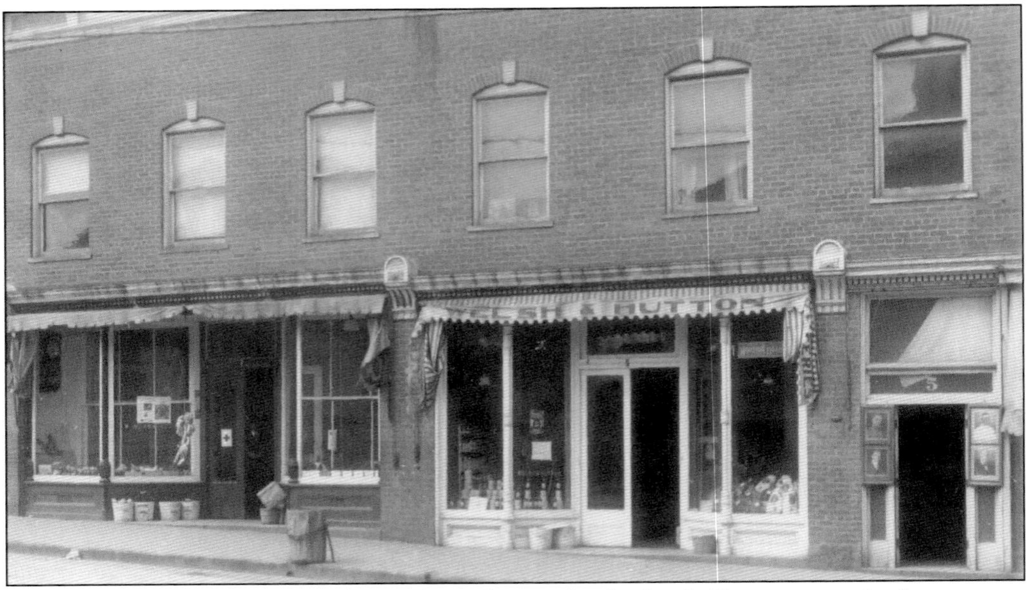

This modest storefront building has real significance for this book. Hanging outside the entrance to No. 5 are four portraits, the only advertisements or markings for Miley's photographic studio, which was located upstairs. The Welsh & Hutton grocery occupied the street level of the building. Bananas are hanging outside and there are baskets with produce on the ground. The trashcan by the street is chained down. The building, which no longer exists, was at the corner of Nelson and Main Streets, across the street from the Lexington Presbyterian Church.

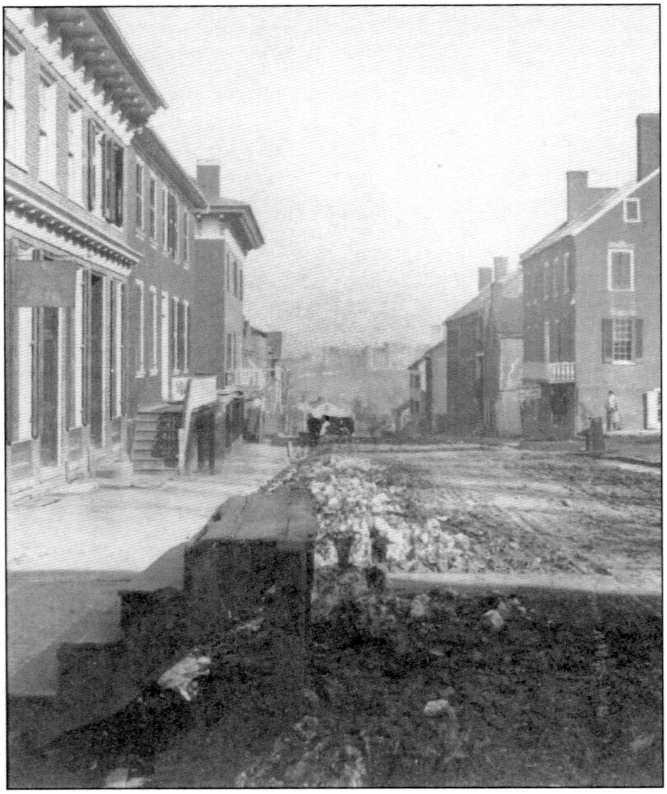

In this interesting shot taken around 1867 by Miley, some important features of the time can be noted. The damaged buildings of VMI can just be made out in the far distance. Buggy steps to assist passengers alighting from carriages are in the foreground, the Dold Building is on the right, and there is just a small corner of the courthouse square showing. Following the lowering of the street levels in the center of town in 1851, many buildings had to reorient their entranceways and several gained new ground floors under their original ground floors. While some complained of the expense and trouble, in the end, the improvements to the streets facilitated the continued growth and prosperity of the village.

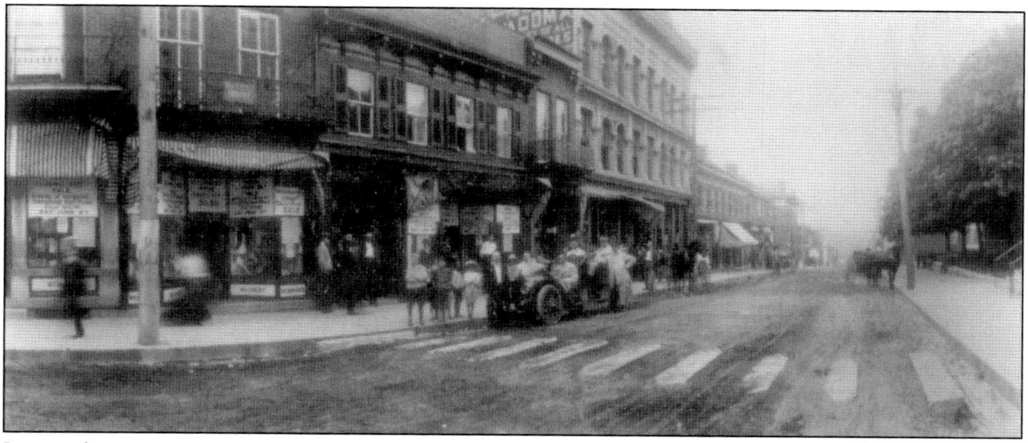

It was always exciting when an automobile came to town. In the early 20th century, automobiles were still quite rare. They were expensive, difficult to maintain, uncomfortable to ride in, and noisy. But they always drew a crowd, as this one on Main Street in Lexington did. The automobile is likely a Ford from 1905 to 1907. Notice the crosswalk in the foreground of the photograph.

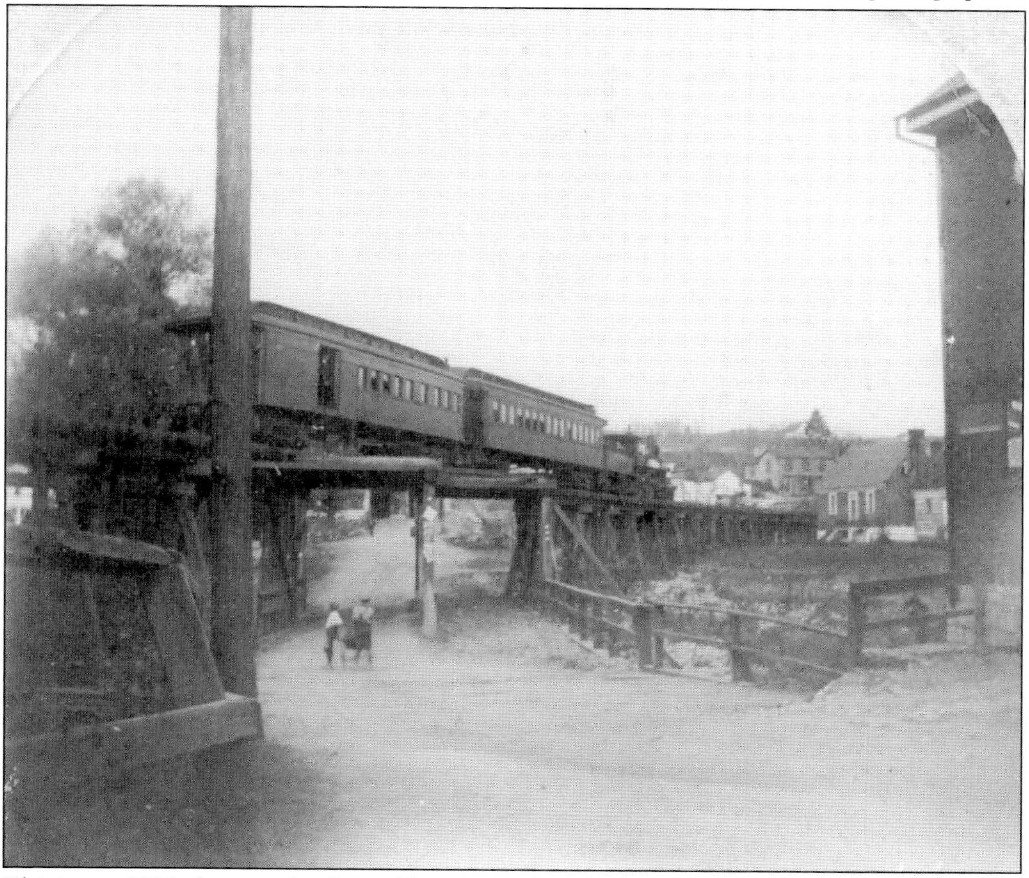

This is a c. 1900 photograph of the old train trestle at Jordon's Point in East Lexington. It looks as though the train has stopped. The young boys seem to be looking up and talking to a man who is standing in the doorway of the train car. The boys seem to be pushing some kind of cart. In the distance is the entrance to the covered bridge.

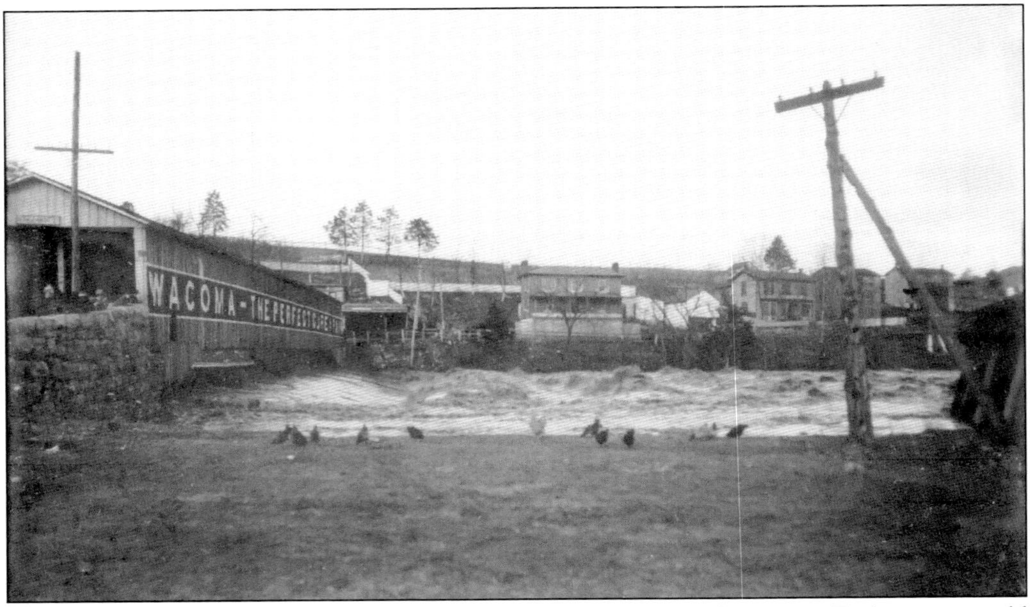

Floodwaters have plagued river towns like Lexington from their earliest years. Each spring would bring new damage and newly washed-out bridges. In this dramatic photograph, Miley captures the force of the flood as well as the curiosity that such disasters always bring with them. Even the chickens seem to be interested. This is more than likely the third bridge at Jordan's Point, as the first was burned during the Civil War and the second was washed away in 1870. The one in this photograph, from around 1900, seems close to its own demise.

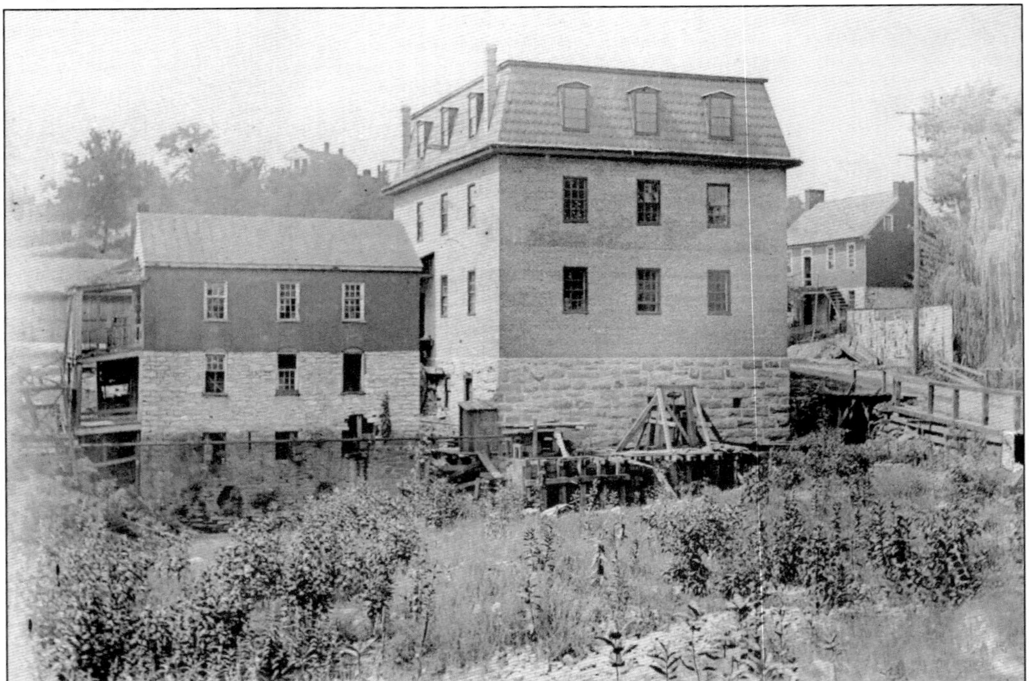

In this 1908 photograph, the Moses Brothers mill is shown as it stood on Jordan's Point. The mill was built in 1900 and served as both a gristmill, grinding grain into flour, and as a lumber mill.

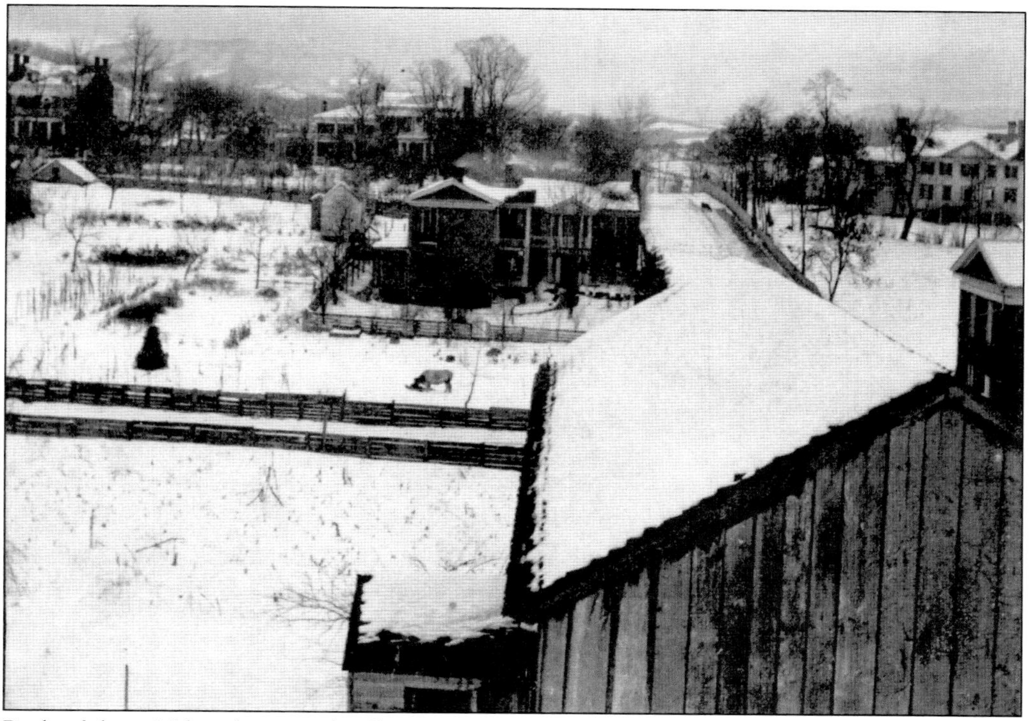

Both of these Miley photographs illustrate beautifully the rural nature of town life in late-19th-century America. In the photograph above, which shows Nelson Street looking west, several important Lexington landmarks are visible. The Hopkins house is in the center of the photograph. The house beside it, facing the camera, was torn down. In the upper right of the photograph is the Anne Smith Academy. Where the cow is standing is Hopkins Green, with Jefferson Street running parallel to it. This is a Miley and Boude photograph from around 1867. The photograph below, from the 1880s, creates a scene somewhat more cluttered and modern in appearance. The identities of the houses is unknown.

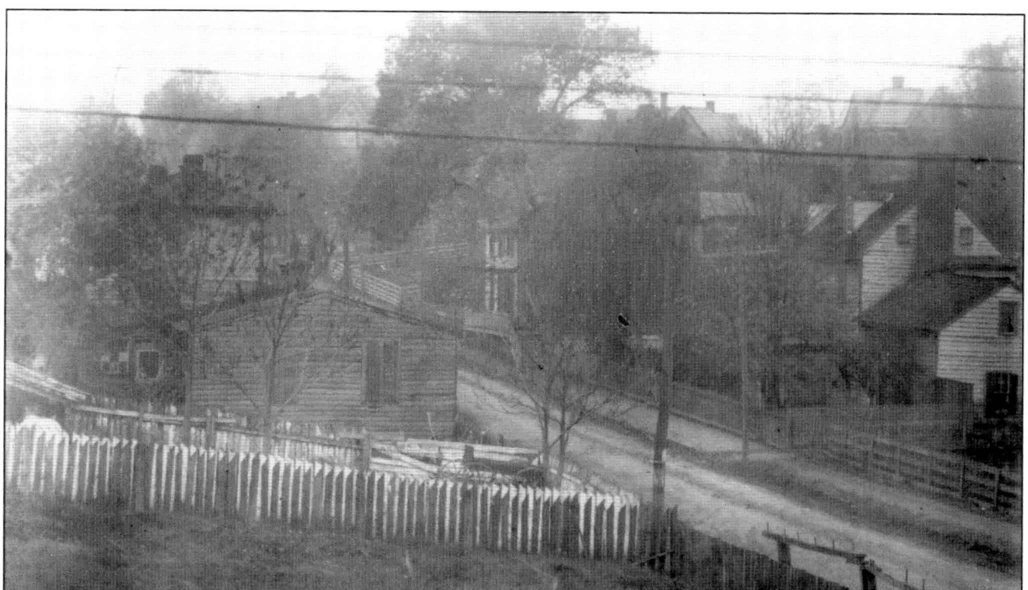

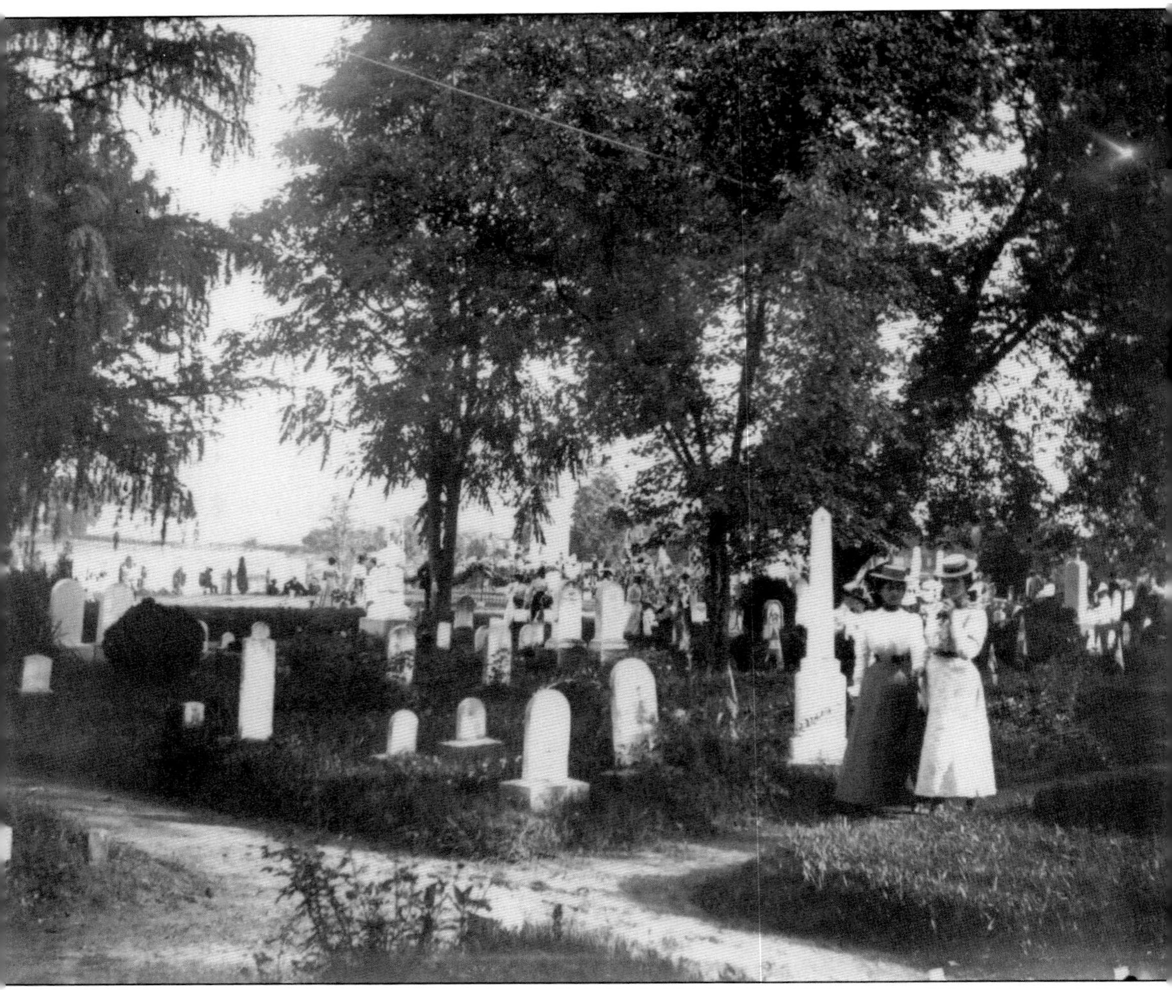

The history of the Presbyterian church cemetery in Lexington is woven into the fabric of the town, and even the South, in many fascinating ways. It was originally the church cemetery for the Lexington Presbyterian Church, which was organized in Lexington in 1847. Church membership grew over the years, as did the cemetery. After Stonewall Jackson was buried there in 1863, a movement began to rename it the Stonewall Jackson Memorial Cemetery. Eventually, the town took it over and enlarged it. A huge number of people, perhaps as many as 30,000, attended the celebration marking the dedication of the Stonewall Jackson statue and memorial on July 21, 1891, and this photograph may show part of that crowd, although there is no way to know that definitively. Michael Miley did attend that day, and took photographs of several of the events. In addition to Jackson, two governors of Virginia are buried there, along with notables of the town and the colleges such as Annie Joe White (1853–1938), who was the librarian at W&L for many years and the founder of the Fancy Dress Ball tradition. Her full name was Anne Robertson White, but everyone called her "Miss Annie Joe." The name on her grave marker is listed as Annie Joe White. The spelling of "Joe" is a bit of a mystery.

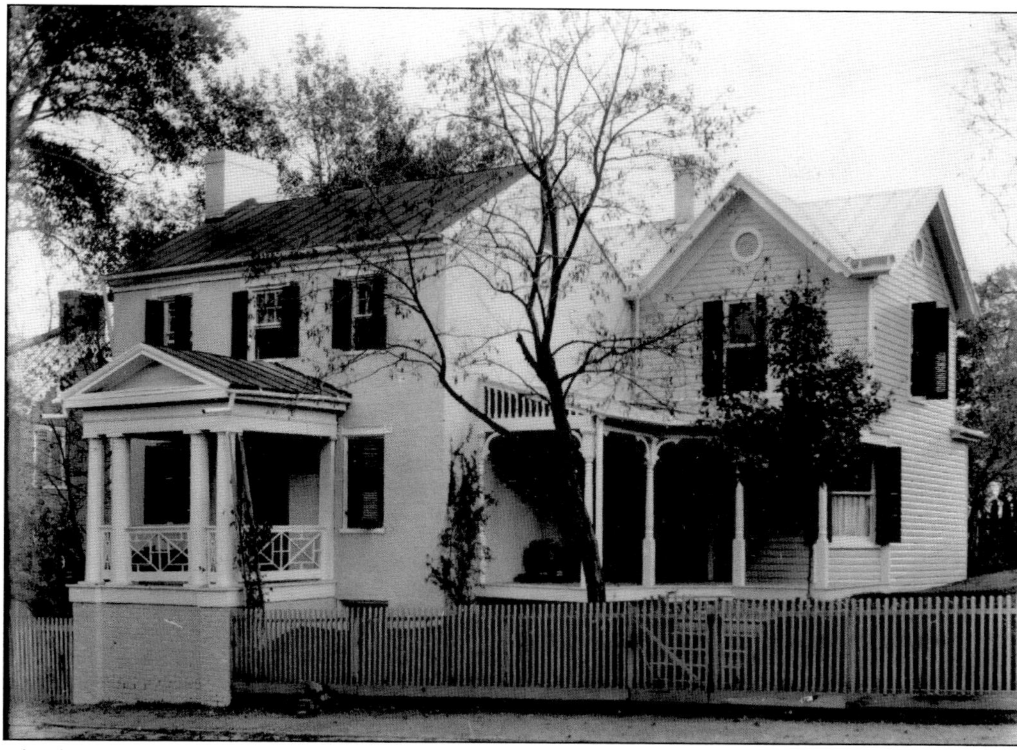

This beautiful residence was probably built around 1824, with additions put on later. It sits at 312 South Main Street in Lexington and served for many years as the local branch of the Botetourt-Rockbridge Regional Library. It is located beside the cemetery.

In 1891, plans were announced in Lexington for the construction of a magnificent hotel that would occupy the crest of Castle Hill. It was built and named the DeHart Hotel, and while it possessed many modern conveniences, including an elevator, it was never used as a hotel. Hard times struck the town at that time, and the DeHart was sold and then used briefly by W&L students as a residence hall before it burned to the ground in 1922.

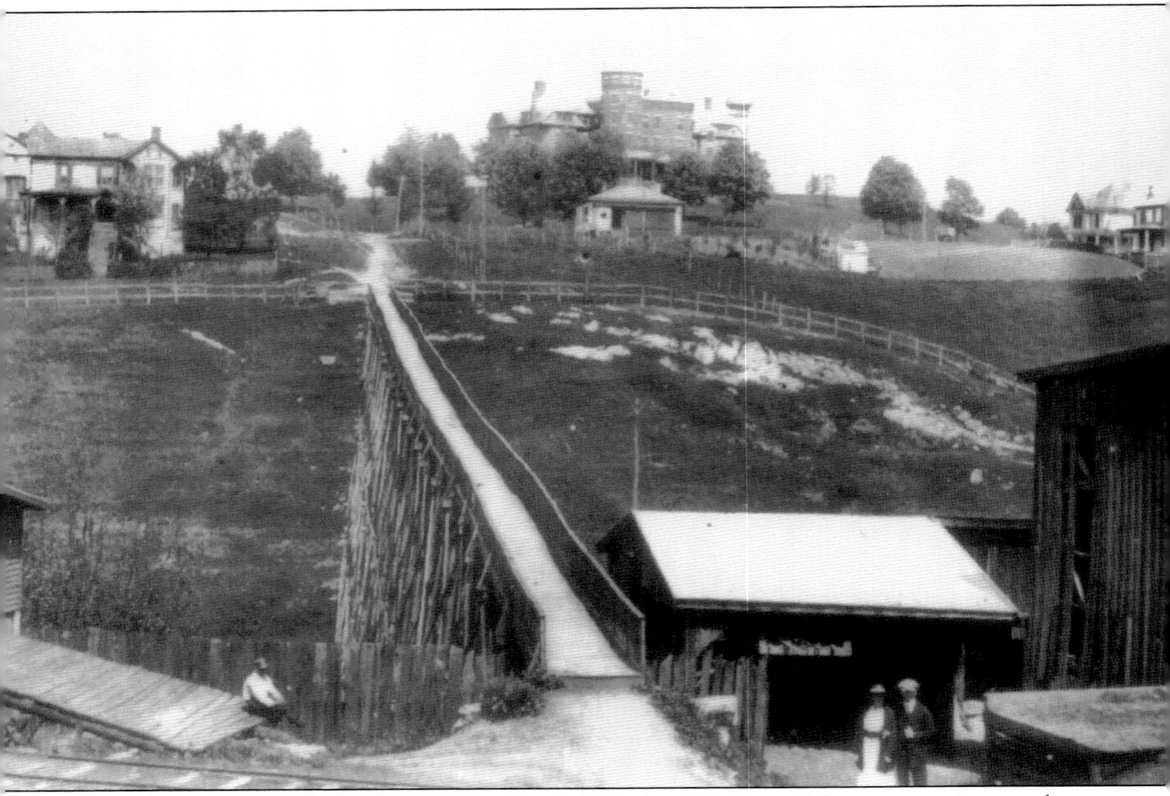

In this view of the DeHart Hotel on Castle Hill, the full effect of the construction can be seen. According to Charles Bodie in *Remarkable Rockbridge*, original plans for the hotel called for the construction of a large iron bridge to cross Wood's Creek and connect with Washington Street. Obviously, this was never completed, as the wooden bridge that can be seen in this Miley photograph is the only bridge that was built. As was the case in other locales that tried to generate business by constructing a large, first-class hotel, the DeHart was placed in proximity to the railroad station. Railroad tracks are just visible in the lower left corner of the photograph. In fact, Miley was probably standing next to the station when he took the photograph. Standing in the foreground are Carrie and Marion Beeton. Mr. Beeton was Lexington's postmaster at the time. In 1908, Washington and Lee offered students rooms in the DeHart, and the university purchased the building in 1911. It was no longer being used for this purpose in 1917, however, and it had been abandoned by the time it burned down five years later.

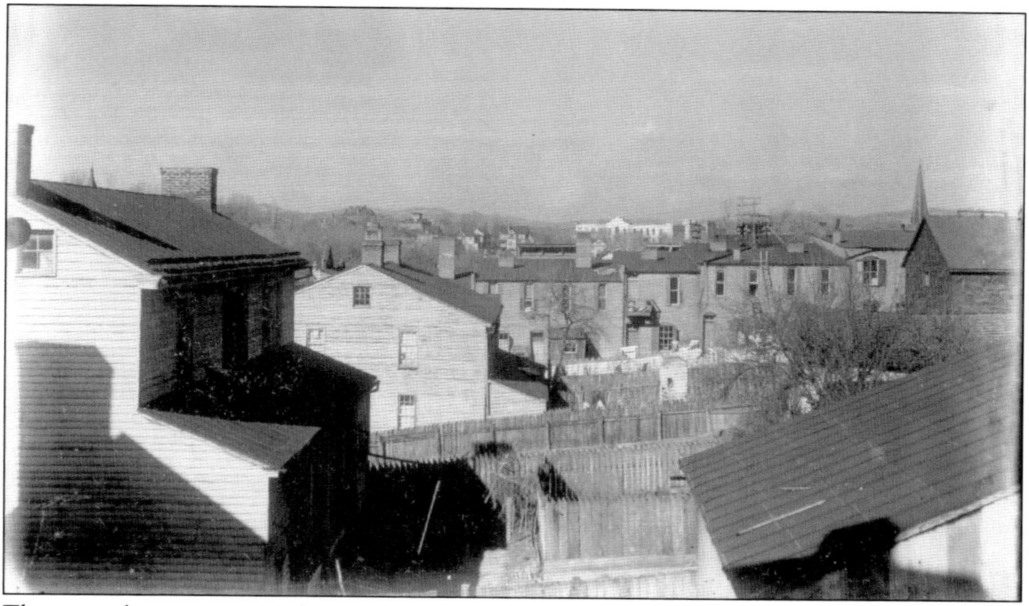

The view, the perspective, the lighting, and the attention to the clouds all seem to point to this being one of Miley's own photographs, made by Miley the artist rather than Miley the commercial photographer. It is a beautiful shot that takes full advantage of shadow and interesting angles and lines. Rather than being a photograph of anything in particular (though many buildings are identifiable), it seems to be more a study in light and lines.

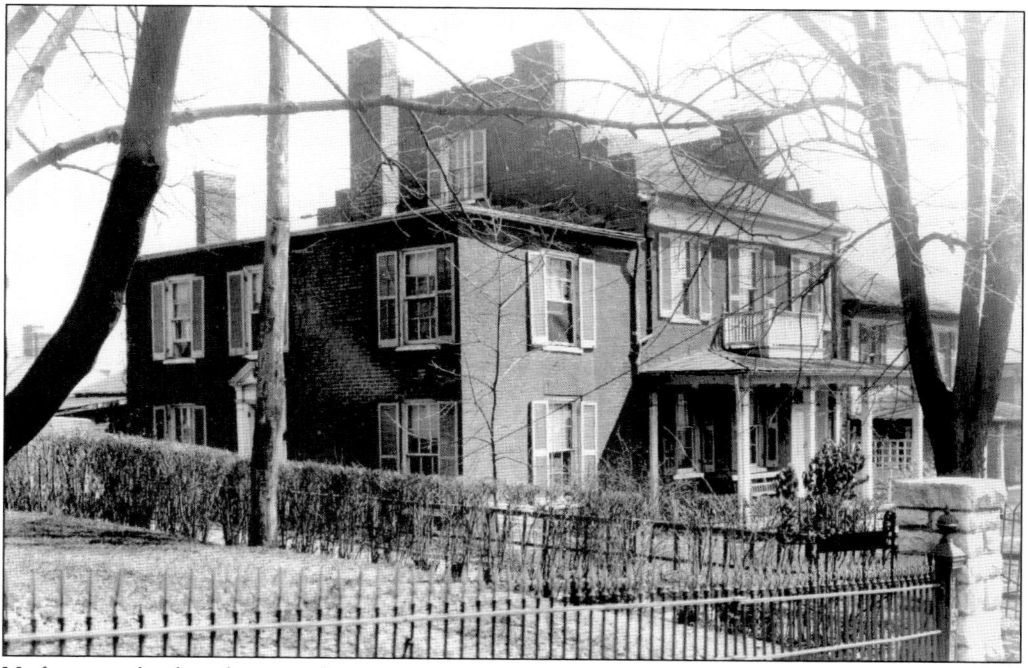

Unfortunately, this photograph is unidentified, so it is unknown why or when Miley shot it. The house is certainly the residence of a respectable middle-class family, a shopkeeper or a professional person perhaps. The side portion of the house is certainly a later addition to a house that was probably built in the first half of the 19th century. Beautiful homes from this era abound in Lexington, and this is a great example of just one.

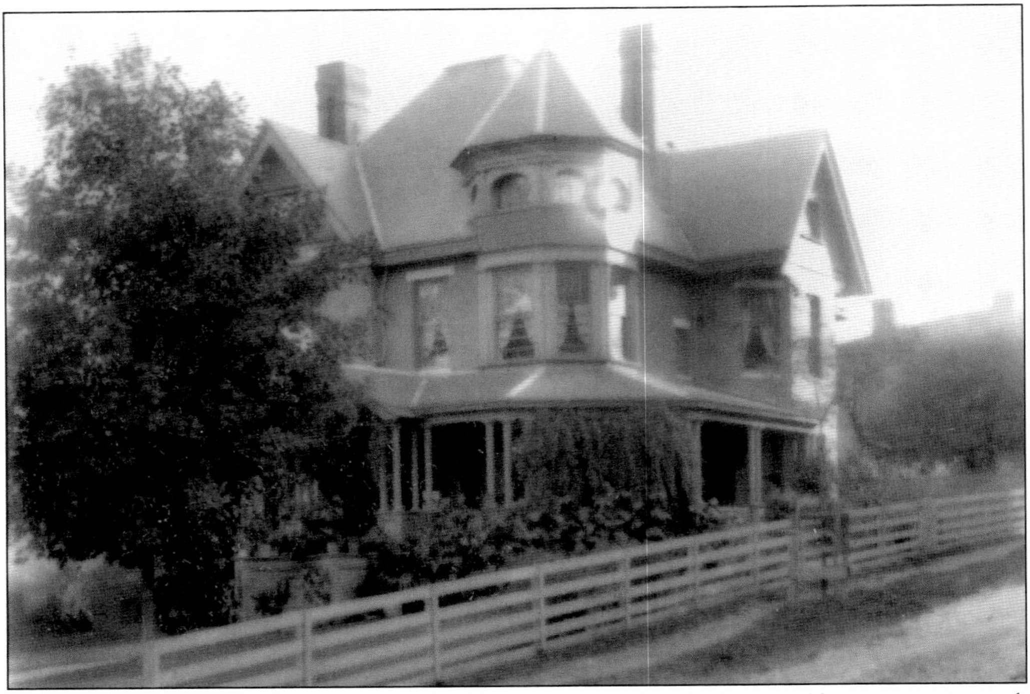

In these Miley photographs from around 1880, two beautiful and substantial homes are pictured. The photograph above shows a lovely Queen Anne–style home that belonged to the Paxton family. It sits on the southeast corner of Lee and Nelson Streets in Lexington and was built in 1895 by local architect William G. McDowell. Lexington experienced a building boom in the 1880s and 1890s that resulted in a startling number of large and stately homes being constructed around town. The town population increased, as did the areas in which people lived. Houses of this nature, relatively common in the town by 1900 and still impressive today, were and are visible evidence of prosperity.

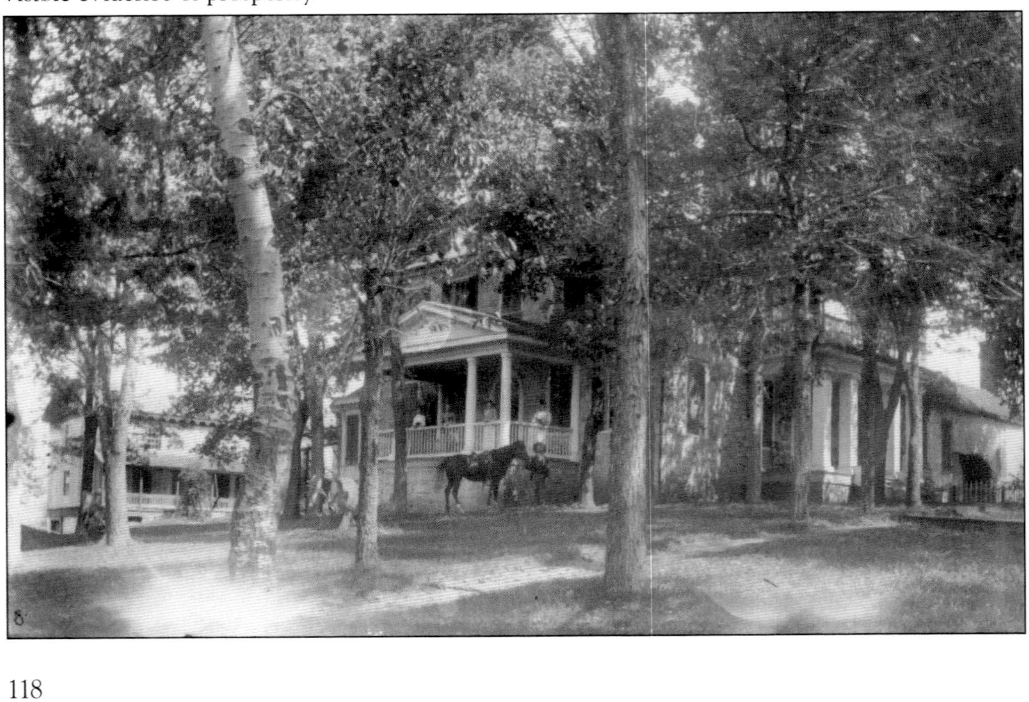

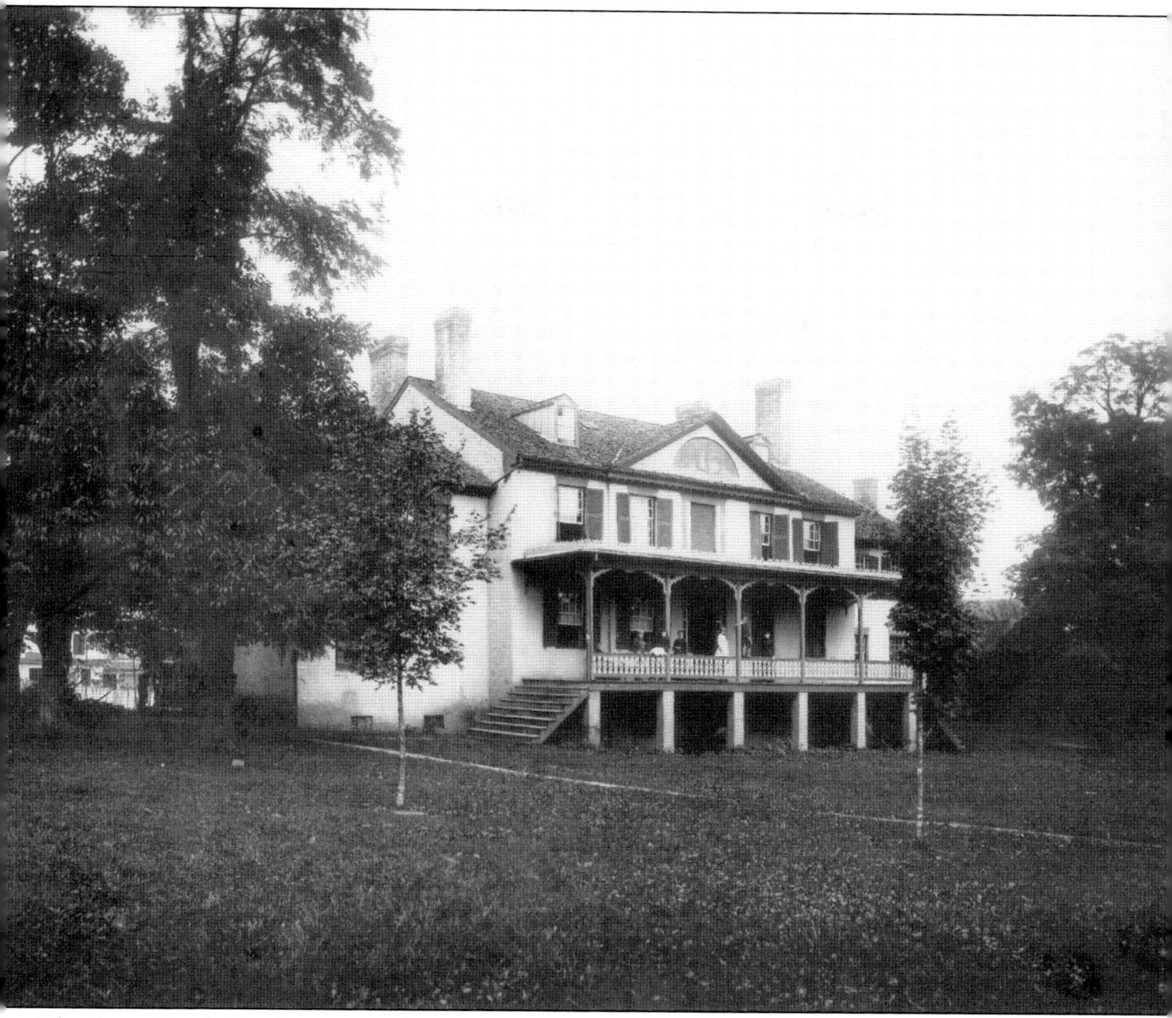

The Anne Smith Academy was a classical school for young women that existed in Lexington from 1808 to 1910. This large house on the corner of Nelson Street and Lee Avenue, which served the needs of the students, was demolished in 1910. In many ways, this photograph reflects the same impulses guiding Miley's camera that are seen in his environmental portraits. The camera is far enough away to capture the entire scene, but the girls on the porch seem completely relaxed and at home and do not have the stiff posture one would expect to see in a posed or formal photograph. Whether it is true or not, the photograph gives the impression that Miley just happened to be passing by and decided to take this photograph. The school closed for a while during the Civil War and, while it reopened afterwards, it struggled financially and enrollments dropped. In 1903, the town began to rent the academy building for a public high school. In 1907, the academy formally transferred its assets to the town, which soon demolished the old building and erected the new Lexington High School, which opened in 1909.

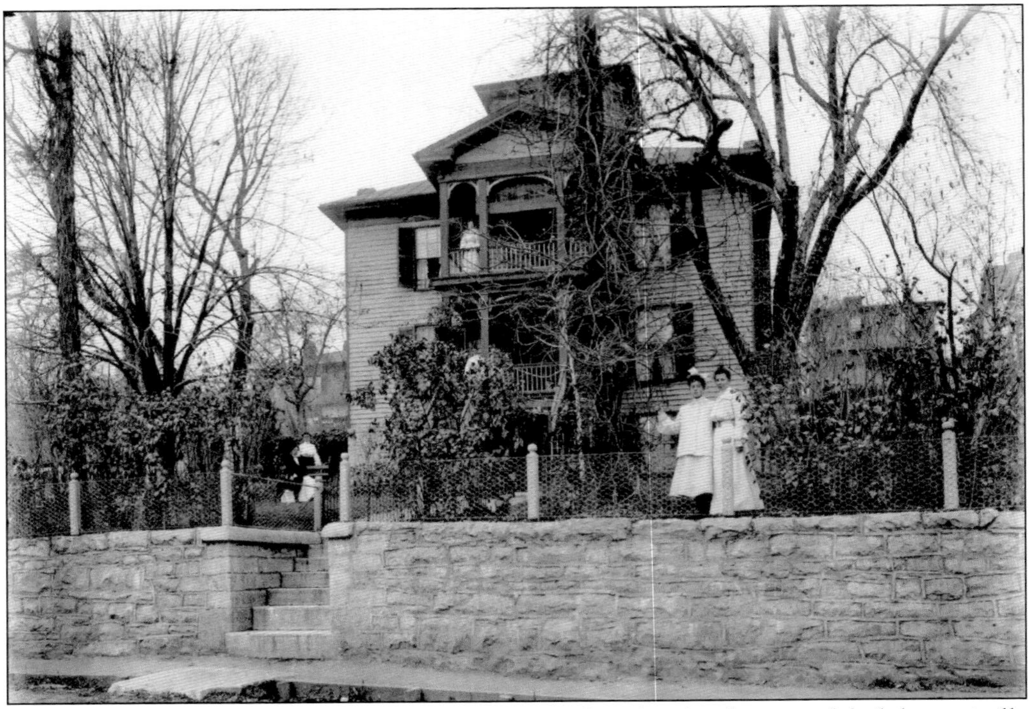

This house, on Virginia Military Institute property, though it has been modified dramatically in several different ways, still serves as a residence today. The house was built between 1869 and 1870 and was sold to VMI in 1946 during a period of expansion for the institute. A very interesting feature of this photograph is that there are only women pictured and they are dressed remarkably alike.

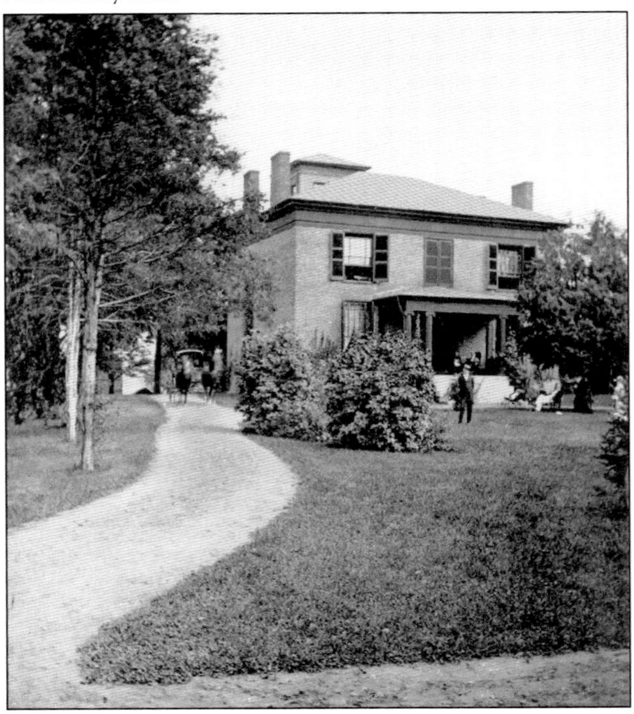

This is Col Alto, located on the eastern edge of Lexington on what is today East Nelson Street. It was built in 1827 for James McDowell, who would be the governor of Virginia and a member of the US House of Representatives. It is possible to date this photograph as post-1895 because a dormer that had been on the visible portion of the roof in this photograph was removed prior to that date. The house has undergone many, many alterations and additions over the decades.

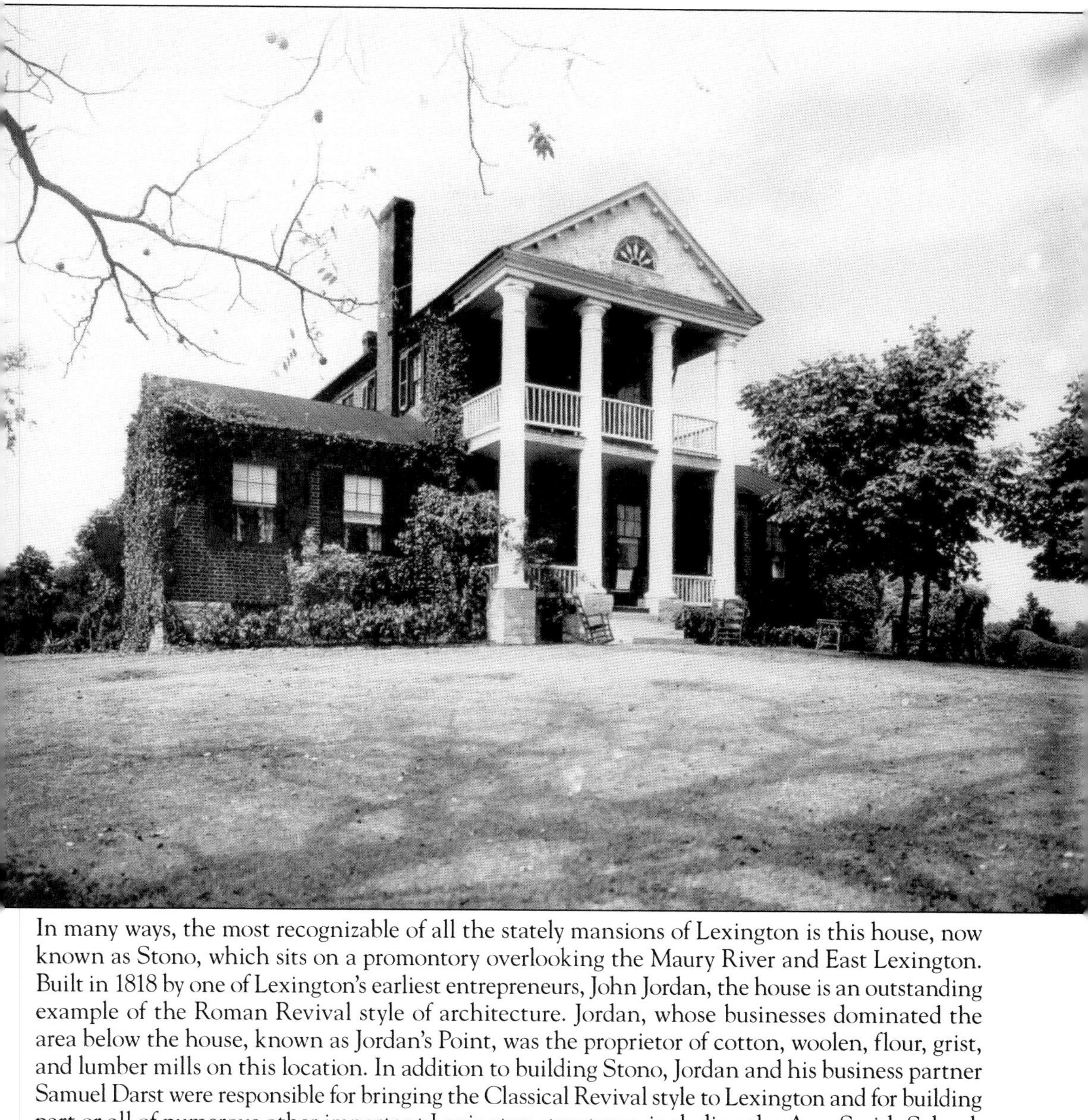

In many ways, the most recognizable of all the stately mansions of Lexington is this house, now known as Stono, which sits on a promontory overlooking the Maury River and East Lexington. Built in 1818 by one of Lexington's earliest entrepreneurs, John Jordan, the house is an outstanding example of the Roman Revival style of architecture. Jordan, whose businesses dominated the area below the house, known as Jordan's Point, was the proprietor of cotton, woolen, flour, grist, and lumber mills on this location. In addition to building Stono, Jordan and his business partner Samuel Darst were responsible for bringing the Classical Revival style to Lexington and for building part or all of numerous other important Lexington structures, including the Ann Smith School. According to *The Architecture of Historic Lexington*, Jordan also built roads and canals—including work on the canal from Richmond that eventually terminated just below his house at Jordan's Point—and the first covered bridge over the Maury River at East Lexington.

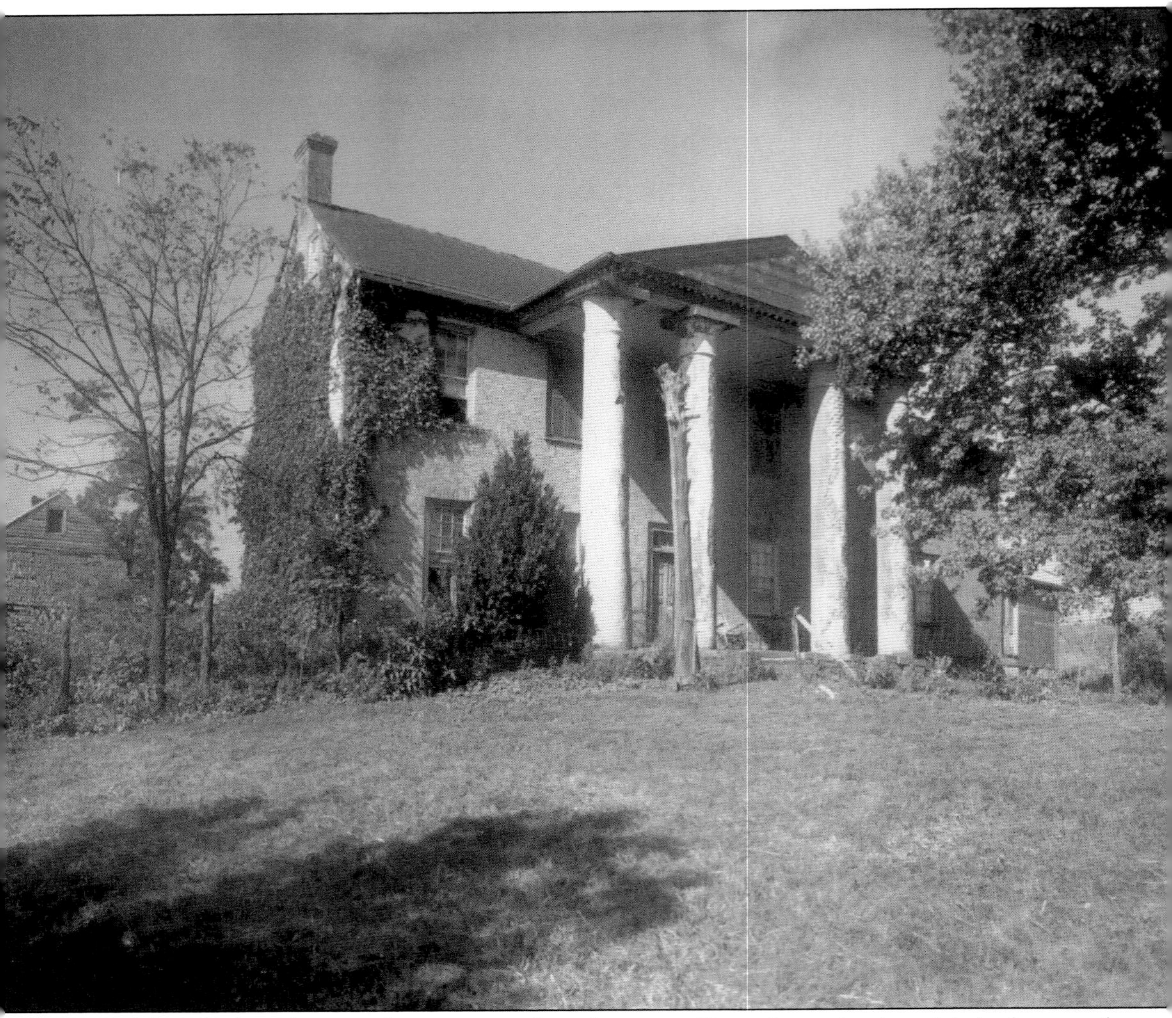

Although this photograph in no way does this magnificent home justice, this is the way the impressive Georgian estate known as Thorn Hill looked when Miley photographed it late in the 19th century. The house shows clear signs of neglect and deterioration. Thorn Hill was the first of the impressive country houses that dot the landscape around Lexington. Thorn Hill was built in 1792 for Col. John Bowyer and remained in his family until 1860. The house and its surroundings possessed all of the trappings of a majestic Georgian plantation house. The house had many outbuildings and gardens, lovely trees and lanes. According to *The Architecture of Historic Lexington*, the enormous columned portico that is its distinguishing feature was probably added in the 1850s. The house is a listed Virginia Landmark and is also in the National Register of Historic Places. While the house did suffer through some years of neglect, it now retains many original architectural and design features. As of this writing, the restored estate is for sale with an asking price of nearly $2 million.

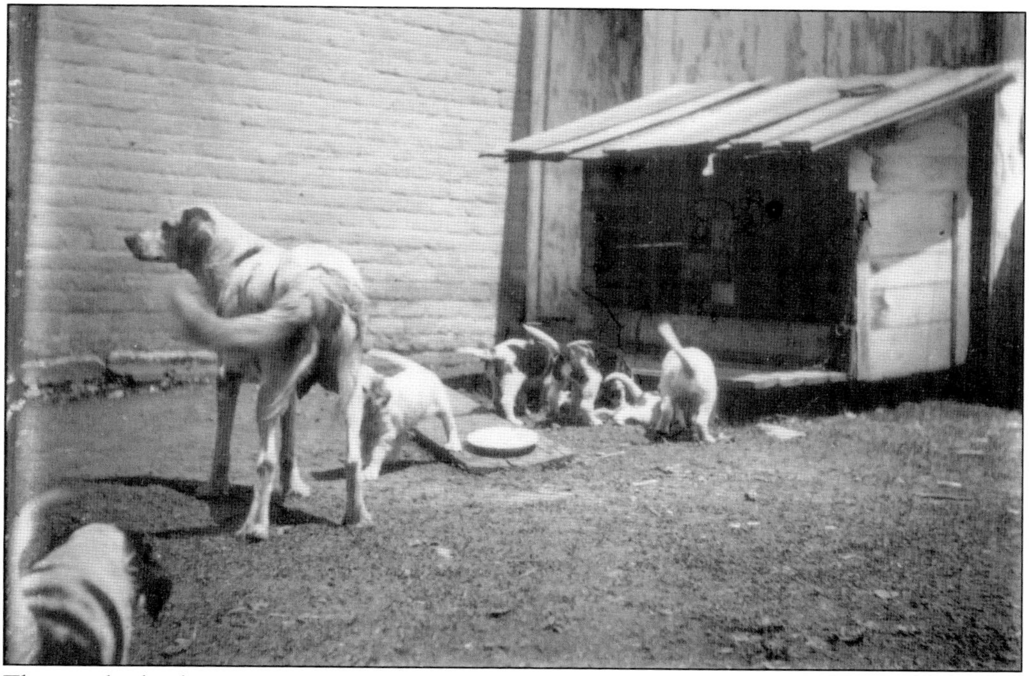

There is absolutely no information available about either of these two Miley photographs, but they had to be included in this collection simply because they are so full of joy and are just fun to look at—a veritable dog and pony show. They represent favorite photographs from the hundreds Miley took around Lexington of houses, industry, businesses, and famous and ordinary people. Visually exciting, imaginative, and sensitive, they show Miley's artistic talents at their best. Spontaneous and delightful, these photographs suggest the power of the photographic image to reveal life.

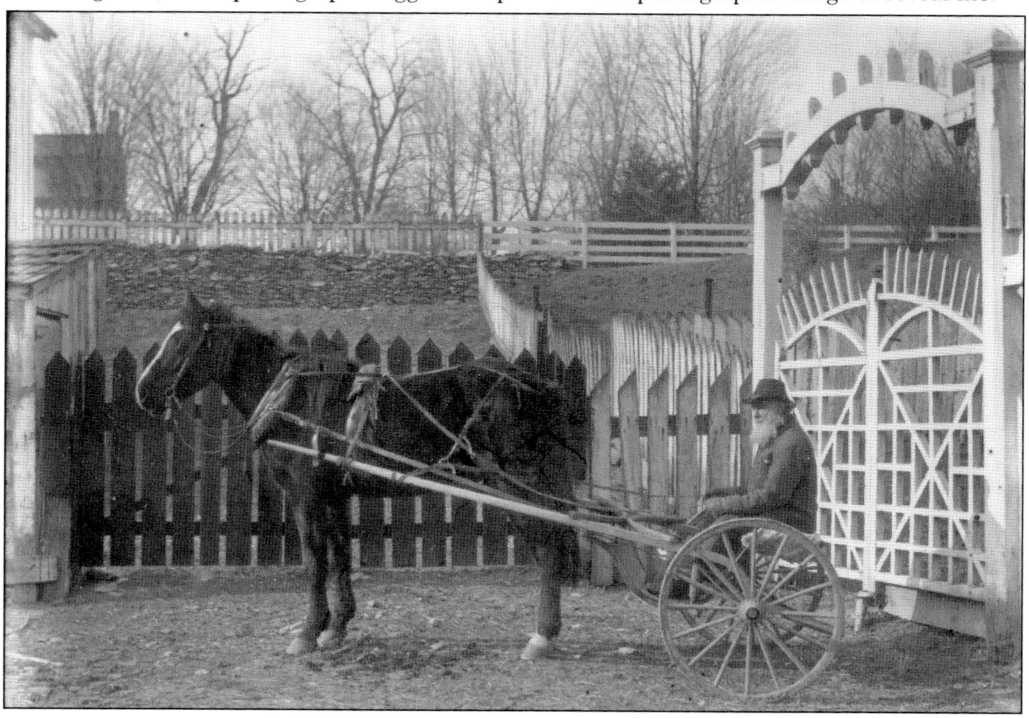

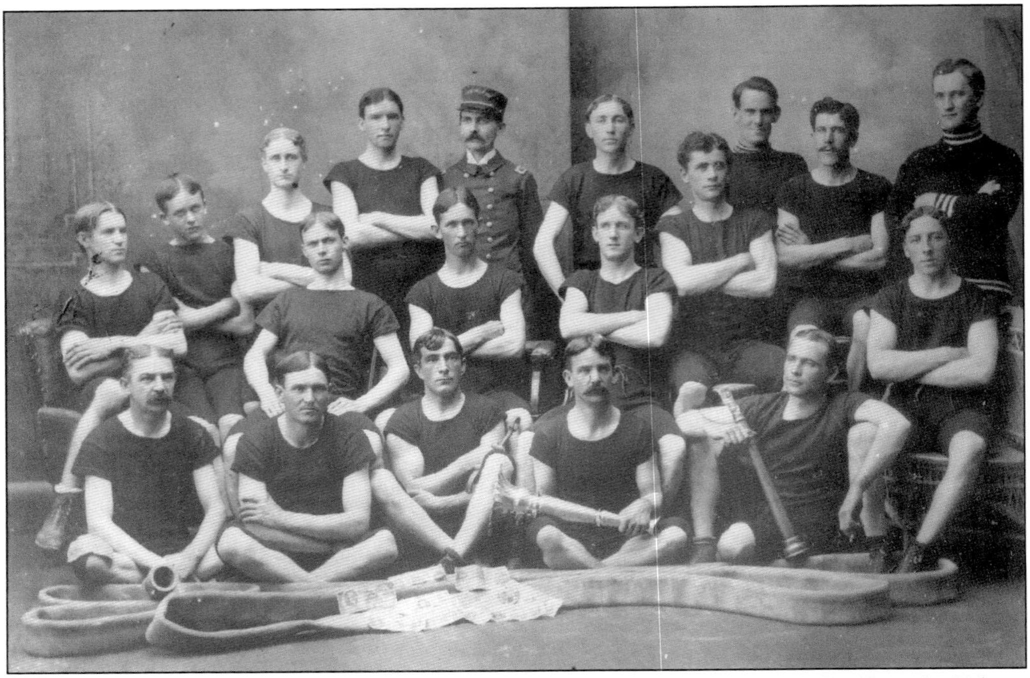

Looking like a sports team, these gentlemen are the members of the Lexington Fire Brigade. Taking their appearance as a guide, this photograph was probably taken around 1900. It is interesting to note that piled on the hoses in the foreground of the photograph are quite a few pieces of US paper currency. It looks like they are all $20 bills. Based on their outfits and the trophy-like object one man is holding, perhaps they had won the money in some type of contest.

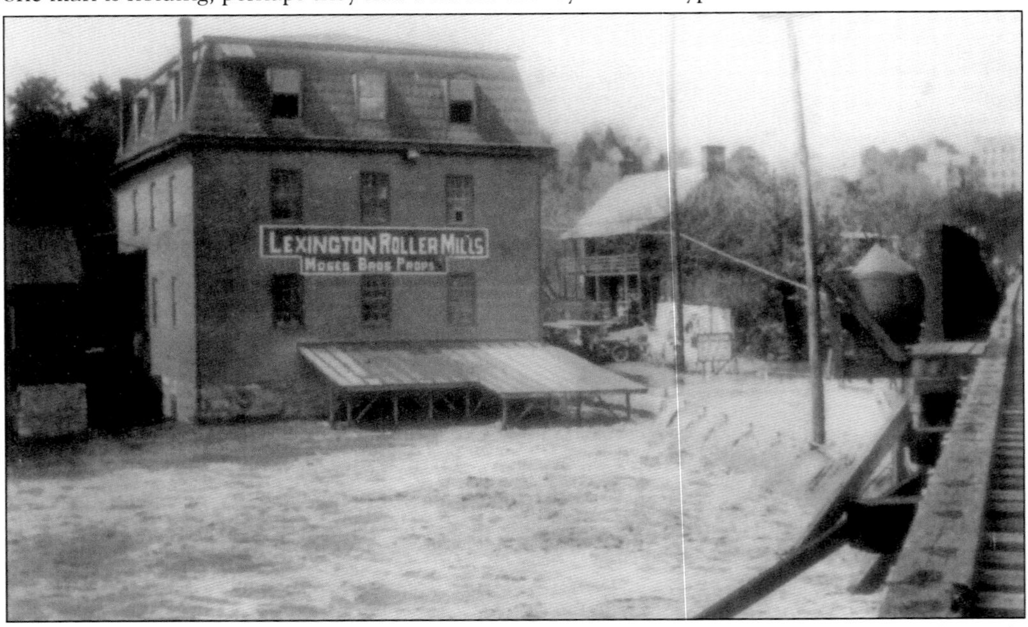

This photograph of the raging floodwaters of the Maury River at Jordan's Point was obviously taken from a rather precarious position on the train trestle. Based on an automobile that is just barely visible in the background, the photograph is probably from the mid-1920s, and therefore would have been the work of Henry Miley, not this father.

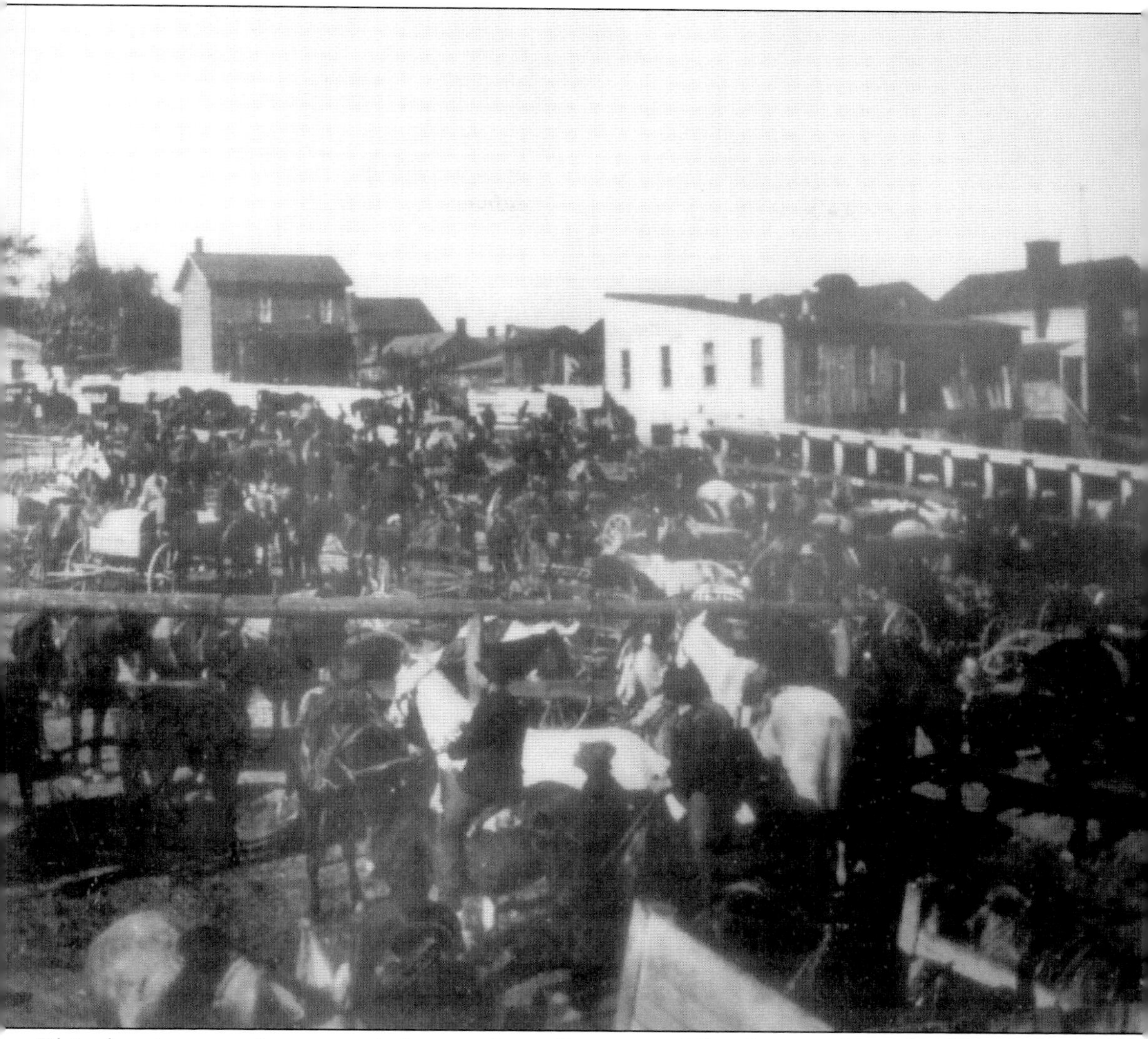

This chaotic scene shows a typical court day in Lexington. The photograph, probably taken by Henry Miley, dates from 1915–1920. The crowd is gathered in the open lot next to Manley Brown's, on the corner of Preston and Randolph Streets. Court day was held on the first Monday of each month, and it was typically a festive occasion. Men would come to town from all over the county to hear testimony in court or have their own cases adjudicated. Frequently, when the weather cooperated, people would camp out for one or two nights, which gave them time to carry out other business while in town. Horse-trading was a favorite form of entertainment and commerce on court days, as was general barter. Some local chronicles report that the degree of fighting and drinking that occurred during the court session assured a full docket for the judges in the coming months.

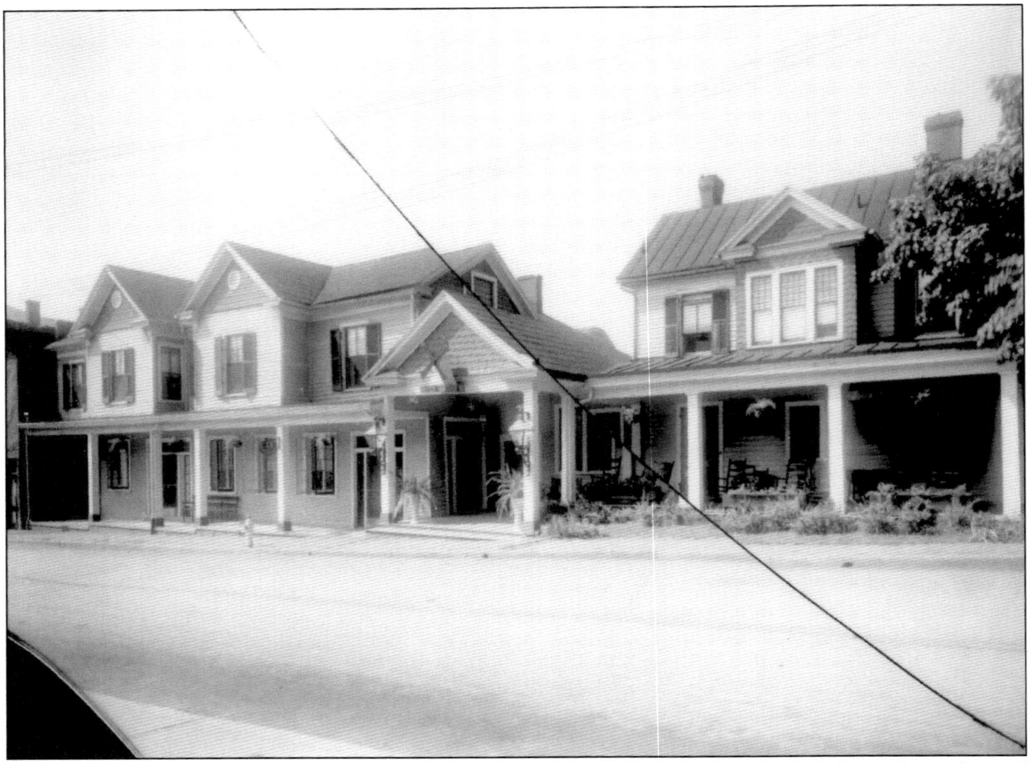

There is considerable evidence that a building has stood on this spot since the earliest days of Lexington. In 2007, the Dutch Inn, seen here in the 1920s, underwent considerable restoration and regeneration. Timbers found inside were dated to between 1795 and 1807. Paint chips discovered were used to restore the exterior to its appearance in the 1920s. It has served many functions in its lifetime and currently includes both residential and commercial space.

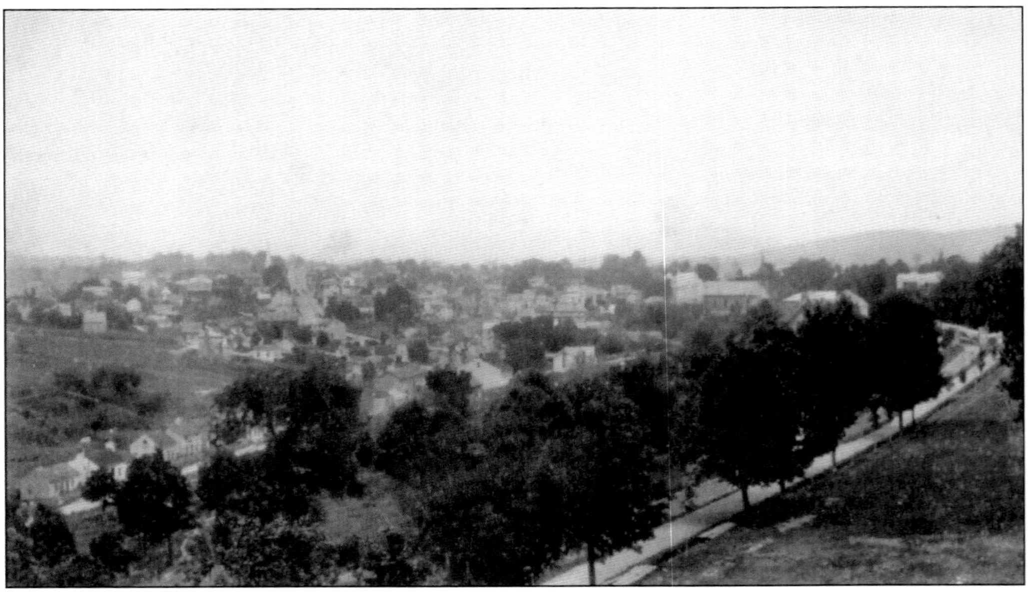

The grace and charm of the village of Lexington can easily be felt through Miley's lens as he takes in nearly the whole town from VMI in this view from 1875.

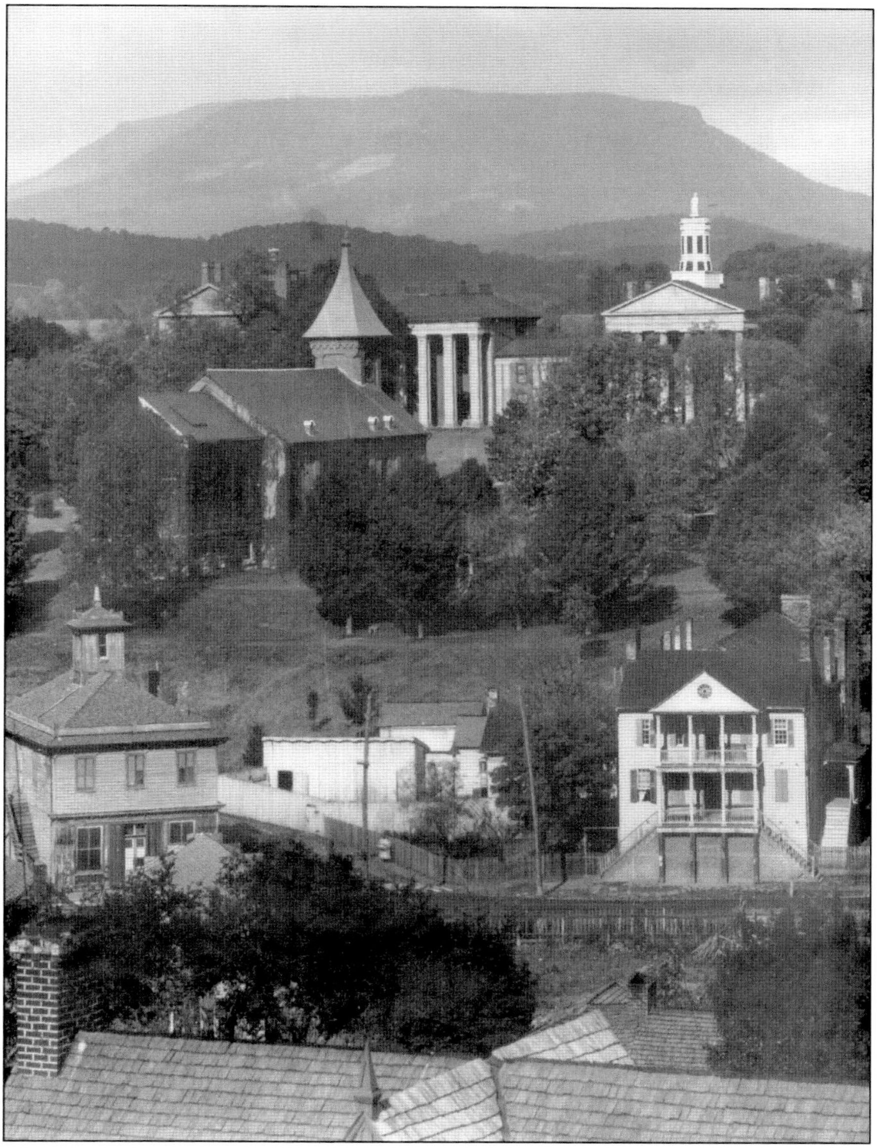

In this majestic view of parts of the town and parts of the W&L campus, Miley captures the quintessential peacefulness and calm of this academic village about 1883. In the lower right of the photograph is the building known at various times as Clyce's Old Tavern, the Blue Hotel, and Old Blue. The building dates from between 1785 and 1816, and, like other undistinguished structures, it experienced a multitude of owners and uses. W&L bought it in 1881 and used it as student housing for a time before abandoning it and then demolishing it in 1947. Rendered beautifully by Miley's perspective in this photograph is the statue atop Washington Hall, dubbed Old George by W&L students. This wooden statue of the school's namesake and original benefactor has been restored and rests in the Special Collections department of the Leyburn Library. All of the images contained in this volume come from their superb collection, and I want to take this opportunity to thank the staff there again for their generous assistance and all the small and large kindnesses they extended to me during my work on this book.